the australian and new zealand
bartenders guide

(Fifth Edition)

Publishers

The Australian and New Zealand
Bartenders Guide (Fifth Edition)

ISBN 1 740221 06 0
First published in Australia 2000
4cPublishers Pty Limited
Copyright © 4cPublishers Pty Limited
This book is copyright, apart from any fair dealings for the
purpose of study, research, criticism or review, as permitted
under the copyright act, no part may be reproduced by any
process without written permission.
Enquiries should be addressed to the publisher.
4cPublishers Pty Ltd
154 Upper Washington Drive,
Bonnet Bay, NSW. 2226. Australia.
Printed and bound in China by Everbest Printing Company.

Introduction

METHODS OF MIXING COCKTAILS

The four methods below are the most common processes of mixing cocktails:-

1. Shake   **2.** Stir

3. Build   **4.** Blend

1. SHAKE: To shake is to mix a cocktail by shaking it in a cocktail shaker by hand. First, fill the glass part of the shaker three quarters full with ice, then pour the ingredients on top of the ice. Less expensive ingredients are more frequently poured before the deluxe ingredients. Pour the contents of the glass into the metal part of the shaker and shake vigorously for ten to fifteen seconds. Remove the glass section and using a Hawthorn strainer, strain contents into the cocktail glass.

Shaking ingredients that do not mix easily with spirits is easy and practical (juices, egg whites, cream and sugar syrups).

Most shakers have two or three parts. In a busy bar, the cap is often temporarily misplaced. If this happens, a coaster or the inside palm of your hand is quite effective. American shakers are best.

To sample the cocktail before serving to the customer, pour a small amount into the shaker cap and using a straw check the taste.

2. STIR: To stir a cocktail is to mix the ingredients by stirring them with ice in a mixing glass and then straining them into a chilled cocktail glass. Short circular twirls are most preferred. (NB. The glass part of the American shaker will do well for this.) Spirits, liqueurs and vermouths that blend easily together are mixed by this method.

3. BUILD: To build a cocktail is to mix the ingredients in the glass in which the cocktail is to be served, floating one on top of the other.

Hi-Ball, long fruit juice and carbonated mixed cocktails are typically built using this technique. Where possible a swizzle stick should be put into the drink to mix the ingredients after being presented to the customer. Long straws are excellent substitutes when swizzle sticks are unavailable.

4. BLEND: To blend a cocktail is to mix the ingredients using an electric blender/mixer. It is recommended to add the fruit (fresh or tinned) first. Slicing small pieces gives a smoother texture than if you add the whole fruit. Next, pour the alcohol. Ice should always be added last. This order ensures that the fruit is blended freely with the alcoholic ingredients allowing the ice to gradually mix into the food and beverage, chilling the flavour. Ideally, the blender should be on for at least 20 seconds. Following this procedure will prevent ice and fruit lumps that then need to be strained.

If the blender starts to rattle and hum, ice may be obstructing the blades from spinning. Always check that the blender is clean before you start. Angostura Bitters is ammonia based which is suitable for cleaning. Fill 4 to 5 shakes with hot water, rinse and then wipe clean.

TECHNIQUES IN MAKING COCKTAILS

1. SHAKE AND POUR: After shaking the cocktail, pour the contents straight into the glass. When pouring into Hi-Ball glasses and sometimes old fashioned glasses the ice cubes are included. This eliminates straining.

2. SHAKE AND STRAIN: Using a Hawthorn strainer (or knife) this technique prevents the ice going into the glass. Straining protects the cocktail ensuring melted ice won't dilute the flavour and mixture.

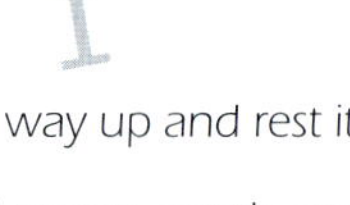

3. FLOAT INGREDIENTS: Hold the spoon right way up and rest it with the lip slightly above the level of the last layer. Fill spoon gently and the contents will flow smoothly from all around the rim. Use the back of the spoons dish only if you are experienced.

4. FROSTING (sugar and salt rims): This technique is used to coat the rim of the glass with either salt or sugar. First, rub lemon/orange slice juice all the way around only the glass rim. Next, holding the glass by the stem upside down, rest on a plate containing salt or sugar and turn slightly so that it adheres to the glass. Pressing the glass too deeply into the salt or sugar often results in chunks sticking to the glass. A lemon slice is used for salt and an orange slice is used for sugar.

To achieve colour affects, put a small amount of grenadine or coloured liqueur in a plate and coat the rim of the glass, then gently place in the sugar. The grenadine absorbs the sugar and turns it pink. This is much easier than mixing grenadine with sugar and then trying to get it to stick to the glass.

Introduction

HELPFUL HINTS

Cocktail mixing is an art which is expressed in the preparation and presentation of the cocktail.

HOW TO MAKE A BRANDY ALEXANDER CROSS

Take two short straws and, with a sharp knife, slice one of the straws half way through in the middle and wedge the other uncut straw into the cut straw to create a cross.

STORING FRUIT JUICES

Take a 750mL bottle and soak it in hot water to remove the label and sterilise the alcohol. The glass has excellent appeal and you'll find it easier to pour the correct measurement with an attached nip pourer.

SUGAR SYRUP RECIPE

Fill a cup or bowl (depending on how much you want to make) with white sugar, top it up with boiling water until the receptacle is just about full and keep stirring until the sugar is fully dissolved. Refrigerate when not in use. Putting a teaspoon of sugar into a cocktail is being lazy, it does not do the job properly as the sugar dissolves.

JUICE TIPS

Never leave juices, Coconut Cream or other ingredients in cans. Pour them into clean bottles, cap and refrigerate them. All recipes in this book have been tested with premium fruit juices.

ICE

Ice is probably the most important part of cocktails. It is used in nearly all cocktails. Consequently ice must be clean and fresh at all times.

The small squared cubes and flat chips of ice are superior for chilling and mixing cocktails. Ice cubes with holes are inefficient. Wet ice, ice scraps and broken ice should only be used in blenders.

CRUSHED ICE

Take the required amount of ice and fold into a clean linen cloth. Although uncivilised, the most effective method is to smash it against the bar floor. Shattering with a bottle may break the bottle. Certain retailers sell portable ice crushers. Alternatively a blender may be used. Half fill with ice and then pour water into the blender until it reaches the level of the ice. Blend for about 30 seconds, strain out the water and you have perfectly crushed ice. Always try and use a metal scoop to collect the ice from the ice tray.

Never pick up the ice with your hands. This is unhygienic. Shovelling the glass into the ice tray to gather ice can also cause breakages and hence should be avoided where possible.

Introduction

It is important that the ice tray is cleaned each day. As ice is colourless and odourless, many people assume wrongly it is always clean. Taking a cloth soaked in hot water, wipe the inside of the bucket warm. The blenders used for all of our bar requirements are Moulinex blenders with glass bowls. We have found these blenders to be of exceptional quality.

GLASSES

Cordial (Embassy):	30mL	Fancy Hi-Ball Glass:	220mL, 350mL, 470mL
Cordial (Lexington):	37mL	Hurricane Glass:	230mL, 440mL, 650mL
Tall Dutch Cordial:	45mL	Irish Coffee Glass:	250mL
Whisky Shot:	45mL	Margarita Glass:	260mL
Martini Glass:	90mL	Hi-Ball Glass:	270mL, 285mL, 330mL
Cocktail Glass:	90mL, 140mL	Footed Hi-Ball Glass:	270mL, 300mL
Champagne Saucer:	140mL	Salud Grande Glass:	290mL
Champagne Flute:	140mL, 180mL	Fiesta Grande Glass:	350mL, 490mL
Wine Goblet:	140mL, 190mL	Poco Grande Glass:	380mL
Old Fashioned Spirit:	185mL, 210mL, 290mL		
Fancy Cocktail:	210mL, 300mL	Brandy Balloon:	650mL

A proven method to cleaning glasses is to hold each glass individually over a bucket of boiling water until the glass becomes steamy and then with a clean linen cloth rub in a circular way to ensure the glass is polished for the next serve

Cocktails can be poured into any glass but the better the glass the better the appearance of the cocktail.

One basic rule should apply and that is, use no coloured glasses as they spoil the appearance of cocktails. All glasses have been designed for a specific task, e.g.,

1. Hi-Ball glasses for long cool refreshing drinks.

2. Cocktail glasses for short sharp, or stronger drinks.

3. Champagne saucers for creamy after-dinner style drinks, etc.,

The stem of the glass has been designed so you may hold it whilst polishing, leaving the bowl free of marks and germs so that you may enjoy your drink. All cocktail glasses should be kept in a refrigerator or filled with ice while you are preparing the cocktails in order to chill the glass. An appealing affect on a 90mL cocktail glass can be achieved by running the glass under cold water and then placing it in the freezer.

GARNISHES AND JUICES

Banana	Onions
Celery	Oranges
Cucumber	Pineapple
Lemons	Red Maraschino Cherries
Limes	Rockmelon
Mint leaves	Strawberries
Olives	Canned fruit
Celery salt	Nutmeg
Chocolate flake	Pepper, Salt
Cinnamon	Tomato

Introduction

Fresh eggs	Sugar and sugar cubes
Fresh single cream	Tabasco sauce
Fresh milk	Worcestershire sauce
Apple	Orange and Mango
Carbonated waters	Pineapple
Coconut Cream	Sugar syrup
Lemon – pure	Canned nectars
Orange	Canned pulps
Jelly Babies	Crushed Pineapple
Almonds	Blueberries
Apricot Conserve	Red Cocktail Onions
Vanilla Ice Cream	Flowers (assorted)

Simplicity is the most important fact to keep in mind when garnishing cocktails. Do not overdo the garnish; make it striking, but if you can't get near the cocktail to drink it then you have failed. Most world champion cocktails just have a lemon slice, or a single red cherry.

Tall refreshing Hi-Balls tend to have more garnish as the glass is larger. A swizzle stick should be served nearly always in long cocktails. Straws are always served for a lady, but optional for a man.

Plastic animals, umbrellas, fans and a whole variety of novelty goods are now available to garnish with, and they add a lot of fun to the drink.

ALCOHOL RECOMMENDED FOR A COCKTAIL BAR

Spirits

Aphrodite Ouzo

Bourbon – Rebel Yell

Brandy – Milne

Campari

Canadian Club

Gin – Gilbey's

Malibu

Pernod

Rum – Bacardi

Rum – Bundaberg

Scotch – Ballantine's

Scotch – Bell's

Scotch – Johnnie Walker

Southern Comfort

Tennessee Whiskey – Jack Daniel's

Tequila – El Toro

Tequila – Pepe Lopez

Vandermint

Vodka – Smirnoff

Liqueurs

Advocaat

Amaretto

Bailey's Irish Cream

Benedictine

Blue Curacao

Cassis

Galliano

Grand Marnier

Kahlúa

Kirsch

Lena Banana

Mango

Introduction

Chartreuse – Green	Midori
Chartreuse – Yellow	Peach
Cherry Advocaat	Pimm's
Cherry Brandy	Sambuca – di Galliano
Clayton's Tonic (Non-alcoholic)	Sambuca – Lago Nera
Cointreau	Sambuca – Opal Nera
Creme de Menthe Green	Sambuca – Romana
Dark Creme de Cacao	Strawberry
Drambuie	Tia Maria
Frangelico	

Vermouth

Cinzano Bianco Vermouth	Martini Bianco Vermouth
Cinzano Dry Vermouth	Martini Dry Vermouth
Cinzano Rosso Vermouth	Martini Rosso Vermouth

ESSENTIAL EQUIPMENT FOR A COCKTAIL BAR

Cocktail shaker	Waiter's friend corkscrew
Hawthorn Strainer	Bottle openers
Mixing glass	Ice scoop

Spoon with muddler

Moulinex Electric blender

Knife, cutting board

Measures (jiggers)

Can opener

Hand cloths for cleaning glasses

Ice bucket

Free pourers

Swizzle sticks, straws

Coasters and napkins

Scooper spoon (long teaspoon)

DESCRIPTION OF LIQUEURS AND SPIRITS

Advocaat: A combination of fresh egg whites, yolks, sugar, brandy and spirit. Limited shelf life, Recommend shelf life 12-15 months from manufacture.

Amaretto: A rich subtle liqueur with a unique almond flavour.

Angostura Bitters: An essential part of any bar or kitchen. A unique additive whose origins date back to 1824. A mysterious blend of natural herbs and spices, both a seasoning and flavouring agent, in both sweet and savoury dishes and drinks. Ideal for dieters as it is low in sodium and calories.

Baileys Irish Cream: The largest selling liqueur in the world. It is a blend of Irish Whiskey, softened by Irish Cream and other flavourings. It is a natural product.

Benedictine: A perfect end to a perfect meal. Serve straight, with ice, soda, or as part of a favourite cocktail.

Bourbon – Rebel Yell: Has a deep flavour of one of America's authentic bourbon whiskies.

Campari: A drink for many occasions, both as a long or short drink, or as a key ingredient in many fashionable cocktails.

Introduction

Cassis: Deep, rich purple promises and delivers a regal and robust flavour and aroma. Cassis lends itself to neat drinking or an endless array of delicious sauces and desserts.

Chartreuse: A liqueur available in either yellow or green colour. Made by the monks of the Carthusian order. The only world famous liqueur still made by monks.

Cherry Advocaat: Same as Advocaat, plus natural cherry flavours and colour is added.

Cherry Brandy: Is made from concentrated, morello cherry juice. Small quantity of bitter almonds and vanilla is added to make it more enjoyable as a neat drink before or after dinner. Excellent for mixers, topping, ice cream, fruit salads, pancakes, etc.

Coconut: A smooth liqueur, composed of exotic coconut, heightened with light-bodied white rum.

Cointreau: Made from a neutral grain spirit, as opposed to Cognac. An aromatic flavour of natural citrus fruits. A great mixer or delightful over ice.

Creme de Cacao Dark: Rich, deep chocolate. Smooth and classy. Serve on its own, or mix for all kinds of delectable treats.

Creme de Cacao White: This liqueur delivers a powerfully lively, full bodied chocolate flavour. Excellent ingredient when absence of colour is desired.

Creme de Grand Marnier: A blend of Grand Marnier and smooth French cream. A premium product, a very smooth taste with the orange/cognac flavour blending beautifully with smooth cream.

Creme de Menthe Green: Clear peppermint flavour, reminiscent of a fresh, crisp, clean winter's day in the mountains. Excellent mixer, a necessity in the gourmet kitchen.

Creme de Menthe White: As Creme de Menthe Green, when colour is not desired.

Curacao Blue: Same as Triple Sec, brilliant blue colour is added to make some cocktails more exciting.

Curacao Orange: Again, same as above, but stronger in orange, colouring is used for other varieties of cocktail mixers.

Curacao Triple Sec: Based on natural citrus fruits. Well known fact is citrus fruits are the most important aromatic flavour constituents. Interesting to know citrus fruit was known 2,000 years before Christ. As a liqueur one of the most versatile. Can be enjoyed with or without ice as a neat drink, or used in mixed cocktails more than any other liqueur. Triple Sec – also known as White Curacao.

Galliano: The distinguished taste! A classic liqueur that blends with a vast array of mixed drinks.

Gin – Gilbey's: Its aroma comes from using the highest quality juniper berries and other rare and subtle herbs. Perfect mixer for both short and long drinks.

Kirsch: A fruit brandy distilled from morello cherries.

Delicious drunk straight and excellent in a variety of food recipes.

Drambuie: A Scotch whisky liqueur. Made from a secret recipe dating back to 1745. "Dram Buidheach" the drink that satisfies.

Frangelico: A precious liqueur imported from Italy. Made from wild hazelnuts with infusions of berries and flowers to enrich the flavour.

Grand Marnier: An original blend of fine old Cognac and an extract of oranges. The recipe is over 150 years old

Kahlúa: A smooth, dark liqueur made from real coffee and fine clear spirits. Its origins are based in Mexico.

Lena Banana: Fresh ripe bananas are the perfect base for the definitive daiquiri and a host of other exciting fruit cocktails.

Malibu: A clear liqueur based on white rum with the subtle addition of coconut. Its distinctive taste blends naturally with virtually every mixer available.

Midori: Soft green, exudes freshness. Refreshing and mouthwatering honeydew melon. Simple yet complex. Smooth on the palate, serve on the rocks, or use to create summertime cocktails.

Ouzo: The traditional spirit aperitif of Greece. The distinctive flavour is derived mainly from the seed of the anise plant. A neutral grain spirit, flavoured with anise.

Peach: The flavour of fresh peaches and natural peach juice make this cocktail lover's dream.

Peachtree Schnapps: Crystal clear, light liqueur, bursting with the taste of ripe peaches. Drink chilled or on the rocks or mix with any soft drink or juice.

Pineapple: A just ripe, sun-filled delight. Delicious neat, a necessity for summertime cocktails.

Rum – Bacardi: A smooth, dry, light bodied rum, especially suited for drinks in which you require subtle aroma and delicate flavour.

Rum – Bacardi Gold: Matured in charred oak barrels to give a dry smooth taste and a clear golden colour. Use in Bacardi drinks where you want a fuller, mellow flavour.

Rum – Bundaberg: The most popular Australian rum, mixes well with all juices and splits.

Rye Whiskey – Canadian Club: The largest selling Canadian Whiskey in North America and Australia. Distilled from corn, rye and malted barley. A light, mild and delicate Whiskey, ideal for drinking straight or in mixed cocktails.

Sabra: A unique flavour which comes from tangy jaffa oranges, with a hint of chocolate.

Sambuca: The Italian electric taste experience. Made from elderberries with a touch of anise.

Sambuca – Lago Nera: An exciting encounter between Sambuca di Galliano and extracts of black elderberry.

Sambuca – Opal Nera: The black Sambuca. Perfect after dinner or as an aperitif. The delicate oil from the Elderbush. The rich flavour of anise, with the subtle essence of lemon. Mingled, they are the dark secret of Opal Nera's delightful flavour.

Scotch Whisky – Ballantine's: One of the top three scotch whiskies in the world. It is a blended whisky and is one of the very few "bottled in Scotland" products available in Australia.

Scotch Whisky – Johnnie Walker: Established 1820, distilled, blended and bottled in Scotland. Australia's largest selling scotch whisky.

Southern Comfort: A liqueur not a bourbon as often thought. It is unique, full-bodied liquor with a touch of sweetness. Its recipe is a secret, but it is known to be based on peaches and apricots. It is the largest selling liqueur in Australia.

Strawberry: Fluorescent red, unmistakable strawberry bouquet. Natural liqueur delivers a true to nature, fresh strawberry flavour.

Tennessee Whiskey – Jack Daniel's: Contrary to popular belief, Jack Daniel's is not a bourbon, it is a distinctive product called Tennessee Whiskey. Made from the 'old sour mash' process. Leached through hard maple charcoal, then aged in charred white oak barrels, at a controlled temperature, acquiring its body, bouquet and colour, yet remaining smooth.

Tequila – El Toro: A clear tequila imported from Mexico, with a scented clean character and slight burn, perfect for drinking straight, and is also a great mixer.

Tequila – Pepe Lopez: Distilled from the Mexcal variety of the agave plant – not Cacti. Pepe Lopez was named after a 19th Century Mexican bandit. A perfect mixer or drink straight with salt and lemon.

Tia Maria: A liqueur with a cane spirit base, and its flavour derived from the finest Jamaican coffee. It is not too sweet with a subtle taste of coffee.

Vandermint: A rich chocolate liqueur with the added zest of mint.

Vermouth: By description, Vermouth is a herbally infused wine. Three styles are most prevalent, these are:

Rosso: A bitter sweet herbal flavour, often drunk as an aperitif.

Bianco: Is light, fruity and refreshing. Mixes well with soda, lemonade and fruit juices.

Dry: Is crisp, light and dry and is used as a base for many cocktails.

Vodka: The second largest selling spirit in the world. Most Vodkas are steeped in tanks containing charcoal, but Smirnoff is pumped through ten columns of best hardwood charcoal for seven hours, removing all odours and impurities, making a superior quality product

A-Z

A.R.B.D.

20mL (0.66 oz) Southern Comfort

20mL (0.66 oz) Tia Maria

20mL (0.66 oz) blue curaçao

20mL (0.66 oz) cherry advocaat

Method
Layer in a Test Tube or shot glass
and serve.

ABBEY

60mL (2 oz) gin

1 dash sweet vermouth

30mL (1 oz) orange juice

garnish:

maraschino cherry

1 dash Angostura bitters

Method
Shake and strain into a 140mL
(5 oz) cocktail glass and serve.

ABC

5 ice cubes

*champagne or sparkling white
wine*

20mL (0.66 oz) Armagnac

garnish:

lemon slice

20mL (0.66 oz) Benedictine

orange segments

1 dash Angostura bitters

maraschino cherries

Method
Crack 2 ice cubes and place them
into a shaker with Armagnac,
Benedictine and Angostura bitters
and shake well. Crush remaining ice
cubes and empty into a goblet.
Drain contents of shaker of the
crushed ice and top with
champagne. Serve garnished
with lemon slice, orange segments
and cherries.

ABERDEEN ANGUS

Ingredients

Glass:

130mL Cocktail Glass

Mixers:

30mL (1 oz) scotch whisky

10mL (0.33 oz) Drambuie

1 tablespoon honey

10mL (0.oz) fresh lime juice

Method
Mix honey into scotch whisky and
add lime then warm Drambuie over
a low flame and pour. Garnish with
a plastic bull. Comments: A
traditional flambé.

ABORTION

30mL (1 oz) vodka

30mL (1 oz) sambuca

30mL (1 oz) Bailey's Irish cream

3 drops grenadine

Method
Layer into an 85mL (3 oz) cocktail
glass and serve.

ABSINTH

50mL (1.66 oz) Pernod

1 tsp anisette

2 tbsp water

1 dash orange bitters

Method
Shake ingredients with ice and strain into a chilled cocktail glass.

ACAPULCO I

30mL (1 oz) tequila

30mL (1 oz) dark rum

30mL (1 oz) Tia Maria

150mL (5 oz) coconut cream

Method
Shake ingredients and strain over ice into a 285mL (10 oz) cocktail glass and serve.

ACAPULCO II

30mL (1 oz) light rum

1 tsp sugar

15mL (0.25 oz) Cointreau or triple sec

½ egg white

15 mL (0.5 oz) lime juice

garnish:

mint leaves

Method
Shake all ingredients except mint leaves and strain over ice into an 3 oz cocktail glass and serve. Garnish with mint.

ADAM & EVE OLD-FASHIONED

1 sugar cube

3 ice cubes

1 dash Angostura bitters

40mL (1.5 oz) Tennessee whiskey

soda water

15 mL (0.5 oz) Galliano Liverno

Method
Place the sugar cube in the bottom of an Old Fashioned glass. Add bitters and cover sugar cube with soda water. Add ice, whiskey, Galliano Liverno, and serve.

ADIOS MOTHER

60mL (2 oz) vodka

1 dash triple sec

60mL (2 oz) white rum

90mL (3 oz) lemon juice

60mL (2 oz) melon liqueur

3 tsp sugar

1 dash blue curaçao

Method
Pour ingredients over ice into a 285mL (10 oz) tulip champagne glass and serve.

ADMIRAL CANNON

45mL (1.25 oz) bourbon

15mL (0.25 oz) lemon juice

30mL (1 oz) white rum

1 tsp maple syrup

Method
Shake and strain into a 140mL (5 oz) cocktail glass over cracked ice and serve.

ADONIS

30mL (1 oz) sweet sherry
1 dash Angostura bitters
20mL (0.66 oz) sweet vermouth
3 ice cubes

Method
Shake and strain into an 85mL
(3 oz) cocktail glass.

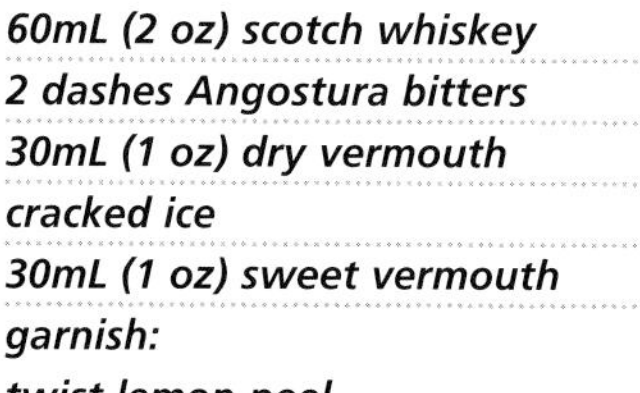

AFFINITY

60mL (2 oz) scotch whiskey
2 dashes Angostura bitters
30mL (1 oz) dry vermouth
cracked ice
30mL (1 oz) sweet vermouth
garnish:
twist lemon peel

Method
Half fill a mixing glass with cracked
ice, add liquid ingredients and stir.
Strain into a 140mL (5 oz)
champagne glass, garnish with
lemon peel and serve.

AFRICAN COFFEE

hot black coffee
sugar (optional)
30mL (1 oz) Afrikoko
marshmallow cream

Method
Fill a goblet with hot coffee and
add Afrikoko. Add sugar, if desired,
stirring well. Float marshmallow
cream on top and serve.

AFRICAN NIGHTS

20mL (0.66 oz) melon liqueur
20mL (0.66 oz) cream
20mL (0.66 oz) Kahlúa
20mL (0.66 oz) milk
20mL (0.66 oz) Afrikoko
garnish:
grated chocolate

Method
Shake ingredients and strain into
a 140mL (5 oz) cocktail glass.
Sprinkle with grated chocolate
and serve.

AFRICAN NIPPLE

30mL (1 oz) vodka
1 tsp grenadine
30mL (1 oz) Afrikoko
60mL (2 oz) cream

Method
Shake and strain into a champagne
saucer and serve.

AFTER EIGHT

15mL (0.5 oz) Kahlúa
20mL (0.66 oz) Bailey's Irish cream
*10mL(0.33 oz) crème de
menthe*

Method
Layer ingredients in order into a
tall Dutch cordial glass or shot
glass and serve.

A

AGENT 99

15mL (0.5 oz) parfait amour
15mL(0.5 oz) ouzo
15mL (0.5 oz) Bailey's Irish cream

Method
Layer ingredients in order into a tall Dutch cordial glass or shot glass and serve.

AIDA'S CURSE

30mL (1 oz) melon liqueur
45mL (1.5 oz) pineapple juice
30mL (1 oz) Cointreau
10mL (0.33 oz) banana liqueur
15mL (0.5oz) lemon juice

Method
Shake first 4 ingredients. Pour banana liqueur in side of a 5 oz cocktail glass. Add shaken ingredients and serve.

ALABAMA SLAMMER

30mL (1 oz) amaretto
15mL (0.5 oz) sloe gin
30mL (1 oz) Southern Comfort
1 dash orange juice

Method
Shake and strain into a 3 oz cocktail glass and serve.

ALASKA

60mL (2 oz) gin
3 ice cubes
20mL (0.66 oz) yellow Chartreuse
garnish:
lemon peel

Method
Mix ingredients in a mixing glass. Strain into a 3 oz cocktail glass. Garnish with lemon peel and serve.

ALEXANDER

45mL (1.5 oz) gin
3 ice cubes
20mL (0.66 oz) crème de cacao
nutmeg
15mL (0.5 oz) fresh cream

Method
Shake liquid ingredients and strain into a 3 oz cocktail glass. Cross two straws over glass, sprinkle nutmeg over the top. Remove straws and serve.

ALFONSO

15mL (0.5 oz) dry gin
4 dashes sweet vermouth
15mL (0.5 oz) French vermouth
1 dash Angostura bitters
30mL (1 oz) Grand Marnier
4 ice cubes

Method
Shake and strain into a 3 oz cocktail glass and serve.

ALICE

30mL (1 oz) scotch whiskey
30mL (1 oz) kümmel liqueur
30mL (1 oz) sweet vermouth
cracked ice

Method
Half fill mixing glass with ice and
add liquid ingredients. Stir and
strain into 5 oz champagne glass.
Garnish with lemon peel and serve.

ALICE IN WONDERLAND

Glass:
170mL Champagne Flute
Mixers:
100mL (3.3 oz) grapefruit juice
30mL (1 oz) green tea
20mL (0.66 oz) lemon juice
15mL (0.5 oz) sugar syrup
top up with soda

Method
Build over ice and top up with
soda. Garnish with white grapes.

ALL NIGHT

30mL (1 oz) tequila
1 dash grenadine
20mL (0.66 oz) lime juice
3 ice cubes
1 egg white
garnish:
1 maraschino cherry

Method
Shake ingredients and strain into a
3 oz cocktail glass. Garnish with
cherry and serve.

ALMOND ORANGE FROST

Glass:
240ml Champagne Sherbert Glass
Mixers:
15mL (0.5 oz) Amaretto di Galliano
15mL (0.5 oz) Frangelico
15mL (0.5 oz) Chambord
10mL (0.33 oz) fresh lime juice
10mL (0.33 oz) fresh lemon juice
1 teaspoon chopped almonds
2 scoops orange sherbert

Method
Blend with ice. Garnish with orange
slice and chopped almonds.

ALMOND JOY

30mL (1 oz) amaretto
90mL (3 oz) milk
1 dash crème de cacao
30mL (1 oz) coconut syrup
1 scoop ice cream
garnish:
1 pineapple wedge

Method
Blend ingredients and pour into a
10 oz tulip glass, garnish with a
pineapple wedge, straws and serve.

ALTERED STATES SHOOTER

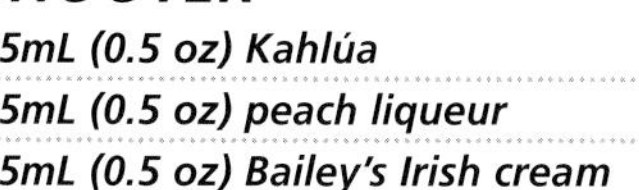

15mL (0.5 oz) Kahlúa
15mL (0.5 oz) peach liqueur
15mL (0.5 oz) Bailey's Irish cream

Method
Layer in a shot glass and serve.

AMARETTO CHOCO CREAM

Glass:
240ml Champagne Sherbert Glass
Mixers:
30ml (1 oz) Amaretto di Galliano
30ml (1 oz) Kahlúa
30ml (1 oz) Chocolate Syrup
2 scoops of vanilla ice cream

Method
Blend without ice and pour over ice. Garnish with aerosol whipped cream.

AMARETTO SOUR

45mL (1.5 oz) amaretto
1/2 lemon, squeezed
soda water
3 ice cubes

Method
Shake amaretto, lemon juice and ice, pour into a sour glass and top with soda. Garnish with a strip of lemon peel and serve.

AMARETTO STINGER

45mL (1.5 oz) amaretto
3 ice cubes
25mL (0.83 oz) white crème de menthe

Method
Shake well, strain into a 3 oz cocktail glass and serve.

AMERICAN BEAUTY

15mL (0.5 oz) brandy
15mL (0.5 oz) grenadine
15mL (0.5 oz) dry vermouth
15 mL (0.5 oz) orange juice
port wine
3 dashes white crème de menthe

Method
Shake all ingredients except port wine. Strain into a 5 oz glass, top with port wine and serve.

AMERICANO

30mL (1 oz) Campari
soda water
60mL (2 oz) sweet vermouth
garnish:
1 twist lemon
3 ice cubes

Method
Place all ingredients except soda into a 10 oz highball glass and stir well. Top with soda and serve.

AMSTERDAM

30mL (1 oz) gin
4 dashes orange bitters
15mL (0.5 oz) orange juice
15mL (0.5 oz) Cointreau
cracked ice

Method
Shake ingredients and strain into a 3 oz cocktail glass and serve.

ANABOLIC STEROID SHOOTER

30mL (1 oz) Midori

30mL (1 oz) Cointreau

30mL (1 oz) blue curaçao

Method
Layer in a shot glass and serve.

ANDY WILLIAMS

60mL (2 oz) Clayton's Tonic

15mL (0.5 oz) lime juice

dash sugar syrup

top up with soda water

Method
Shake with ice and pour.
Garnish with a thin lime slice
floated in the drink.

ANGEL DEW

15mL (0.5 oz) Benedictine

15mL (0.5 oz) Bailey's Irish cream

Method
Layer in a shot glass and serve.

ANGEL TIP SHOOTER

15mL (0.5 oz) crème de cacao

15mL (0.5 oz) Bailey's Irish cream

Method
Layer in a shot glass. Garnish with
an Impaled cherry and serve.

ANGEL PUNCH

100mL (3.33 oz) apple juice

30mL (1 oz) green tea

20mL (0.66 oz) lemon juice

15mL (0.5 oz) sugar syrup

top up with soda

Method
Build over ice and top up with soda.
Garnish with sprinkled tea leaves.

ANGEL WING SHOOTER

15mL (0.5 oz) crème de cacao

15mL (0.5oz) Bailey's cream

15mL (0.5oz) brandy

Method
Layer in order in a shot glass
and serve.

ANGEL'S DELIGHT

30mL (1 oz) Cointreau

50mL (1.66 oz) cream

30mL (1 oz) gin

1 dash grenadine

Method
Shake and strain into a 5 oz
cocktail glass and serve.

ANGEL'S FACE

20mL (0.66 oz) apricot brandy

10mL (0.33 oz) Calvados

20mL (0.66 oz) gin

3 ice cubes

Method
Shake and strain into 3 oz cocktail
glass and serve.

ANGEL'S KISS NO. 1

20mL (0.66 oz) apricot liqueur

1 tsp Thickened cream

Method
Place apricot liqueur in a
90mL cocktail glass, float cream
and serve.

ANGEL'S KISS NO. 2

10mL (0.33 oz) crème de cacao

10mL (0.33 oz) Prunelle

10mL (0.33 oz) crème de Violette

10mL (0.33 oz) fresh cream

Method
Layer in a liqueur glass and serve.

ANGEL'S KISS NO. 3

10 mL (0.33 oz) maraschino liqueur

10 mL (0.33 oz) Benedictine

10 mL (0.33 oz) parfait amour

10 mL (0.33 oz) cognac

10 mL (0.33 oz) yellow Chartreuse

10 mL (0.33 oz) cream

Method
Layer in order in a Mousse Cafe
glass and serve.

ANGEL'S KISS NO. 4

30mL (1 oz) crème de cacao

30mL (1 oz) gin

30mL (1 oz) cream

30mL (1 oz) brandy

Method
Layer in order in a 150mL cocktail
glass and serve.

ONGELIQUE

30mL (1 oz) ouzo

30mL (1 oz) fresh cream

30mL (1 oz) advocaat

30mL (1 oz) orange juice

30mL (1 oz) Strega

garnish:

1 maraschino cherry

Method
Shake and strain into a champagne
saucer. Garnish with cherry and serve.

ANGRY FIJIAN

30mL (1 oz) banana liqueur

30mL (1 oz) Bailey's Irish cream

30mL (1 oz) Malibu

Method
Layer in a 3 oz cocktail glass and
serve.

ANWAR SADAT

30mL (1 oz) Sabra liqueur

mineral water

30mL (1 oz) advocaat

Method
Place Sabra and advocaat in a 5oz
cocktail glass. Top with mineral water.
Garnish with Umbrella and serve.

APOLLO 13

60mL (2 oz) white rum
1 dash grenadine
15mL (0.5 oz) Galliano Liverno
60mL (2 oz) fresh cream
15mL (0.5 oz) Grand Marnier
cracked ice

Method
Shake and strain into a 5 oz champagne saucer. Garnish with a maraschino cherry and serve.

APOTHEKE

20mL brandy
15mL (0.5 oz) Fernet-Branca
15mL (0.5 oz) crème de menthe

Method
Place ingredients in a 3 oz cocktail glass and serve.

APPEASE ME

30mL (1 oz) mango liqueur
60mL (2 oz) orange juice
20mL (0.66 oz) advocaat
30mL (1 oz) cream
20mL (0.66 oz(vodka
2 slices mango

Method
Blend ingredients with ice and pour into a 10 oz highball glass. Garnish with the pulp of half a passionfruit and serve with straws.

APPLE À LA MODE

Glass:
285mL Tulip Wine Glass
Mixers:
30mL (1 oz) Bacardi
2 sprinkles Cinnamon powder
1/2 ripe apple (seedless)
60mL (2 oz) apple cider
2 scoops vanilla ice cream

Method
Blend without ice and pour into glass over ice. Garnish with apple slice and sprinkle of cinnamon.

APPLE ANGEL

30mL (1 oz) brandy
1 maraschino cherry
30mL (1 oz) Calvados
garnish:
1 slice apple
1 dash grenadine
3 ice cubes
15mL (0.5 oz) lemon juice

Method
Shake and strain into a 3 oz cocktail glass. Garnish with apple, cherry and serve.

APPLE JACK

Glass:
210mL Old Fashioned Spirit Glass
Mixers:
30mL (1 oz) Jack Daniel's
top up with fresh apple juice

Method
Build over ice. Garnish with an apple slice.

APPLE JACKRABBIT

30mL (1 oz) Calvados
1 tsp sugar syrup
20mL (0.66 oz) orange juice
1 dash orange bitters
10mL (0.33 oz) lemon juice
2-3 ice cubes

Method
Shake and strain into a 3 oz
cocktail glass and serve.

APPLE MAGIC

30mL (1 oz) Midori
10mL (0.33 oz) orange
15mL (0.5 oz) Southern Comfort
90mL (3 oz) apple juice
15mL (0.5 oz) Grand Marnier

Method
Blend and pour into a colada glass.
Garnish with a slice of apple and
strawberry and serve.

APPLE SPECIAL

60mL (2 oz) brandy
1 slice apple
15mL (0.5 oz) Cointreau
3 ice cubes
dry apple cider (top up)
garnish:
1 apple slice

Method
Shake ice, brandy and Cointreau.
Strain into a 10 oz highball glass
and top with soda. Garnish with
apple slice and serve with straws.

APPLE STRAWBERRY CORDIAL

1 apple, peeled and cored
3 strawberries
30mL (1 oz) scotch whisky
1 teaspoon brown sugar
allspice, nutmeg

Method
Blend over ice and pour into a
210mL Old Fashioned Spirit Glass.
Garnish with a strawberry and
sprinkle of nutmeg

APRES SKI

30mL (1 oz) crème de menthe
15mL (0.5 oz) Pernod
15mL (0.5 oz) vodka
lemonade

Method
Third fill a 10 oz highball glass with
ice and pour ingredients over ice. Top
with lemonade and serve with straws.

APRICOT

30mL (1 oz) gin
2 drops Angostura bitters
15mL (0.5 oz) apricot brandy
1/2 tsp lemon juice
2 dashes grenadine

Method
Shake and strain into a 3 oz
cocktail glass and serve.

APRICOT MARIA

30mL (1 oz) Tia Maria
60mL (2 oz) apricot nectar
15mL (0.5 oz) vodka
3 ice cubes

Method
Blend and pour into a 5 oz cocktail glass and serve.

APRICOT RICKEY

30mL (1 oz) Apricot Liqueur
top up with soda
squeeze of lime, optional

Method
Build over ice and top up with soda. Garnish with a slice of lime.

APRIL SHOWER

30mL (1 oz) brandy
60mL (2 oz) orange juice
30mL (1 oz) Benedictine
2 ice cubes
soda water (top up)

Method
Pour ingredients except soda into a 10 oz highball glass. Stir, top with soda and serve with straws.

AQUAVIT FIZZ

45mL (1.5 oz) Aquavit
30mL (1oz) lemon juice
15mL (0.5 oz) Cherry Heering
10mL (0.33 oz) sugar syrup
1 egg white
top up with soda

Method
Shake over ice and strain then top up with soda. Garnish with a red cherry.

AQUA THUNDER

10mL (0.33 oz) blue curaçao
10mL (0.33 oz) lemon juice
10mL (0.33 oz) banana liqueur
soda water (top up)
30mL (1 oz) Midori

Method
Build ingredients over ice in a 5 oz cocktail glass. Garnish with swizzle stick, a slice of lemon and serve.

ARCADIA No. 1

25mL (0.83 oz) Lochan Ora
garnish:
1 spiral lemon peel
60mL (2 oz) saki (hot)
1 spiral orange peel
15mL (0.5 oz) boiling water

Method
Pour Lochan Ora into a 4 oz cocktail glass. Stir and Ignite, pour remaining ingredients over the top. Garnish with a spiral of orange peel and lemon peel and serve.

After Eight
(Recipe page 24)

Bananarama
(Recipe page 41)

Banana Split
(Recipe page 41)

Bee Sting
(Recipe page 42)

B&B
(Recipe page 36)

Blue Hawaiian
(Recipe page 51)

ARCADIA No. 2

45mL (1 oz) Midori
1 dash grenadine
15mL (0.5 oz) lemon juice
30mL (0.5 oz) orange juice

Method
In a 10 oz highball glass place a scoop of crushed ice. Blend ingredients except grenadine and pour over ice. Add grenadine and serve with straws.

ARGYLE TAVERN

60mL (2 oz) brandy
15mL (0.5 oz) almond liqueur
15mL (0.5 oz) Galliano Liverno
garnish: 1 maraschino cherry
30mL (1 oz) dry vermouth
cracked ice

Method
Half fill a mixing glass with cracked ice and add ingredients. Stir and strain into a 5 oz cocktail glass, garnish with cherry and serve.

ASPIRATION

30mL (1 oz) Midori
30mL (1 oz) pineapple juice
15mL (0.5 oz) Galliano Liverno
1 slice kiwifruit
5mL (0.17 oz) white curaçao
1 dash coconut cream

Method
Blend and pour into a colada glass. Garnish with a slice of kiwifruit and serve.

ASTRONAUT

30mL (1 oz) Coruba Rum
30mL (1 oz) Smirnoff Vodka
10mL (0.33 oz) fresh lemon juice
6 drops of passionfruit pulp

Method
Shake over ice and strain. Garnish with 1/2 scoop of passionfruit.

ATOMIC BOMB SHOOTER

30mL (1 oz) Tia Maria
15mL (0.5 oz) gin

Method
Layer in a shot glass and serve.

AUSSIE SLINGER

45mL (1.5 oz) any white Spirit
lemonade
30mL (1 oz) grenadine
1 dash Angostura bitters
60mL (2 oz) lemon juice
1 cracked ice

Method
Half fill a 10 oz highball glass with cracked ice, add ingredients and top with lemonade. Garnish with 1/2 orange slice, 1/2 lemon slice, 1 maraschino cherry, swizzle stick, straws and serve.

AUSTRALIA III

30mL (1 oz) Midori
1 egg yolk
15mL (0.5 oz) Grand Marnier
1/2 kiwifruit
15mL (0.5 oz) pineapple juice
4 ice cubes

Method
Blend ingredients and pour into a 5 oz tulip glass. Garnish with a slice of kiwifruit and serve.

AUSTRALIAN CRAWL

15mL (0.5 oz) Bundaberg rum
15mL (0.5 oz) scotch whiskey
15mL (0.5 oz) gin
Coca-Cola
15mL (0.5 oz) vodka
cracked ice

Method
Build ingredients except Coca-Cola over ice in a 10 oz highball glass. Top with Coca-Cola, garnish with a lemon wheel, straws and serve.

AUSTRALIAN GOLD

30mL (1 oz) Bundaberg rum
30mL (1 oz) Galliano Liverno
30mL (1 oz) mango liqueur
garnish:
pineapple wedge

Method
Build over ice in a 5 oz cocktail glass. Garnish and serve.

AUSTRALIS

20mL (0.66 oz) white rum
15mL (0.5 oz) cream
20mL (0.66 oz) melon liqueur
20mL (0.66 oz) pineapple juice
20mL (0.66 oz) blue curaçao
garnish:
1 slice pineapple
3 ice cubes
1 maraschino cherry

Method
Shake and strain into a 5 oz cocktail glass. Garnish and serve.

A

AUTUMN LEAF

30mL (1 oz) Arrak
30mL (1 oz) Dazzinger goldwasser
30mL (1 oz) crème de cacao

Method
Mix in mixing glass with cracked
ice, strain into 3 oz cocktail glass
and serve.

AVALANCHE

30mL (1 oz) Cointreau
30mL (1 oz) orange juice
30mL (1 oz) Tia Maria
50 mL (1.66 oz) cream

Method
Shake and strain into a
champagne glass and serve.

B&B

30mL (1 oz) brandy
30mL (1 oz) Benedictine

Method
Pour over ice in a brandy Balloon
and serve.

B&G

30mL (1 oz) Benedictine
30mL (1 oz) Grand Mariner

Method
Pour over ice in an Old Fashioned
glass.

B&P

30mL (1 oz) Benedictine
60mL (2 oz) port

Method
Pour over ice in a brandy Balloon
and serve.

B.B.C. SHOOTER

15mL (0.5 oz) Benedictine
15mL (0.5 oz) Cointreau
15mL (0.5 oz) Bailey's Irish cream

Method
Layer in order in a shot glass and
serve.

B.B.G. SHOOTER

15mL (0.5 oz) Benedictine
15mL (0.5 oz) Grand Marnier
15mL (0.5 oz) Bailey's Irish cream

Method
Layer in order in a shot glass and
serve.

B52

30mL (1 oz) Kahlúa
30mL (1 oz) Bailey's Irish cream
30mL (1 oz) Grand Marnier
crushed ice

Method
Place a scoop full of crushed ice in
a 5 oz cocktail glass. Layer
ingredients and serve.

B53 SHOOTER

10mL (0.33 oz) Kahlúa
10mL (0.33 oz) tequila
10mL (0.33 oz) Bailey's Irish cream

Method
Layer in order in a shot glass and
serve.

B54 SHOOTER

10mL (0.33 oz) Kahlúa
10mL (0.33 oz) Grand Marnier
15mL (0.5 oz) Bailey's Irish cream
10mL (0.33 oz) tequila

Method
Layer in order in a shot glass and serve.

BACARDI

45mL (1.5 oz) Bacardi rum
1 dash egg white
1 dash grenadine
3 ice cubes
15mL (0.5 oz) lemon juice
garnish:
1 maraschino cherry

Method
Shake and strain into a 3 oz cocktail glass. Garnish with cherry on a toothpick and serve.

BACARDI BLOSSOM

40mL (1.33 oz) Bacardi rum
3 ice cubes
10mL (0.33 oz) orange juice
10mL (0.33 oz) lemon juice
1 tsp sugar

Method
Shake and strain into a 3 oz cocktail glass and serve.

BACARDI NO. 2

60mL (2 oz) Bacardi rum
1 egg white
5 mL (0.17 oz) grenadine
ice
20mL (0.66 oz) lemon or lime juice

Method
Shake and strain into a 5 oz cocktail glass and serve.

BACCILE BALL

30mL (1 oz) amaretto
30mL (1 oz) soda water
60mL (2 oz) orange juice

Method
Pour ingredients over ice in a rocks glass and serve.

BAD GIRL

15mL (0.5 oz) Malibu
10mL (0.33 oz) Galliano Liverno
15mL (0.5 oz) banana liqueur
30mL (1 oz) cream
15mL (0.5 oz) advocaat

Method
Blend ingredients, pour into a 5 oz champagne glass and serve.

BAHAMA MAMA

15mL (0.5 oz) Bacardi Gold Rum
15mL (0.5 oz) Malibu
15mL (0.5 oz) Banana Liqueur
15mL (0.5 oz) Grenadine
100mL (3.33 oz) orange juice
60mL (2 oz) pineapple juice

Method
Blend over ice. Garnish with a
pineapple wedge and leaves.

BAILEY'S COCONUT CREAM

30mL (1 oz) Bailey's Irish cream
30mL (1 oz) cream
15mL (0.5 oz) Malibu
60mL (2 oz) orange juice

Method
Shake ingredients and pour over
cracked ice in a 5 oz wine glass.
Add a dash of grenadine and serve
with straws.

BALALANKA

40mL (1.33 oz) vodka
garnish:
1 spiral orange peel
15mL (0.5 oz) Cointreau
3 ice cubes
15mL (0.5 oz) lemon juice

Method
Shake and strain into a 3 oz
cocktail glass. Garnish with orange
peel and serve.

BALI HI

30mL (1 oz) advocaat
orange soft drink
10mL (0.33 oz) orange curaçao
garnish:
1 slice orange
10mL (0.33 oz) Mandarin liqueur
1 maraschino cherry

Method
Mix ingredients except soft drink
with cracked ice in a 10 oz highball
glass. Top with soft drink, garnish
and serve with straws.

BALL OF FIRE

50mL (1.66 oz) white rum
lemonade
60mL (2 oz) advocaat
cracked ice
30mL (1 oz) Pernod
garnish:
maraschino cherry
grenadine

Method
Half fill a 10 oz highball glass with
cracked ice. Add rum, Pernod and
advocaat. Top with lemonade and
float grenadine. Garnish with cherry,
swizzle stick. straws and serve.

BALLET RUSSE

30mL (1oz) Smirnoff Vodka
15mL (0.5 oz) Creme de Cassis
15mL (0.5 oz) fresh lime juice
15mL (0.5 oz) fresh lemon juice

Method
Shake with ice and strain. Garnish
with an orange slice and a red cherry.

BALTIMORE ZOO

15mL (0.5 oz) Coruba Rum
15mL (0.5 oz) Gilbey's Gin
15mL (0.5 oz) Cointreau
60mL (2 oz) cranberry juice
top with draft beer

Method
Shake with ice and strain then top
with draft beer.

BAMBOO

30mL (1 oz) dry vermouth
2 ice cubes
30mL (1 oz) dry sherry
1 dash orange bitters
2 dashes Angostura bitters
garnish:
1 maraschino cherry

Method
Mix ingredients in a mixing glass,
strain into a 5 oz cocktail glass.
Garnish with cherry and serve.

BANANA BENDER

30mL (1 oz) Cointreau
60mL (2 oz) cream
30mL (1 oz) banana liqueur
1/2 banana

Method
Blend ingredients until smooth,
pour into a 5 oz champagne glass
and serve.

BANANA BENDER NO. 2.

30mL (1 oz) banana liqueur
30mL (1 oz) cream
30mL (1 oz) Cointreau
2 slices banana
30mL (1 oz) pineapple juice
1/2 Scoop crushed ice

Method
Blend until smooth, pour into a
6 oz flute glass and serve.

BANANA BLISS

30mL (1 oz) cognac
crushed ice
30mL (1 oz) banana liqueur

Method
Fill a 6 oz Old Fashioned glass
with crushed ice, Build liquid
ingredients and serve.

BANANA COLADA

45mL (1.5 oz) Bacardi light rum
1 dash cream
15mL (0.5 oz) banana liqueur
1/2 banana
15mL (0.5 oz) Malibu
60mL (2 oz) pineapple juice
30mL (1 oz) coconut cream
1 Scoop ice cream

Method
Blend until smooth and pour into
a colada glass. Garnish with a
pineapple wedge, straws and serve.

BANANA JAFFA

15mL (0.5 oz) Kahlúa
30mL (1 oz) cream
15mL (0.5 oz) brandy
1/2 banana
30mL (1 oz) orange juice

Method
Blend until smooth, pour into a 10
oz highball glass. Garnish with an
orange wheel. pineapple wedge,
straws and serve.

BANANA COW

30mL (1 oz) white rum
45mL (1.5 oz) cream
30mL (1 oz) crème de banana
garnish:
nutmeg
1 dash grenadine

Method
Shake and pour into a 5 oz cocktail
glass. Sprinkle with nutmeg and
serve.

BANANA MARGARITA

30mL (1 oz) tequila
30mL (1 oz) lemon juice
15mL (0.5 oz) Cointreau
1/2 small banana
15mL (0.5 oz) banana liqueur
cracked ice

Method
Blend until smooth, pour into a salt
rimmed margarita glass and serve.

BANANA PEEL

45mL (1.5 oz) vodka
60mL (2 oz) orange juice
45mL (1.5oz) banana liqueur

Method
Shake and strain over ice in a 5 oz
Old Fashioned glass and serve.

BANANA CREAMY

30mL (1 oz) banana liqueur
15mL (0.5 oz) cream
90mL (3 oz) milk
1 banana

Method
Blend until smooth, pour into a
5 oz champagne glass and serve.

BANANA SPLIT

30mL (1 oz) banana liqueur
15mL (0.5 oz) cream
30mL (1 oz) crème de cacao

Method
Shake and strain into a 3 oz
cocktail glass. Garnish with a
banana wheel and serve.

BANANA SPLIT SHOOTER

15mL (0.5 oz) Kahlúa
10mL (0.33 oz) grenadine
15 mL (0.5 oz) banana liqueur
whipped cream

Method
Layer in order in a shot glass and
serve.

BANANA WONDER

20mL (0.66 oz) Kahlúa
30mL (1 oz) cream
20mL (0.66) Bailey's Irish cream
1/2 banana

Method
Blend until smooth, pour into a 5
oz cocktail glass. Garnish with a
slice of banana and serve.

BANANARAMA

30mL (1 oz) vodka
1 banana
30mL (1 oz) Kahlúa
60mL (2 oz) cream
15mL (0.5 oz) Bailey's Irish cream

Method
Blend with ice and pour into a 5 oz
cocktail glass. Garnish with two
banana wheels and serve.

BANGER

30mL (1 oz) Bacardi rum
180mL (6 oz) orange juice
15mL (0.5 oz) Galliano Liverno
cracked ice

Method
Pour into 10 oz highball glass.
Garnish with orange wheel, straws
and serve.

BANGO

45mL (1.5 oz) mango liqueur
slice pineapple
20mL (0.66 oz) Malibu
1/2 banana
60mL (2 oz) pineapple juice

Method
Blend until smooth, pour into a
flute glass and serve.

BANSHEE

30mL (1 oz) rum
60mL (2 oz) cream
20mL (0.66 oz) crème de cacao
1 banana
15mL (0.5 oz) banana liqueur

Method
Blend until smooth, pour into a
brandy Balloon and serve.

BANSHEE NO. 2

30mL (1 oz) banana liqueur
60mL (2 oz) cream
30mL (1 oz) white crème de cacao
ice

Method
Shake and strain into a 5 oz
cocktail glass. Garnish with a cherry
and serve.

BEAR HUG

30mL (1 oz) Bailey's Irish cream
60mL (2 oz) cream
20mL (0.66 oz) vodka.

Method
Shake and strain into a 5 oz
cocktail glass and serve.

BEE STING SHOOTER

20mL (0.66 oz) tequila
10mL (0.33 oz) yellow Chartreuse

Method
Layer in order in a shot glass, Ignite
and serve.

BELLINI

champagne
1 large peach
1 dash amaretto
garnish:
1 slice peach

Method
Liquidise the peach in a blender,
pour into a flute glass. Add dash of
amaretto and top with chilled
champagne. Garnish with peach
slice, straws and serve.

BELLINI NO. 2

45mL (1.5 oz) peach juice
90mL (1.5 oz) champagne (chilled)

Method
Place peach juice in a tulip flute,
lop with champagne and serve.

BELLY DANCER

Ingredients
Glass:
90mL Cocktail Glass – Frosted
Mixers:
30mL (1oz) cream
15mL (0.5 oz) lime juice
60mL (2 oz) coconut cream
15mL (0.5 oz) Grenadine

Method
Shake over ice and strain. Garnish with grated coconut.

BERLIN

20mL (0.66 oz) gin
20mL (0.66 oz) orange juice
20mL (0.66 oz) Madeira
3 ice cubes
1 dash Angostura bitters

Method
Crush ice and shake with other ingredients. Pour into a 5 oz cocktail glass and serve with straws.

BERLIN BINGE

30mL (1 oz) bourbon
30mL (1 oz) vodka
30mL (1 oz) gin
garnish:
1 green olive
30mL (1 oz) cognac

Method
Mix ingredients in a 4 oz cocktail glass, garnish with olive and serve.

BERMUDA ROSE

Ingredients
Glass:
90mL Cocktail Glass
Mixers:
30mL (1 oz) Gilbey's Gin
10mL (0.33 oz) lime juice
5ml Grenadine
4-5 drops of Apricot Brandy

Method
Shake over ice and strain. Garnish with a slice of lime.

BERMUDA TRIANGLE

30mL (1 oz) blue curaçao
60mL (2 oz) pineapple juice
30mL (1 oz) Bacardi rum
crushed ice
20mL (0.66 oz) amaretto
garnish:
pineapple wedge

Method
Blend until smooth, pour into a 5 oz cocktail glass.
garnish with pineapple wedge and serve.

BERRY A RET TO

30mL (1 oz) amaretto

60mL (2 oz) milk

1 scoop ice cream

3-6 strawberries

Method
Blend and pour into a 6 oz tulip
glass. garnish with a strawberry,
straws and serve.

BESSIE & JESSIE

60mL (2 oz) Blended whiskey

180mL (6 oz) milk

30mL (1 oz) advocaat

ice

Method
Shake ice, whiskey and milk. Pour
into a 10 oz highball glass, Float
advocaat and serve with straws.

BETWEEN THE SHEETS

10mL (0.33 oz) brandy

juice 1/2 lemon

10mL (0,33 oz) rum

ice

10mL (0.33 oz) triple sec

Method
Shake ingredients, strain into a
3 oz cocktail glass and serve.

BETWEEN THE SHEETS. NO. 2

30mL (1 oz) brandy

15mL (0.5 oz) lemon juice

30mL (1 oz) white rum

cracked ice

30mL (1 oz) Cointreau

Method
Shake and strain into a 5 oz
cocktail glass and serve.

BIKINI

90mL (3 oz) vodka

30mL (1 oz) milk

15mL (0.5 oz) lemon juice

Method
Shake and strain into a 5 oz
cocktail glass and serve.

BILL BAILEY

60mL (2 oz) Bailey's Irish cream

soda water

30mL (1 oz) vodka

ice

Method
Pour ingredients over ice in a
colada glass and serve.

BILL BRONX

45mL (1.5 oz) gin
15mL (0.5 oz) orange juice
15mL (0.5 oz) sweet vermouth
garnish:
orange and lemon slices
15mL (0.5 oz) dry vermouth
ice

Method
Shake ingredients and strain into 5 oz cocktail glass, garnish with orange and lemon and serve.

BLACK DREAM SHOOTER

20mL (0.66 oz) Opal Nera
10mL (0.33 oz) Bailey's Irish cream

Method
Layer in a shot glass and serve.

BLACK FOREST

30mL (1 oz) vodka
90mL (3 oz) apple juice
30mL (1 oz) Cointreau
1 tbsp Raspberries
15mL (0.5 oz) Blackberry liqueur

Method
Blend until smooth, pour over ice in a 10 oz highball glass.
Serve with straws.

BLACK HELL SHOOTER

30mL (1 oz) Opal Nera
30mL (1 oz) strawberry liqueur
30mL (1 oz) Midori

Method
Layer in a shot glass and serve.

BLACKJACK

30mL (1 oz) Kirsch
40mL (1.33 oz) ice coffee
5mL (0.17 oz) Milne Brandy

Method
Stir with ice and pour into a 130ml Cocktail Glass. Garnish with coffee granules.

BLACK JACK SHOOTER

30mL (1 oz) Kahlúa
25mL (0.87 oz) ouzo

Method
Layer in a shot glass and serve.

BLACK MAGIC

30mL (1 oz) Jamaican rum
30mL (1 oz) pineapple juice
15mL (0.5 oz) Kahlúa
15mL (0.5 oz) lemon juice
30mL (1 oz) mango liqueur
2 slices mango
30mL (1 oz) orange juice
1 Scoop ice

Method
Blend and pour into a brandy Balloon, add two black straws and serve.

BLACK NIPPLE SHOOTER

45mL (1.5 oz) Opal Nera
45mL (1.5 oz) Bailey's Irish cream

Method
Layer in a shot glass and serve.

BLACK NUTS

30mL (1 oz) Frangelico
crushed ice
30mL (1 oz) Opal Nera

Method
Build ingredients over ice in a 3 oz cocktail glass and serve.

BLACK ON BLUE SHOOTER

15mL (0.5 oz) Opal Nera
15mL (0.5 oz) Blue sambuca

Method
Layer in a shot glass and serve.

BLACK ON GREEN SHOOTER

15mL (0.5 oz) Opal Nera
15mL (0.5 oz) green sambuca

Method
Layer in a shot glass and serve.

BLACK ON RED SHOOTER

15mL (0.5 oz) Opal Nera
15mL (0.5 oz) red sambuca

Method
Layer in a shot glass and serve.

BLACK ON WHITE SHOOTER

15mL (0.5 oz) Opal Nera
15mL (0.5 oz) sambuca

Method
Layer in a shot glass and serve.

BLACK OPAL

1 Mug hot coffee
30mL (1 oz) Galleon Liverno
whipped cream

Method
Float Galleon Liverno over the top of the coffee and ignite. When serving extinguish the flame by putting cream on top.

BLACK RUSSIAN

30mL (1 oz) Smirnoff Vodka
30mL (1 oz) Kahlúa

Method
Build over ice. Place a swizzle stick in the glass. Add milk to make a White Russian.

BLACK VELVET

champagne

stout

Method
Half fill a champagne flute with chilled stout. Top with chilled champagne and serve.

BLACK WIDOW SHOOTER

30mL (1 oz) Opal Nera

30mL (1 oz) cream

30mL (1 oz) strawberry liqueur

Method
Layer in a shot glass and serve.

BLINKER

15mL (0.5 oz) Canadian whiskey

25mL (0.87 oz) grapefruit juice

7mL (0.23 oz) grenadine

cracked ice

Method
Shake and strain into a 3 oz cocktail glass and serve.

BLOOD AND SAND

30mL (1 oz) scotch whiskey

30mL (1 oz) orange juice

30mL (1 oz) cherry brandy

cracked ice

30mL (1 oz) sweet vermouth

garnish:

1 twist orange peel

Method
Half fill mixing glass with cracked ice, add liquid ingredients and stir. Strain into a 5 oz champagne saucer, garnish with orange peel and serve.

BLOOD CLOT SHOOTER

30mL (1 oz) sambuca

30mL (1 oz) cream

30mL (1 oz) Opal Nera

3-4 drops grenadine

Method
Layer in a shot glass and serve.

BLOOD SHOT

30mL (1 oz) vodka

15mL (0.5 oz) lemon juice

60mL (2 oz) condensed consommé

15mL (0.5 oz) tomato sauce (catsup)

15mL (0.5 oz) Worcestershire sauce

Method
Shake and strain into a 5 oz cocktail glass. Garnish with a sprinkle of celery salt and a slice of Cucumber and serve.

BLOOD TYPE 0-NEGATIVE SHOOTER

30mL (1 oz) strawberry liqueur
30mL (1 oz) gin
30mL (1 oz) red crème de menthe

Method
Layer in a shot glass and serve.

BLOOD TYPE 0-POSITIVE SHOOTER

30mL (1 oz) triple sec
30mL (1 oz) strawberry liqueur
30mL (1 oz) sambuca

Method
Layer in order in a 3 oz shot or port glass and serve.

BLOOD TYPE A-POSITIVE SHOOTER

30mL (1 oz) red crème de menthe
30mL (1 oz) sambuca
30mL (1 oz) strawberry liqueur

Method
Layer in a shot glass and serve.

BLOODBATH SHOOTER

30mL (1 oz) tequila
30mL (1 oz) strawberry liqueur

Method
Layer in a shot glass and serve.

BLOODHOUND

15mL (0.5 oz) dry vermouth
3 dashes strawberry liqueur
15mL (0.5 oz) gin
4 strawberries (Two for garnish)
15mL (0.5 oz) sweet vermouth
4 ice cubes

Method
Blend two ice cubes. gin, vermouths, strawberry liqueur and two strawberries. Pour into a 5 oz cocktail glass over remaining ice cubes. Garnish with remaining strawberries and serve.

BLOODHOUND NO. 2

15mL (0.5 oz) gin
15mL (0.5 oz) Rubis
15mL (0.5 oz) dry vermouth
5 strawberries (Two for garnish)
15mL (0.5 oz) sweet vermouth
1 scoop crushed ice

Method
Blend all ingredients except 3 strawberries until smooth. Pour into an old fashioned glass, garnish with remaining strawberry and serve.

Black Russian
(Recipe page 46)

Blue French
(Recipe page 50)

Brandy Alexander
(Recipe page 60)

Between the Sheets
(Recipe page 44)

Black Widow
(Recipe page 47)

Banana Daiquiri
(Recipe page 80)

BLOODY LOVELY

30mL (1 oz) Midori
30mL (1 oz) cream
30mL (1 oz) Bailey's Irish cream
4 strawberries
30mL (1 oz) Malibu
ice

Method
Blend and pour into a 6 oz tulip glass and serve.

BLOODY MARY

60mL (2 oz) vodka
1 dash Worcestershire Sauce
10mL (0.33 oz) lemon juice
2-3 drops Tabasco Sauce
tomato juice
3 ice cubes
Salt
pepper

Method
In a 10 oz highball glass or equivalent place vodka, Sauces, lemon juices and a sprinkle of salt and pepper. Top with tomato juice and serve with swizzle stick and straws. (white rum or tequila may be used instead of vodka)

BLOSSOM

30mL (1 oz) white rum
15mL (0.5 oz) orange juice
15mL (0.5 oz) apple juice
cracked ice
15mL (0.5 oz) sugar syrup

Method
Half fill shaker with cracked ice, add ingredients, shake and strain into a 5 oz champagne saucer and serve.

BLOW JOB SHOOTER

15mL (0.5 oz) Kahlúa
15mL (0.5 oz) Bailey's Irish cream
10mL (0.33 oz) banana liqueur
whipped cream

Method
Layer in order in a shot glass and serve.

BLOW UP

30mL (1 oz) Bacardi rum
5 drops green crème de menthe
30mL (1 oz) Chartreuse
5 drops grenadine
15mL (0.5 oz) parfait amour
cracked ice

Method
Half fill a mixing glass with cracked ice and add Bacardi rum, Chartreuse and parfait amour. Stir and strain into a 5 oz cocktail glass, add other ingredients and serve.

BLUEBERRY DELIGHT

20mL (0.66 oz) Opal Nera
60mL (2 oz) cream
20mL (0.66 oz) strawberry liqueur
ice
20mL (0.66 oz) Malibu

Method
Shake and strain into a 5 oz cocktail glass and serve.

BLUEBERRY DELIGHT NO. 2

15mL (0.5 oz) Galleon Liverno
15mL (0.5 oz) blue curaçao
15mL (0.5 oz) dry vermouth
lemonade
30 mL (1 oz) gin

Method
Shake ingredients except lemonade and strain into a 10 oz highball glass. Top with lemonade, garnish with an lemon wheel, mint leaves, straws and serve.

BLUE BLAZER

60mL (2 oz) scotch whiskey
garnish:
lemon peel
60mL (2 oz) boiling water
2 Mugs (silver or copper)
sugar

Method
Pour whiskey into one mug and water into the other. Ignite whiskey and pour into water mug. Pour ingredients from one mug to the other a few times. Add sugar to taste, garnish with lemon peel and serve.

BLUE DAY

40mL (1.33 oz) vodka
garnish:
1 lemon slice
20mL (0.66 oz) blue curaçao
peel 1/2 lemon
3 ice cubes

Method
Crack ice and place in shaker with liquid ingredients, shake and strain into a 3 oz cocktail glass. Squeeze 1/2 lemon peel over the top, garnish with the lemon slice and serve.

BLUE DOVE

30mL (1 oz) blue curaçao
lemonade
20mL (0.66 oz) vodka
whipped cream

Method
Pour blue curaçao and vodka over ice in a 10 oz highball glass. Top with lemonade, add whipped cream to top and serve.

BLUE FRENCH

30mL (1 oz) Pernod
5mL (0.17 oz) lemon juice
5mL (0.17 oz) blue curaçao
Bitter lemon soft drink

Method
Build over ice in a 10 oz highball glass. Top with Bitter lemon soft drink. Garnish with lemon wheel, straws and serve.

BLUE HAWAIIAN

15mL (0.5 oz) white rum
90mL (3 oz) pineapple juice
15mL (0.5 oz) blue curaçao
3 tbsp cream
3 tbsp coconut milk
ice

Method
Mix ingredients in a 10 oz highball glass, top with cream. Add straws and serve.

BLUE HAZE

30mL (1 oz) Bacardi rum
15mL (0.5 oz) Cointreau
15mL (0.5 oz) sweet vermouth
15mL (0.5 oz) Rossi vermouth
4 drops blue curaçao
15mL (0.5 oz) parfait amour

Method
Add all ingredients except blue curaçao in mixing glass. Strain into a 5 oz champagne saucer, add blue curaçao and serve.

BLUE HEAVEN

60mL (2 oz) vodka
150mL (5 oz) lemonade
30mL (1 oz) blue curaçao

Method
Shake vodka and blue curaçao. Pour over ice in a 10 oz highball glass. Top with lemonade and serve with straws.

BLUE LADY

25mL (0.87 oz) gin
garnish:
1 maraschino cherry
15mL (0.5 oz) blue curaçao
3 ice cubes
15mL (0.5 oz) lemon juice

Method
Shake and strain into a 3 oz cocktail glass. Garnish with cherry and serve.

BLUE LAGOON

30mL (1 oz) blue curaçao
lemonade
Galleon Liverno
cracked ice

Method
Pour blue curaçao over ice in a 10 oz highball glass. Top with lemonade, float Galleon Liverno. Serve with straws.

BLUE LAGOON NO. 2

30mL (1 oz) vodka
15mL (0.5 oz) lemon juice
5mL (0.17oz) blue curaçao
ice

Method
Shake and strain into a 5 oz cocktail glass and serve.

BLUE LAGOON NO. 3

30mL (1 oz) vodka
lemonade
15mL (0.5 oz) blue curaçao
ice

Method
Half fill a 10 oz highball glass with
ice. Add vodka and blue curaçao,
top with lemonade and serve.

BLUE MALLET

30mL (1 oz) gin
15mL (0.5 oz) lemon juice
15mL (0.5 oz) blue curaçao
ice

Method
Shake and strain into a 3 oz
cocktail glass and serve.

BLUE MONDAY

30mL (1 oz) vodka
ice
15mL (0.5 oz) Blue Curaco

Method
Shake and strain into a 3 oz
cocktail glass and serve.

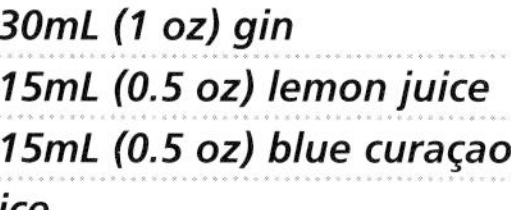

BLUE MOON

30mL (1 oz) dry gin
15mL (0.5 oz) lemon juice
15mL (0.5 oz) crème Yvette
cracked ice

Method
Shake and strain into a 3 oz
cocktail glass and serve.

BLUE NEGLIGÉE

15mL (0.5 oz) ouzo
garnish:
1 maraschino cherry
15mL (0.5 oz) Chartreuse
ice
15mL (0.5 oz) Parfait Armour

Method
Shake and strain into a 3 oz
cocktail glass. Garnish with cherry
and serve.

BLUE PACIFIC

60 mL (2 oz) dry gin
cracked ice
30mL (1 oz) blue curaçao
1 tsp castor sugar
1 dash orange bitters
garnish:
1 orange wheel

Method
Half fill shaker with ice, add liquid
ingredients and shake. Rim a 5 oz
champagne saucer with sugar.
Strain liquid ingredients into
glass. Garnish with orange wheel
and serve.

BLUE SEAS

15mL (0.5 oz) blue curaçao
lemonade
30mL (1 oz) vodka
Galliano Liverno (float)

Method
Build over ice in a 10 oz highball
glass. Top with lemonade.
Float Galleon Liverno and serve
with straws.

B

BLUE SEAS NO. 2

30mL (1 oz) vodka
lemonade
15mL (0.5 oz) Blue sambuca
Galliano Liverno (float)

Method
Build over ice in a 10 oz highball
glass. Top with lemonade.
Float Galleon Liverno and serve
with straws.

BLUE TRAIN

45mL (1.5 oz(brandy
45mL (1.5 oz) pineapple juice
30mL (1 oz) blue curaçao
champagne
cracked ice
garnish:
1 maraschino cherry

Method
Layer brandy, curaçao and
pineapple juice over cracked ice.
Top with champagne, garnish with
cherry and serve.

BLUE VEIN

30mL (1 oz) Malibu
30mL (1 oz) blue curaçao
30mL (1 oz) Cointreau

Method
Layer in a 3 oz cocktail glass and
serve.

BOBBY BURNS

15mL (0.5 oz) scotch whiskey
1 dash Benedictine
7mL (0.23) sweet vermouth
garnish:
lemon peel
7mL (0.23 oz) dry vermouth
ice

Method
Stir ingredients in a mixing glass,
strain into a 3 oz cocktail glass.
Garnish with lemon peel and serve.

BODY HEAT

30mL (1 oz) Malibu
30mL (1 oz) pineapple juice
30mL (1 oz) banana liqueur
30mL (1 oz) orange juice
1 dash grenadine
8 mL (0.27 oz) lemon juice

Method
Blend all ingredients with ice until
smooth, pour into a 10 oz highball
glass. Add grenadine and serve
with straws.

BOILERMAKER

Serve 30-60 mL (1-2 oz) scotch
Whiskey with a beer Chaser.

BOLSHOI PUNCH

30mL (1oz) Smirnoff Vodka
10mL (0.33 oz) Coruba Rum
10mL (0.33 oz) Creme de Cassis
15mL (0.5 oz) lime juice
15mL (0.5 oz) lemon juice
top up with bitter lemon

Method
Blend with ice and strain then top up with bitter lemon. Garnish with an orange slice and red cherry.

BOMBAY

60mL (2 oz) brandy
3 dashes crème de cacao
7mL (0.23 oz) dry vermouth
ice
7mL (0.23 oz) sweet vermouth

Method
Shake and strain into a 3 oz cocktail glass and serve.

BOND 7 & JAMES

30mL (1 oz) Bond 7 whiskey
garnish:
orange peel
1 dash sweet vermouth
1 maraschino cherry
Spa water

Method
Pour whiskey and vermouth into highball glass over ice.
Top with spa water, garnish with orange peel and cherry and serve.

BONDI BLUE

45mL (1.5 oz) Bacardi rum
1/2 egg white
30mL (1 oz) blue curaçao
cracked ice
30mL (1 oz) banana liqueur
lemonade

Method
Shake all ingredients except lemonade, strain over ice in a 10 oz highball glass. Top with lemonade, add straws and serve.

BOOMERANG

30mL (1 oz) Canadian whiskey
23mL (0.77 oz) Swedish punch
23mL (0.77 oz) dry vermouth
2 dashes lemon juice
ice

Method
Shake and strain into 3 oz cocktail glass and serve.

BORN TO BE ALIVE

30mL (1 oz) Bacardi rum
15mL (0.5 oz) Peter Herring
15mL (0.5 oz) advocaat
15mL (0.5 oz) blue curaçao
15mL (0.5 oz) green Chartreuse
5 mL Galliano Liverno
15mL (0.5 oz) yellow Chartreuse

Method
Gently layer ingredients in a 5 oz cocktail glass with advocaat in the centre. Serve.

BOSOM CARESSER

45mL (1.5 oz) brandy
1 egg yolk
15mL (0.5 oz) blue curaçao
1 tsp grenadine

Method
Shake and strain into 3 oz cocktail glass and serve.

BOSOM CARESSER NO. 2

30mL (1 oz) brandy
1 egg yolk
15mL (0.5 oz) orange curaçao
ice
5mL (0.17 oz) grenadine

Method
Shake and strain into a 5 oz cocktail glass and serve.

BOSSA NOVA

30mL (1 oz) Galleon Liverno
60mL (2 oz) pineapple juice
30mL (1 oz) light dark rum
10mL (0.33 oz) lemon juice
10 mL (0.33 oz) apricot brandy
15mL (0.5 oz) egg white

Method
Shake and pour over ice in a highball glass.
garnish with fruit and serve.

BOSTON COCKTAIL

30mL (1 oz) Gilbey's Gin
30mL (1 oz) Apricot Brandy
5mL (0.17 oz) lemon juice
5mL (0.17 oz) Grenadine

Method
Shake over ice and strain then add Grenadine. Garnish with a red cherry.

BOSTON CREAM

30mL (1 oz) cream
15mL (0.5 oz) lime juice
30mL coconut cream
15mL Grenadine

Method
Shake over ice and strain. Garnish with a chocolate cross.

BOURBON BANANA

30mL (1 oz) bourbon
30mL (1 oz) orange juice
30mL (1 oz) Kahlúa
30mL (1 oz) cream
1 banana

Method
Blend ingredients with ice and serve in a brandy Balloon.

BRAIN DEAD BLASTER SHOOTER

10mL (0.33 oz) Southern Comfort
10mL (0.33 oz) tequila
10mL (0.33 oz) Galliano Liverno
10mL (0.33 oz) Tia Maria
10mL (0.33 oz) blue curaçao

Method
Layer in a Test Tube or shot glass
and serve.

BRANDY ALEXANDER

30mL (1 oz) crème de cacao
30mL (1 oz) fresh cream
30mL (1 oz) brandy
garnish:
Ground nutmeg

Method
Shake ingredients and strain into a
champagne saucer. Cross two
straws over glass and sprinkle with
nutmeg. Remove straws and serve.

BRANDY BOOSTER

30mL (1 oz) brandy
30mL (1 oz) orange juice
2 tsp lemon juice
1 egg yolk
1/2 tsp Icing sugar
ice

Method
Blend and pour into a rocks glass
and serve.

BRANDY BOSS

30mL (1 oz) brandy
15mL (0.5 oz) Tia Maria
15mL (0.5 oz) Vandermint
60mL (2 oz) cream

Method
Shake and strain into a champagne
saucer and serve.

BRANDY CIDER

60mL (2 oz) brandy
apple cider

Method
Pour brandy over ice in a 10 oz
brandy Balloon. Top with cider and
serve.

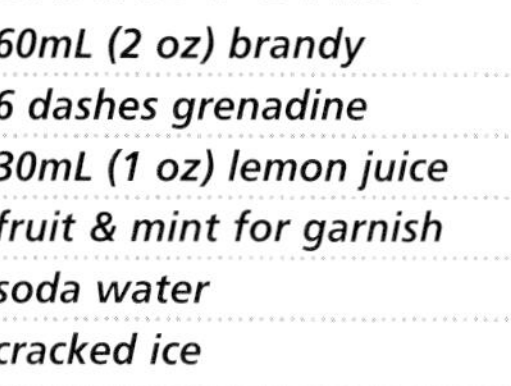

BRANDY DAISY

60mL (2 oz) brandy
6 dashes grenadine
30mL (1 oz) lemon juice
fruit & mint for garnish
soda water
cracked ice

Method
Fill a Goblet with cracked ice, shake
brandy, lemon juice and grenadine.
Strain into Goblet, top soda.
Garnish and serve.

BRANDY EGG NOG

30mL (1 oz) brandy
1 egg yolk
5mL (0.17 oz) sugar syrup
milk

Method
Shake all ingredients except milk, strain into a 10 oz highball glass. Top with milk, sprinkle with nutmeg, add straws and serve.

BRANDY FIX

30mL (1 oz) brandy
30mL (1 oz) lemon juice
30mL (1 oz) cherry brandy
1 tsp water
1 tsp sugar
garnish:
1 lemon wheel

Method
Stir ingredients in a 5oz cocktail glass, garnish with lemon wheel and serve.

BRANDY FLIP

60mL (2 oz) brandy
ice
1 tsp sugar
garnish:
nutmeg
I egg

Method
Shake ingredients and strain into a champagne saucer. Sprinkle with nutmeg and serve.

BRANDY ICE

30mL (1 oz) Milne Brandy
15mL (0.5 oz) vanilla extract
2 scoops vanilla ice cream
15mL (0.5 oz) lemon juice
top up with bitter lemon

Method
Blend with ice and strain then top up with bitter lemon. Garnish with an orange slice and a cherry

BRANDY KISS

30mL (1 oz) brandy
30mL (1 oz) lemon juice
30mL (1 oz) Grand Marnier

Method
Shake and strain into a 3 oz cocktail glass and serve.

BRANDY, LIME & SODA

45mL (1.5 oz) brandy
ice
15mL (0.5 oz) lime juice
garnish:
1 lime or lemon wheel
soda water

Method
Pour brandy and lime juice over one scoop of ice in a 10 oz highball glass. Top with soda water, garnish with lime or lemon wheel, straws and serve.

BRANDY RIVIERA

30mL (1 oz) brandy
30mL (1 oz) Vandermint
30mL (1 oz) banana liqueur
cracked ice

Method
Pour ingredients over ice in a
champagne saucer and serve.

BRANDY SMASH

60mL (2 oz) brandy
2 Spring mint
1 tsp sugar
cracked ice
water

Method
Dissolve sugar in a little water.
Muddle with ice and mint in Old
Fashioned glass. Pour brandy
over the top and serve.

BRANDY SNAPS

10mL (0.33 oz) Milne Brandy
10mL (0.33 oz) Peach Schnapps
10mL (0.33 oz) apple juice

Method
Layer Brandy onto Peach Schnapps,
then pour apple juice. Garnish with
floated cream (optional).

BRANDY TODDY

60mL (1 oz) brandy
1 tsp sugar
water
cracked ice

Method
Dissolve sugar in a little water in a
3 oz cocktail glass. Acid ice, brandy
and serve.

BRAVE BULL

60mL (2 oz) Kahlúa
60mL (2 oz) tequila

Method
Place two ice cubes in a 3 oz cocktail
glass and pour ingredients over ice.
Serve with two short straws.

BRAZILIAN MONK

30mL (1oz) Kahlúa
15mL (0.5 oz) Frangelico
15mL (0.5 oz) Dark Creme de Cacao
2 scoops vanilla ice cream

Method
Blend with ice. Garnish with a wild
flower or flower petals.

BREAK SHOOTER

10mL (0.33 oz) Kahlúa
10mL (0.33 oz) ouzo
10mL (0.33 oz) banana liqueur

Method
Layer in order in a shot glass
and serve.

BREATHALYSER BUSTER

12mL (0.4 oz) crème de menthe
12mL (0.4 oz) vodka
12mL (0.4 oz) Cointreau

Method
Pour into a 3 oz cocktail glass
and serve.

BRITTANY

30mL (1 oz) Gilbey's Gin
15mL (0.5 oz) Amer Picon
10mL (0.33 oz) orange juice
10mL (0.33 oz) lemon juice

Method
Build over ice. Garnish with
lemon peel.

BRONX

30mL (1 oz) gin
15mL (0.5 oz) orange juice
1 dash French vermouth
cracked ice
1 dash Italian vermouth

Method
Shake and strain into 3 oz cocktail
glass and serve.

BRONX DISCO

30mL (1 oz) dry gin
15mL (0.5 oz) dry vermouth
30mL (1 oz) Galliano Liverno
30mL (1 oz) orange juice
15mL (0.5 oz) sweet vermouth

Method
Shake and strain into a 5 oz
cocktail glass and serve.

BROWN BETTY

60mL (2 oz) beer or ale
1 tbsp Brown sugar
15mL (0.5 oz) brandy
1 lemon wheel (Garnish)
1 pinch cinnamon
30mL (1 oz) water
nutmeg
Pinch Ground Cloves
1/2 slice toasted bread
1/2 fresh ginger Root

Method
Dissolve sugar in water and allow
to stand for 15 minutes. Add
Cloves, brandy and beer or ale and
stir well. Pour into a 10 oz brandy
Balloon, break toasted bread into
it. Sprinkle with nutmeg and grate
ginger root over top and serve.

BROWN BOMBER

45mL (1.5 oz) Kahlúa
45mL(1.5 oz) Bailey's Irish cream

Method
Pour over ice in a sherry glass and
serve.

BROWN COW

45mL (1.5 oz) Tia Maria

milk

Method
Pour Tia Maria over ice in a 10 oz highball glass, top with milk. Add straws and serve.

BROWN SMOOTHIE

45mL (1.5 oz) Kahlúa

30mL (1 oz) cream

1 banana

ice

Method
Blend until smooth, pour into a flute glass and serve.

BROWN SQUIRREL

30mL (1 oz) amaretto

30mL (1 oz) heavy cream

15mL (0.5 oz) crème de cacao

Method
Shake and strain into a 5 oz champagne saucer and serve.

BRUISE SHOOTER

30mL (1 oz) Kahlúa

30mL (1 oz) Bailey's Irish cream

30mL (1 oz) crème de menthe

Method
Layer in order in a shot glass and serve.

BUBBLE YUM

30mL (1 oz) Cointreau

10mL (0.33 oz) raspberry cordial

30mL (1 oz) banana liqueur

60mL (2 oz) cream

Method
Shake and strain into a 5 oz cocktail glass and serve.

BUCCANEER

45mL (1.5 oz) Bundaberg rum

dry ginger ale

15mL (0.5 oz) advocaat

Method
Shake rum and advocaat and strain over ice in a 10 oz highball glass. Top with dry ginger ale and serve with straws.

BUCKS

60mL (2 oz) champagne

60mL (2 oz) orange juice

Method
Mix together in a flute glass and serve.

BULLSHOT

40mL (1.33 oz) vodka
1 Beef Stock Cube
60mL (2 oz) hot water
1/4 tsp Celery salt or salt
1 squeeze lemon juice
ice
garnish: 1 strip lemon peel

Method
In a mixing glass dissolve stock cube in water, add salt, squeeze of lemon and vodka, Stir rapidly and pour into an Old Fashioned glass. Garnish with lemon peel and serve.

BULLSHOT SHOOTER

10mL (0.33 oz) Kahlúa
10mL (0.33 oz) tequila
10mL (0.33 oz) Bacardi rum

Method
Layer in order in a shot glass and serve.

BURNING DESIRE

30mL (1 oz) Cointreau
50mL (1.66 oz)orange juice
15mL (0.5 oz) Galleon Liverno
5mL (0.17 oz)grenadine
1 dash egg white

Method
Shake and strain into a 5 oz cocktail glass and serve.

BUSH PEAK

20mL (0.66 oz) Cointreau
20mL (0.66 oz) Galleon Liverno
20mL (0.66 oz) Grand Marnier
90mL (3 oz) orange juice
20mL (0.66 oz) brandy
dash of grenadine

Method
Shake all ingredients except grenadine and pour into a 10 oz highball glass. Add grenadine, flexible straws and serve.

BUTTERFLY FLIP

30mL (1 oz) brandy
1 egg yolk
30mL (1 oz) crème de cacao
2-3 ice cubes
1/2 tsp castor sugar
garnish:
nutmeg
25mL (0.83 oz) cream

Method
Shake and strain into a 5 oz cocktail glass, sprinkle with nutmeg and serve.

BYRRH FREEZER

60mL (2 oz) Byrrh
garnish:
1 lemon wheel
15mL (0.5 oz) lemon cordial
1 maraschino cherry
soda water

Method
Pour Byrrh and cordial over ice in a 10 oz highball glass. Top with soda, garnish with lemon wheel, cherry and serve.

CAFÉ DE PARIS

60mL (2 oz) Gilbey's Gin
10mL (0.33 oz) double cream
5mL (0.17 oz) Pernod
1 egg white

Method
Shake over ice and strain. Garnish
with half a slice of lemon.

CAFÉ NERO

30mL (1 oz) Galliano
black coffee
fresh cream
sugar

Method
Firstly, sprinkle white sugar inside
the glass after coating with
Galliano. Set Galliano alight and
twirl the glass so that flames burn
brightly. Pour black coffee gently
into glass then layer cream on top
of the burning coffee. Sprinkle
grated chocolate over the coffee.

CAFÉ OSCAR

20mL (0.66 oz) Kahlúa
20mL (0.66 oz) Amaretto di
Galliano
top up with hot coffee
layer double cream
2 scoops vanilla ice cream

Method
Pour in order then float cream.
Garnish with ice cream.

CAFÉ ROYALE

1 cup black coffee
1 Lump sugar
1 tbsp brandy

Method
Place sugar in spoon and hold over
coffee, fill spoon with brandy and
ignite. When flame starts to fade
place spoon in coffee and serve.

CAFÉ SOCIETY

30mL (1 oz) Cadbury cream liqueur
60mL (2 oz) cream
30mL (1 oz) Frangelico
garnish:
grated chocolate
15mL (0.5 oz) Kahlúa
strawberry

Method
Blend with ice and pour into a 5 oz
colada glass. Garnish with Flake
chocolate and a strawberry, serve
with straws.

CALVADOS

30mL (1 oz) Calvados
garnish:
apple slices
15mL (0.5 oz) Cointreau
1 maraschino cherry
30mL (1 oz) orange juice

Method
Shake liquid ingredients and strain
into 3 oz cocktail glass, garnish with
apple slices and cherry and serve.

C

CAMERON CANNON

30mL (1 oz) Kahlúa
30mL (1 oz) Bailey's Irish cream
90mL (3 oz) vodka
dash crème de menthe
3 drops green Chartreuse
crushed ice

Method
Shake and strain into 5 oz cocktail glass and serve.

CAMPARI

30mL (1 oz) Campari
garnish:
1 slice lemon
30mL (1 oz) sweet vermouth
cracked ice
soda water

Method
Half fill a 10 ox highball glass with ice, pour Campari and vermouth over ice. Top with soda water, garnish with lemon slice, straws and serve.

CAMPINO

15mL (0.5 oz) Campari
2 dashes crème de cassis
15mL (0.5 oz) sweet vermouth
garnish:
1 spiral orange peel
15mL (0.5 oz) dry vermouth
soda water
15mL (0.5 oz) gin

Method
Mix all ingredients except soda water and peel in mixing glass. Pour into small Tumbler and top with soda. Garnish with peel and serve.

CANADIAN DAISY

30mL (3 oz) Canadian Club Whisky
10mL (0.33 oz) Milne Brandy
10mL (0.33 oz) lemon juice
5mL (0.17 oz) raspberry syrup
top up with soda

Method
Shake over ice and strain then top up with soda. Garnish with assorted colourful cherries.

CANADIAN SHERBET

30mL (1 oz) Canadian whiskey
30mL (1 oz) lemon juice
15mL (0.5 oz) Tia Maria
30mL (1 oz) sugar syrup

Method
Blend and pour into chilled margarita glass, garnish with banana slice and strawberry and serve.

CANDY CANE

15mL (0.5 oz) grenadine
15mL (0.5 oz) vodka
15mL (0.5 oz) crème de menthe

Method
Layer in order in shot glass and serve.

CAPE KENNEDY

5mL (0.17 oz) dark rum
20mL (0.66 oz) lemon juice
5mL (0.17 oz) scotch whiskey
20mL (0.66 oz) orange juice
5mL (0.17 oz) Benedictine
2-3 ice Cubes
5mL (0.17 oz) sugar syrup

Method
Shake and strain into 3 oz cocktail glass and serve.

CAPER'S CAPER

30mL (1 oz) advocaat
1/4 Avocado
30mL (1 oz) Frangelico
1 scoop ice cream
4-5 strawberries
garnish:
coffee Bean

Method
Blend ingredients with ice and pour into a 10 oz colada glass. Float coffee Bean and serve with straws.

CAPER'S CAPER NO. 2

30mL (1 oz) Frangelico
90mL (3 oz) cream
30mL (1 oz) vodka
3-4 strawberries
15mL (0.5 oz) Cointreau

Method
Blend ingredients with ice and pour into an 8 oz colada glass.
garnish with strawberries and straws and serve.

CAPER'S TRAFFIC LIGHT

30mL (1 oz) strawberry liqueur
30mL (1 oz) Midori
6 strawberries
1 slice honeydew melon
30mL (1 oz) banana liqueur
1/2 banana

Method
Blend each liqueur and corresponding fruit with ice and layer in a 10 oz colada glass in recipe order. Garnish with fruits and straws and serve.

CARDINAL

45mL (1.5 oz) gin
1 twist lemon
45mL (1.5 oz) dry vermouth
cracked ice
45mL (1.5 oz) Campari

Method
Shake and strain into 5 oz cocktail glass, garnish with lemon peel and serve.

CARELESS WHISPER

30mL (1 oz) strawberry liqueur
10mL (0.33 oz) cream
10mL (0.33 oz) Cheri-Suisse
garnish:
grated chocolate
20mL (0.66 oz) Amanda
1 maraschino cherry

Method
Shake and strain into a 3 oz cocktail glass, garnish with chocolate, cherry and serve.

CARIBBEAN CHAMPAGNE

100mL (3.33 oz) Champagne
10mL (0.33 oz) Bacardi
10mL (0.33 oz) Banana Liqueur
5mL (0.17 oz) Orange Bitters

Method
Stir without ice and strain. Garnish with a slice of banana.

CARLTON

30mL (1 oz) Canadian whiskey
10mL (0.33 oz) orange juice
15mL (0.5 oz) Cointreau
cracked ice

Method
Shake and strain into a 3 oz cocktail glass and serve.

CAT WALK

30mL (1 oz) Bacardi rum
15mL (0.5 oz) lemon juice
20mL Cointreau
4 strawberries
15mL (0.5 oz) Malibu

Method
Blend until smooth, pour into a 3 oz cocktail glass and serve.

CATCH ME

45mL (1.33 oz) vodka
30mL (1 oz) lemon juice
15mL (0.5 oz) red curaçao

Method
Shake and strain into a 3 oz cocktail glass and serve.

CATERPILLAR

15mL (0.5 oz) gin
15mL (0.5 oz) yellow Chartreuse
15mL (0.5 oz) blue curaçao
ice

Method
Pour ingredients over ice in a 3 oz cocktail glass and serve.

CHA CHA

30mL (1 oz) Frangelico
15mL (0.5 oz) cream
30mL (1 oz) crème de cacao

Method
Float ingredients in a 3 oz cocktail glass and serve.

CHABLIS CUP

20mL (0.66 oz) Grand Marnier

15mL (0.5 oz) Kirsch

1 peach slice

1 bananas slice

1 orange slice

1 lemon slice

1 mint sprig

top 60mL (2 oz) Chablis wine

Method
Blend over ice and then top up
with Chablis. Garnish with an
assorted fruit arrangement.

CHAMPAGNE 69

15mL (0.5 oz) Cointreau

chilled champagne

15mL (0.5 oz) Grand Marnier

Method
Build Cointreau and Grand Marnier
in a champagne saucer. Top with
champagne and serve.

CHAMPAGNE COCKTAIL

15mL (0.5 oz) brandy

1 sugar Cube

chilled champagne

garnish:

1 twist lemon

Angostura bitters

Method
Place sugar Cube in a champagne
saucer and saturate with Angostura
bitters. Add brandy and fill with
champagne, stir until sugar is
dissolved. Garnish with twist of
lemon and serve.

CHAMPAGNE COCKTAIL NO. 2.

15mL (0.5 oz) brandy

1 sugar Cube

chilled champagne

1 dash Angostura bitters

1 dash orange curaçao

garnish:

1 strip orange peel

Method
Place sugar Cube in a champagne
saucer, add Angostura bitters and
curaçao. Fill almost to top with
champagne, float brandy on top.
Garnish with orange peel and serve.

CHAMPAGNE COCKTAIL NO. 3

30mL (1 oz) cogna

10 mL Angostura bitters

chilled champagne

garnish:

1 strawberry

1 sugar Cube

Method
Place sugar Cube in a champagne
saucer and saturate with Angostura
bitters. Add cognac and top with
champagne. Garnish with
strawberry and serve.

CHAMPAGNE COCKTAIL NO. 4

15mL (0.5 oz) Grand Marnier
20mL orange juice
chilled champagne
1 egg yolk

Method
Shake Grand Marnier, orange juice and egg yolk with ice. Strain into a champagne saucer, top with champagne and serve.

CHAMPAGNE PICK-ME-UP

30mL (1 oz) brandy
30mL (1 oz) orange juice
chilled champagne
ice
5mL (0.17 oz) grenadine

Method
Shake ingredients except champagne and strain into a flute glass. Top with champagne and serve.

CHAMPAGNE ST. MORITZ

10mL (0.33 oz) Beefeater Dry Gin
10mL (0.33 oz) Apricot Brandy
10mL (0.33 oz) orange juice
top up with Champagne

Method
Shake over ice and strain then top up with Champagne. Garnish with a slice of orange.

CHAMPAGNE TORY

15mL (0.5 oz) Midori
15mL (0.5 oz) Rubis
15mL (0.5 oz) banana liqueur
chilled champagne

Method
Pour ingredients into a champagne saucer, top with champagne and serve.

CHANNEL 64 SHOOTER

10 mL (0.33 oz) advocaat
10 mL (0.33 oz) Bailey's Irish cream
10 mL (0.33 oz) banana liqueur

Method
Layer in order in a shot glass and serve.

CHASTITY BELT SHOOTER

20mL (0.66 oz) Tia Maria
10mL (0.33 oz) Bailey's Irish cream
10mL (0.33 oz) Frangelico
5mL (0.17 oz) cream

Method
Layer in order in a shot glass and serve.

CHEE CHEE

30mL (1 oz) vodka
60mL (2 oz) pineapple juice
30mL (1 oz) coconut milk
garnish:
1 pineapple wedge

Method
Shake and strain into a champagne
saucer, garnish with pineapple
wedge and serve.

CHERRIES JUBILEE

30mL (1 oz) cherry advocaat
15mL (0.5 oz) milk
30mL (1 oz) white crème de cacao
grated chocolate (Garnish)
15mL (0.5 oz) Malibu
garnish:
1 strip coconut Rind
40mL (1.33 oz) cream
1 maraschino cherry

Method
Shake and strain into a 5 oz
cocktail glass. Garnish and serve.

CHERRY

15mL (0.5 oz) cherry brandy
15mL (0.5 oz) Double cream
1 tsp white rum
garnish:
2 small sprigs mint
90mL (3 oz) sparkling white wine

Method
Stir all ingredients except wine in a
10 oz highball glass. Top with wine,
garnish with mint, straws and serve.

CHERRY ALEXANDER

30mL (1 oz) cherry brandy
60mL (2 oz) cream
30mL (1 oz) crème de cacao
ice

Method
Shake and strain into a 5 oz
cocktail glass and serve.

CHERRY BOMB

30mL (1 oz) Smirnoff Vodka
15mL (0.5 oz) Cherry Brandy
5mL (0.17 oz) Grenadine
top up with lemonade

Method
Colour sugar with Grenadine and
prepare glass by sugar coating rim.
Blend over ice and pour then top
up with lemonade. Garnish with an
orchid.

CHERYL

30mL (1 oz) vodka
1 scoop vanilla ice cream
30mL (1 oz) Galleon Liverno
garnish:
1 maraschino cherry

Method
Shake and strain into a 5 oz
cocktail glass, garnish with cherry
and serve.

C

CHEVRON'S MOON LANDING

1 pineapple
15mL (0.5 oz) cherry brandy
30mL (1 oz) vodka
1 dash Angostura bitters
30mL (1 oz) dark rum
12 maraschino Cherries
15mL (0.5 oz) apricot brandy
2 lemon slices
2 olives
3 ice cubes

Method
Cut the top off the pineapple approximately two inches from the top and hollow out the bottom section of the pineapple. Cut half the fruit into cubes and replace it in the hollowed shell. In a shaker, place ice cubes, vodka, rum, apricot brandy, cherry brandy and bitters. Shake rapidly and pour unstrained over fruit in pineapple. Place four Toothpicks around top of pineapple Shell and place three Cherries on each toothpick. Place four more toothpicks in top of pineapple so that they match the ones in the shell and replace the top so that the toothpicks line up through the Cherries. Place a slice of lemon on each side of the pineapple with a toothpick and balance two crossed swizzle sticks on each Toothpick and secure them with an olive. Add a Spoon, straws and serve.

CHI CHI

45mL (1.33 oz) vodka
20mL (0.66 oz) coconut cream
20mL (0.66 oz) Malibu
15mL (0.5 oz) lime cordial
15mL (0.5 oz) lemon cordial
1 slice pineapple
60mL (2 oz) pineapple juice
1 dash cream

Method
Blend until smooth and pour into a champagne saucer and serve.

CHICAGO

40mL (1.33 oz) brandy
1 dash Angostura bitters
1 tsp Cointreau
2 ice cubes
Sparkling white wine

Method
Place ingredients in a champagne saucer, top with white wine and serve.

CHIQUITA

45mL (1.5 oz) Smirnoff Vodka
10mL (0.33 oz) Banana Liqueur
10mL (0.33 oz) lime juice
half a sliced banana
pinch of sugar

Method
Blend with ice and pour. Garnish with banana slices.

CHOC MINT

30mL (1 oz) crème de cacao
50mL (1.66 oz) cream
15mL (0.5 oz) white crème de menthe

Method
Shake and strain into a champagne saucer and serve.

CHOCBERRY

30mL (1 oz) Afrikoko
60mL (2 oz) cream
15mL (0.5 oz) Framboise
5 strawberries

Method
Blend until smooth, pour into a champagne saucer and serve.

CHOCOLATE BABY

45mL (1.5 oz) crème de cacao
Coca-Cola

Method
Half fill a 10 oz highball glass with ice, add crème de cacao. Top with Coca-Cola and serve with straws.

CHOCOLATE CHIP MINT

30mL (1 oz) White Creme de Cacao
30mL (1 oz) Green Creme de Menthe
2 scoops vanilla ice cream
15mL (0.5 OZ) lemon juice
2 chocolate chips
top up with lemonade

Method
Blend with ice and strain then top up with lemonade. Serve with chocolate chip cookies on a side plate.

CHOCOLATE CHIP SHOOTER

15mL (0.5 oz) Vandermint
15mL (0.5 oz) Bailey's Irish cream
15mL (0.5 oz) crème de menthe

Method
Layer in a shot glass and serve.

CHOCOLATE NOUGAT SHOOTER

10mL (0.33 oz) Frangelico
10mL (0.33 oz) yellow Chartreuse
10mL (0.33 oz) Bailey's Irish cream

Method
Layer in a shot glass and serve.

CHOCOLATE SOLDIER

25mL (0.83 oz) brandy
1 dash orange bitters
20mL(0.66 oz) dry vermouth
2 ice cubes
10mL (0.33 oz) crème de cacao

Method
Blend and pour into a champagne saucer and serve.

CHOCOLATE STINGER

30mL (1 oz) crème do cacao
30mL (1 oz) crème de menthe

Method
Shake and strain into a 3 oz cocktail glass and serve.

CHOW CHE HUA

30mL (1 oz) Midori
1 peeled Kiwi fruit
30mL (1 oz) Cointreau
garnish:
1 pineapple wedge
90mL (3 oz) pineapple juice

Method
Blend until smooth, pour into a colada glass. Garnish with pineapple wedge and serve.

CHURCHES

30mL (1 oz) scotch whiskey
15mL (0.5 oz) Drambuie
15mL (0.5 oz) sweet vermouth
1 dash Angostura bitters

Method
Shake and strain over ice in a 3 oz cocktail glass and serve.

CIDER CUP

75mL (2.5 oz) sweet apple cider
1/4 tsp sugar
15mL (0.5 oz) brandy
15mL (0.5 oz) pineapple juice
15mL (0.5 oz) sweet sherry
15mL (0.5 oz) lemon juice
soda water
garnish:
nutmeg
crushed ice

Method
Place all ingredients except nutmeg and soda into a 10 oz highball glass and stir until sugar is dissolved. Top with soda, sprinkle with nutmeg. Serve with straws.

CLARET CUP

90mL (3 oz) claret
1 tsp sugar
15mL (0.5 oz) maraschino
crushed ice
soda water
garnish:
nutmeg

Method
Stir all ingredients except soda and nutmeg in a brandy Balloon until sugar is dissolved.
Top with soda, sprinkle with nutmeg and serve.

CLARET FLIP

90mL (3 oz) claret
1 egg yolk
2 tsp sugar syrup
2-3 ice cubes

Method
Shake and strain into a 5 oz cocktail glass and serve.

CLIFF HANGER

40mL (1.33 oz) vodka
15mL (0.5 oz) Peter Herring
15mL (0.5 oz) Galleon Liverno
lemonade

Method
Place 2 ice cubes in a 5 oz cocktail glass, Pour vodka and Peter Herring over top. Top with lemonade, float Galleon Liverno and serve.

CLOVER CLUB

45mL (1.5 oz) gin
1 egg white
4 dashes grenadine
cracked ice
juice 1/2 lemon

Method
Shake and strain into a champagne saucer and serve.

CLUB FORREST

15mL (0.5 oz) port wine
1 egg yolk
15mL (0.5 oz) Chartreuse
5mL (0.17 oz) sugar syrup
5mL (0.17 oz) white curaçao
garnish:
nutmeg

Method
Shake and strain into a 3 oz cocktail glass, sprinkle with nutmeg and serve.

COATHANGER SHOOTER

15mL (0.5 oz) Cointreau
7mL (0.23 oz) grenadine
15mL (0.5 oz) tequila
1 Drop milk

Method
Layer in a shot glass and serve.

COFFEE

30mL (1 oz) brandy
1 tsp sugar
30mL (1 oz) port wine
cracked ice
1 dash curaçao
garnish:
nutmeg
1 egg yolk

Method
Shake and strain into a 5 oz
cocktail glass, sprinkle with nutmeg
and serve.

COFFEE BOMB

15mL (0.5 oz) Cointreau
15mL (0.5 oz) Bailey's Irish cream
hot coffee
cream (float)

Method
Fill a Goblet with hot coffee and
add other ingredients.
Add sugar if desired, float cream
and serve.

COINTREAU CAIPIRINHA

30mL (1 oz) Cointreau
1/4 fresh lime or lemon
crushed ice

Method
Cut lime into pieces and place in a
175mL Prism Rocks Glass. Extract
juice by using the Cointreau Pestle,
fill glass with crushed ice and add
Cointreau and mini pestle. Stir.

COINTREAU MUPPET SHOOTER

30mL (1 oz) Cointreau
30mL (1 oz) Tonic water

Method
Layer on a shot glass and serve.

COLD DUCK

90mL (3 oz) chilled Moselle
1/2 tsp sugar
30mL (1 oz) Sparkling white wine
1 tbsp hot water
garnish: lemon peel

Method
Dissolve sugar in hot water in a
shaker, add other ingredients.
Shake and strain into a 5 oz
cocktail glass, garnish with lemon
peel and serve.

COLORADO

20mL (0.66 oz) cherry brandy
20mL (0.66 oz) cream
20mL (0.66 oz) kirsch
2-3 ice cubes

Method
Shake and strain into a 3 oz
cocktail glass and serve.

COLUMBIA SKIN

1/2 lemon, thinly peeled
30mL (1 oz) scotch whisky
1 cup of boiling water

Method
Pour in order into a 300mL Beer
Mug. Garnish with a slice of lemon.

COLUMBUS

20mL (0.66 oz) rum
20mL (0.66 oz) lemon juice
20mL (0.66 oz) apricot brandy
2-3 ice cubes

Method
Shake and strain into 3 oz cocktail
glass and serve.

COMFORT AND BOURBON

45mL (1.5 oz) Southern Comfort
45mL (1.5 oz) cold water
45 mL (1.5 oz) bourbon
cracked ice

Method
Half fill an Old Fashioned glass
with cracked ice. Add ingredients,
garnish with a twist of lemon and
serve.

COMFORT BABY

45mL (1.5 oz) Southern Comfort
1 Cube sugar
45mL (1.5 oz) fresh milk
2 ice cubes
nutmeg

Method
Place sugar cube in an Old
Fashioned glass and add liquid
ingredients. Stir gently until sugar
is dissolved, sprinkle with nutmeg
and serve.

COMFORTABLE SCREW

30mL (1 oz) vodka
orange juice
15mL (0.5 oz) Southern Comfort
ice

Method
In a 10 oz highball glass, Half fill
glass with ice and build vodka and
Southern Comfort. Top
with orange juice and serve.

COMMODORE

30mL (1 oz) bourbon
30mL (1 oz) lemon juice
30mL (1 oz) crème de cacao
crushed ice

Method
Shake and strain into champagne
glass and serve.

C

COMMONWEALTH

30mL (1 oz) Canadian Club Whisky
15mL (0.5 oz) Vandermint Liqueur
15mL (0.5 oz) lemon juice

Method
Shake over ice and strain. Garnish
with a slice of lemon.

CONCORD

30mL (1 oz) gin
10mL (0.33 oz) dry vermouth
15mL (0.5 oz) orange curaçao

Method
Shake and strain into a 3 oz
cocktail glass and serve.

CONSTELLATION

45mL (1.33 oz) dark rum
1 dash Angostura bitters
45mL (1.33 oz) Italian vermouth
1 dash lime juice
45mL (1.33 oz) green ginger wine
cracked ice

Method
Shake and strain into 5 oz cocktail
glass and serve.

CONTESSA

20mL (0.66 oz) brandy
20mL (0.66 oz) orange juice
20mL (0.66 oz) Cointreau
20mL (0.66 oz) fresh cream
20mL (0.66 oz) Galliano Liverno
1 maraschino cherry

Method
Shake and strain into a 5 oz.
champagne glass. Slit cherry and
place on lip of glass and serve.

COOL CUCUMBER

30mL (1 oz) Benedictine
15mL (0.5 oz) lemon juice
chilled champagne
garnish:
1 long strip cucumber

Method
Pour Benedictine and lemon juice
into a champagne flute. Top with
champagne, add Cucumber and serve.

COOPERSTOWN

25mL (0.83 oz) gin
garnish:
1 sprig mint
15mL (0.5 oz) dry vermouth
crushed ice
15mL (0.5 oz) Bianco vermouth

Method
Place ingredients in mixing glass
and stir, strain into a 3 oz cocktail
glass, garnish with sprig of mint
and serve.

COPACABANA

25mL (0.83 oz) apricot brandy
15mL (0.5 oz) lemon juice
15mL (0.5 oz) brandy
garnish:
1 slice orange
15mL (0.5 oz) Cointreau
crushed ice

Method
Shake and strain into a 3 oz
cocktail glass, garnish with orange
slice and serve over ice.

COPENHAGEN SPECIAL

30mL (1 oz) Aquavit
30mL (1 oz) Arrack
15mL (0.5 oz) lemon juice

Method
Shake over ice and strain. Garnish
with a slice of lemon.

CORONATION

15mL (0.5 oz) gin
15mL (0.5 oz) French vermouth
15mL (0.5 oz) Dubonnet

Method
Stir ingredients in a mixing glass,
strain into a 3 oz cocktail glass
and serve.

CORPSE REVIVER

30mL (1 oz) brandy
30mL (1 oz) white rum
30mL (1 oz) Fernet Branca

Method
Shake and strain into a 3 oz
cocktail glass and serve.

CORPSE REVIVER NO. 2.

30mL (1 oz) brandy
15mL (0.5 oz) sweet vermouth
30mL (1 oz) Fernet Branca

Method
Shake and strain into a 3 oz
cocktail glass and serve.

CORUBA CARIBBEAN

30mL (1 oz) Coruba rum
90 mL (3 oz) orange juice
15mL (0.5 oz) Malibu
30mL (1 oz) cream
1 dash blue curaçao
1 pineapple wedge
lemonade

Method
Shake rum, Malibu, cream and
orange juice and strain into a 10 oz
highball glass. Add blue curaçao
and garnish with the pineapple
wedge. Add straws and serve.

C

COUNTRY

30mL (1 oz) scotch whiskey
15mL (0.5 oz) lime juice
15mL (0.5 oz) cream
crushed ice

Method
Shake and strain into a 3 oz
cocktail glass and serve.

COVENANT'S RING SHOOTER

10mL (0.33 oz) parfait amour
10mL (0.33 oz) advocaat
10mL (0.33 oz) crème de menthe
sambuca (float)

Method
Layer in order in a 4 oz shot glass.
Float sambuca and serve.

COWBOY

40mL (1.33 oz) bourbon
30mL (1 oz) cream
4 ice cubes

Method
Shake ingredients and strain
into a wine glass over crushed ice
and serve.

CROCODILE COOLER

30mL (1 oz) Midori
60mL (2 oz) sweet and sour
30mL (1 oz) lemon vodka
lemonade
15mL (0.5 oz) Cointreau

Method
Build over ice in a 10 oz highball
glass, add straws and serve.

CRUSTA AMOUR

50mL (1.66 oz) tawny port
1 tbsp sugar (glass rim)
5mL (0.17 oz) Cointreau
2 dashes lime juice
2 dashes peach bitters
crushed ice
15mL (0.5 oz) lemon juice
garnish:
1 spiral lemon peel
5mL (0.17 oz) maraschino

Method
sugar rim an champagne glass.
Shake remaining ingredients and
strain into glass. Garnish with
lemon peel and serve.

CRUSTA BRANDY

90mL (3 oz) brandy
1 dash Angostura bitters
3 dashes maraschino
garnish:
1 maraschino cherry

Method
Shake and strain into a champagne
saucer. Garnish with cherry and
serve.

CRUSTA DAWN

40mL (1.33 oz) white rum
15mL (0.5 oz) lemon juice
1 tbsp apricot brandy
15mL (0.5 oz) orange juice
1 dash grenadine
spiral orange peel
1 tbsp castor sugar
2-3 ice cubes

Method
sugar Rim a champagne saucer and place remaining ingredients in a shaker. Shake and strain into the glass and serve

CRUSTA VODKA

40mL (1.33 oz) vodka
15mL (0.5 oz) orange juice
15mL (0.5 oz) sweet vermouth
50mL (1.66 oz) pineapple juice
15mL (0.5 oz) brandy
1 tbsp castor sugar
1 dash Angostura bitters
2-3 ice cubes
1 dash orange bitters
garnish:
1 spiral orange peel

Method
sugar Rim a champagne saucer. Shake remaining ingredients and strain into the glass. Garnish with spiral of orange peel and serve.

CUBE LIBRE

30mL (1 oz) white rum
juice 1/2 lemon
Coca-Cola
ice

Method
Pour ingredients over ice in a 10 oz highball glass, add straws and serve.

CURRENT RUM

60mL (2 oz) rum
soda water
15mL (0.5 oz) blackcurrant juice
ice

Method
Stir rum and juice together in a 5 oz cocktail glass with one ice cube, top with soda water and serve.

CYBER PUNCH

30mL (1 oz) vodka
30mL (1 oz) lemon juice
30mL (1 oz) gin
1 tsp sugar
30mL (1 oz) Bacardi rum
1 dash grenadine
30mL (1 oz) triple sec
180mL (6 oz) beer

Method
Pour ingredients into a 12 oz Hurricane glass. Serve with straws.

CYCLONE

90mL (3 oz) vodka
10mL (0.33 oz) Pernod
30mL (1 oz) dry vermouth
garnish:
1 twist lemon peel

Method
Half fill a mixing glass with cracked
ice and add ingredients. Stir and
strain into a 5 oz cocktail glass,
garnish with lemon peel and serve.

CYCLONE TRACY

30mL (1 oz) Tia Maria
30mL (1 oz) scotch whiskey
30mL (1 oz) Kahlúa
milk
30mL (1 oz) Bailey's Irish cream
crushed ice

Method
Shake ingredients except milk and
strain into an 8 oz highball glass.
Top with milk and serve with straws.

CZAR'S DELIGHT

1 tbsp vodka
75mL (2.5 oz) cream
1 tbsp mint liqueur
garnish:
frosted mint leaves
150mL (5 oz) milk
2 ice cubes

Method
Shake ingredients except mint
leaves and pour into a rocks glass,
garnish with mint leaves and serve.

D.J. SPECIAL

30mL (1 oz) brandy
30mL (1 oz) Benedictine
30mL (1 oz) Cointreau
Coca-Cola

Method
Shake ingredients except Coca-Cola and pour over ice in a brandy Balloon. Top with Coca-Cola and serve with straws.

D'ARTAGNAN

90mL (3 oz) Americano vermouth
garnish:
1 maraschino cherry
30mL (1 oz) orange curaçao
cracked ice

Method
Shake and strain into a 5 oz cocktail glass, garnish with cherry and serve.

DAIQUIRI

American

30mL (1 oz) white rum
1 tsp sugar
1 tsp Cointreau
garnish:
1 slice lime
15mL (0.5 oz) lime juice
1 maraschino cherry

Method
Shake and strain over crushed ice in a 5 oz cocktail glass.

Banana

30mL (1 oz) white rum
30mL (1 oz) orange juice
30mL (1 oz) dark rum
1/2 banana
2 tbsp banana liqueur
30mL (1 oz) orange juice
3 tbsp cream
ice

Method
Blend and pour into a 10 oz highball glass. Garnish with orange and banana wheels. Add straws and serve.

Kings

45mL (133 oz) Bacardi rum
15mL (0.5 oz) lemon juice
15mL (0.5 oz) parfait amour
1/4 tsp sugar
1 dash egg white

Method
Blend until smooth, pour into a champagne saucer and serve.

Death in the Afternoon
(Recipe page 83)

Depth Charge
(Recipe page 84)

Double Jeopardy
(Recipe page 87)

Fruit Tingle
(Recipe page 103)

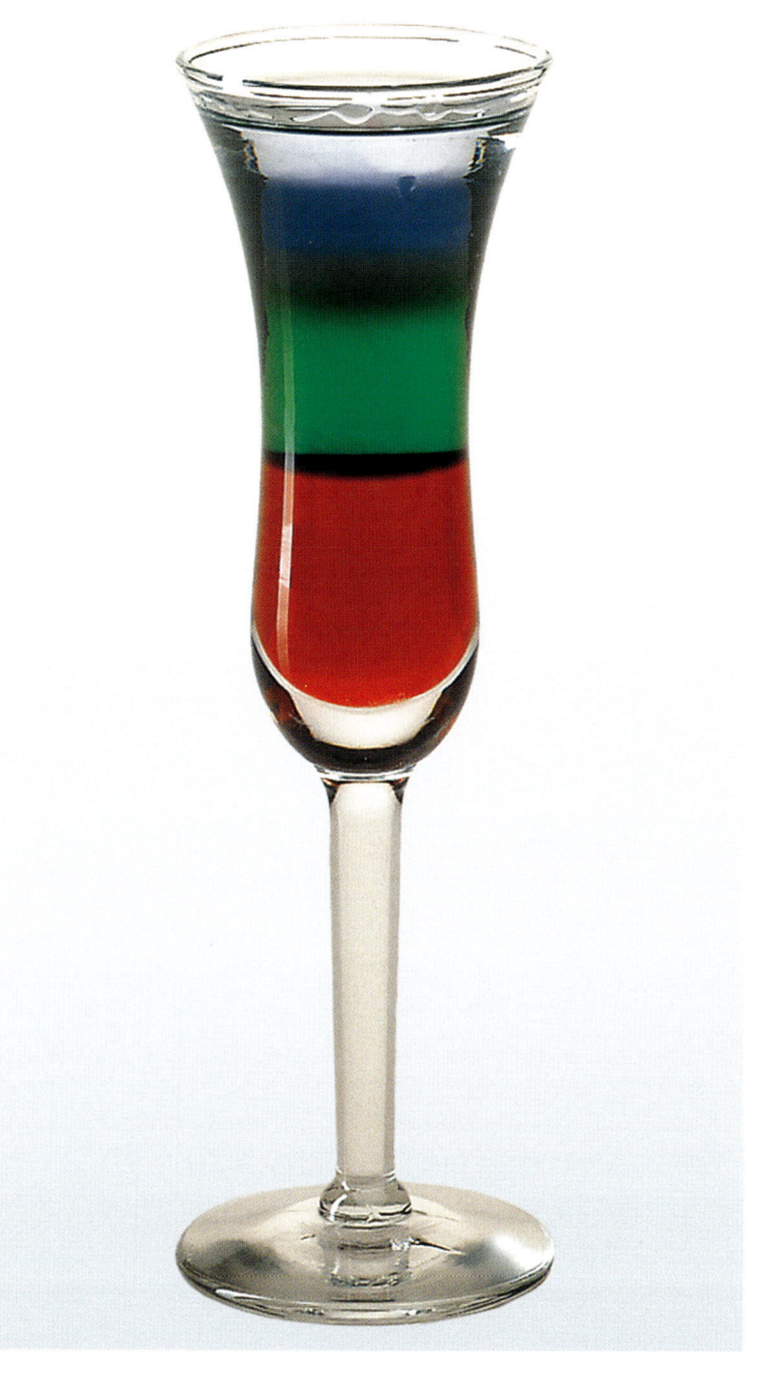

Face off
(Recipe page 94)

Frappé
(Recipe page 99)

Kiwi fruit

30mL (1 oz) Bacardi light rum
30mL (1 oz) lemon juice
30mL (1 oz) Cointreau
15mL (0.5 oz) sugar syrup
30mL (1 oz) Midori
1/2 kiwifruit

Method
Blend ingredients until smooth, pour
Into a champagne saucer and serve.

Lime

45mL (1.5 oz) Bacardi rum
30mL (1 oz) lime juice
20mL (0.66 oz) Cointreau

Method
Shake and strain into a 3 oz
cocktail glass and serve.

Mango

45mL (1.5 oz) Bacardi rum
20mL (0.66 oz) lemon juice
30mL (1 oz) Cointreau
15mL (0.5 oz) sugar syrup
30mL (1 oz) mango liqueur
1/2 mango

Method
Blend until smooth and pour into a
champagne glass and serve.

Midori

30mL (1 oz) Midori
20mL (0.66 oz) lemon juice
40mL (1.33 oz) white rum

Method
Shake and strain into a 3 oz
cocktail glass and serve.

Original

90mL (3 oz) white rum
1 tsp sugar
30mL (1 oz) lemon or lime juice
fruit for garnish

Method
Shake and strain into a chilled
cocktail glass, garnish and serve.

Peach

45mL (1.5 oz) Bacardi rum
20mL (0.66 oz) lemon juice
30mL (1 oz) Cointreau
15mL (0.5 oz) sugar syrup
30mL (1 oz) peach tree
1/2 peach

Method
Blend until smooth, pour into a
champagne glass and serve.

Rockmelon

45mL (1.5 oz) Bacardi rum
20mL (0.66 oz) lemon juice
30mL (1 oz) Cointreau
15mL (0.5 oz) sugar syrup
30mL (1 oz) mango liqueur
1/3 Rockmelon

Method
Blend until smooth and pour into a
champagne glass and serve.

Strawberry

90mL (3 oz) white rum
30mL (1 oz) lemon juice
1 tsp strawberry liqueur
60mL (2 oz) milk
10 strawberries
ice

Method
Blend until smooth, pour into a
colada glass, garnish with a
strawberry and serve.

DAIRY DREAM

15mL (0.5 oz) Galliano Liverno
30mL (1 oz) banana liqueur
20mL (0.66 oz) vodka
60mL (2 oz) cream

Method
Shake and strain into a 5 oz
cocktail glass and serve.

DAME PENNY

45mL (1.5 oz) dry gin
1 dash egg white
30mL (1 oz) dry vermouth
soda water
30mL (1 oz) lemon juice
cracked ice
30mL (1 oz) sugar syrup
garnish:
1/2 slice lemon

Method
Half fill shaker with cracked ice and
add ingredients except soda water.
Shake and strain into a 10 oz
highball glass. Garnish with
lemon slice, straws, swizzle sticks
and serve.

DANGEROUS VIOLETS

30mL (1 oz) parfait amour
30mL (1 oz) Bacardi rum
30mL (1 oz) gin
lemonade

Method
Shake ingredients except lemonade
and pour over ice in a 10 oz
highball glass. Top with lemonade,
add straws and serve.

DAYDREAM ISLAND

60mL (2 oz) dry gin
15mL (0.5 oz) orange juice
15mL (0.5 oz) blue curaçao
garnish:
1 maraschino cherry
30mL (1 oz) Galliano Liverno
cracked ice
1/2 egg white

Method
Shake and strain into a 5 oz
cocktail glass, garnish with cherry
and serve.

DEAD BANANA

60mL (2 oz) banana liqueur
milk
60mL (2 oz) grenadine

Method
Shake banana liqueur, grenadine
and strain into a 10 oz highball
glass, top with milk and serve
with straws.

DEAN'S DELIGHT

30mL (1 oz) tequila
30mL (1 oz) Benedictine
30mL (1 oz) crème de menthe
crushed ice
15mL (0.5 oz) brandy
soda water (Optional)

Method
Shake and strain into an Old
Fashioned glass over crushed ice.
Add soda water if Desired.

DEATH BY CHOCOLATE

30mL (1 oz) Bailey's Irish cream
30mL (1 oz) crème de cacao
30mL (1 oz) Kahlúa
90 mL (3 oz) Thickened cream
30mL (1 oz) Tia Maria
garnish:
grated chocolate

Method
Shake and strain into a champagne saucer, garnish with grated chocolate and serve.

DEATH BY CHOCOLATE NO. 2

30mL (1 oz) Bailey's Irish cream
30mL (1 oz) crème de cacao
30mL (1 oz) Kahlúa
90mL (3 oz) Thickened cream
30mL (1 oz) Afrikoko
garnish:
grated chocolate

Method
Shake and strain into a champagne saucer, garnish with grated chocolate and serve.

DEATH BY CHOCOLATE NO. 3

30mL (1 oz) Bailey's Irish cream
30mL (1 oz) Kahlúa
30mL (1 oz) crème de cacao
90 mL (3 oz) Thicken cream
30mL (1 oz) Cadbury's chocolate liqueur
garnish:
grated chocolate

Method
Shake and strain into a champagne saucer, garnish with grated chocolate and serve.

DEATH IN THE AFTERNOON

15mL (0.5 oz) Pernod
1 sugar Cube
champagne

Method
Place the sugar Cube in a 6 oz tulip glass and add Pernod, top with champagne and serve.

DEEP THROAT SHOOTER

20mL (0.66 oz) Kahlúa
Thickened cream
20mL (0.66 oz) Grand Marnier

Method
Layer in a shot glass and serve.

DEPTH CHARGE

340mL (11.33 oz) beer
30mL (1 oz) Cointreau

Method
Pour beer into a 375mL glass, fill a
1 oz shot glass with Cointreau.
Drop shot glass into beer in front
of Customer.

DE RIGUEUR

30mL (1 oz) scotch whisky
10mL (0.33 oz) grapefruit juice
10mL (0.33 oz) honey

Method
Shake over ice and pour. Garnish
with a swizzle stick.

DESERT COOLER

60mL (2oz) Southern Comfort
75mL (2.5 oz) pineapple juice
15mL (0.5 oz) bourbon
75mL (2.5 oz) grapefruit juice
cracked ice

Method
Half fill a 10 oz glass with cracked
ice, shake remaining ingredients
and strain over ice and serve.

DESERT ISLAND

30mL (1 oz) Bacardi light rum
60mL (2 oz) pineapple juice
45mL (1.5 oz) Midori
cream

Method
Shake all ingredients except cream
and strain into a 5 oz champagne
saucer, top with cream and serve.

DESERT ROSE

30mL (1 oz) Midori
60mL (2 oz) pineapple juice
30mL (1 oz) Bailey's Irish cream
60g rockmelon
15mL (0.5 oz) Glayva
garnish:
pineapple wedge

Method
Blend and pour into a colada glass,
garnish with pineapple wedge and
serve with straws.

DESERT STORM

15mL (0.5 oz) mango liqueur
60mL (2 oz) pineapple juice
15mL (0.5 oz) Bacardi rum
1 dash Tabasco Sauce
15mL (0.5 oz) gin

Method
Shake and strain into a 4 ?/.
cocktail glass and serve.

D

DESHLER

30mL (1 oz) Canadian whiskey
1 dash Angostura bitters
15mL (0.5 oz) Dubonnet
garnish:
1 strip lemon peel
1 dash Cointreau
1 strip orange peel

Method
Shake and strain into a 3 oz
cocktail glass, garnish with lemon
and orange peel and serve.

DESPINA

90mL (3 oz) sweet vermouth
garnish:
1 twist orange peel
30mL (1 oz) Galliano Liverno

Method
Shake and strain into a 5 oz
cocktail glass, garnish with orange
peel and serve.

DEVIL

45mL (1.5 oz) brandy
45mL (1.5 oz) crème de Menthe

Method
Shake and strain into a 3 oz
cocktail glass and serve.

DEVIL'S HANDBRAKE SHOOTER

15mL (0.5 oz) banana liqueur
15mL (0.5 oz) cherry brandy
15mL (0.5 oz) mango liqueur

Method
Layer in order in a shot glass
and serve.

DIPLOMAT

45mL (1.5 oz) vodka
90mL (3 oz) pineapple juice
45mL (1.5 oz) Midori
5mL (0.17 oz) lemon juice

Method
Shake and strain into a 8 oz
highball glass and serve with
straws.

DIRTY MOTHER

30mL (1 oz) tequila
milk
30mL (1 oz) Tia Maria

Method
Shake and strain over ice in a
10 oz highball glass, top with milk
and serve.

DIZZY BLOND

60mL (2 oz) advocaat
lemonade
30mL (1 oz) Pernod
garnish:
1 maraschino cherry

Method
Half fill a 10 oz highball glass with
cracked ice and add advocaat and
Pernod. Top with lemonade,
garnish with cherry and serve.

DIZZY DAME

30mL (1 oz) brandy
30mL (1 oz) cream
15mL (0.5 oz) Kahlúa
1/2 scoop ice
15mL (0.5 oz) cherry brandy

Method
Blend and pour into a flute glass
and serve.

DIZZY WHISTLE

15mL (0.5 oz) Frangelico
10mL (0.33 oz) pineapple juice
*10mL (0.33 oz) Green Creme de
Menthe*
10mL (0.33 oz) cream

Method
Layer pineapple juice onto
Frangelico then shake Green Creme
de Menthe with cream and layer.

DOCTOR DANGEROUS

45mL (1.5 oz) brandy
60mL (2 oz) milk
45mL (1.5 oz) Bailey's Irish cream

Method
Shake and strain into an Old
Fashioned glass and serve.

DOG'S SPECIAL

30mL (1 oz) Midori
30mL (1 oz) pineapple juice
30mL (1 oz) vodka
15mL (0.5 oz) cream

Method
Float ingredients in order in a 4 oz
cocktail glass and serve.

DOLOMINT

30mL (1 oz) Gilbey's Gin
30mL (1 oz) Galliano
25mL (0.83 oz) lime juice
top up with soda
fresh mint leaves

Method
Pour over ice and top up with soda.
Coat rim of glass with sprig of mint
and add 2 fresh mint leaves.

DOROTHY LAMOUR

30mL (1 oz) Bacardi rum
3 slices mango
30mL (1 oz) banana liqueur
1 scoop ice
15mL (0.5 oz) lemon juice

Method
Blend and pour into a flute glass
and serve.

DOUBLE BLAZER

30mL (1 oz) white crème de
menthe
30mL (1 oz) Southern Comfort

Method
Pour crème de menthe into a white
wine glass. Slowly add Southern
Comfort and ignite. Serve and
extinguish flame in front of
Customer.

DOUBLE DATE

15mL (0.5 oz) Midori
15mL (0.5 oz) White Creme de
Menthe
15mL (0.5 oz) DOM Benedectine

Method
Layer in order.

DOUBLE JEOPARDY

45mL (1.5 oz) Frangelico
1 scoop vanilla ice cream
45mL (1.5 oz) Opal Nera
milk

Method
Blend all ingredients except milk,
pour into a 10 oz highball glass.
Top with milk and serve with straws
and a Parfait Spoon.

DRAGON'S FIRE SHOOTER

15mL (0.5 oz) cherry advocaat
15mL (0.5 oz) Galleon Liverno
15mL (0.5 oz) orange curaçao
15mL (0.5 oz) Southern Comfort
15mL (0.5 oz) blue curaçao
15mL (0.5 oz) advocaat

Method
Layer in order in a shot glass and
serve.

DRAMBUIE HIGH

30mL (1 oz) Drambuie
20 mL (0.66 oz) coconut cream
30mL (1 oz) Golden rum
30mL (1 oz) pineapple juice
30mL (1 oz) cream
1/2 banana
1 scoop crushed ice

Method
Blend until smooth, pour into a 10
oz highball glass. Garnish with
pineapple leaves and serve.

DUBONNET

60mL (2 oz) Dubonnet
garnish:
1 twist lemon
60mL (2 oz) gin

Method
Stir ingredients in a 3 oz cocktail glass, garnish with lemon and serve.

DUCHESS

45mL (1.5 oz) dry vermouth
45mL (1.5 oz) Pernod
45mL (1.5 oz) sweet vermouth
garnish:
1 strip orange peel

Method
Stir and strain into a 5 oz cocktail glass, garnish with orange peel and serve.

DUKE OF MARLBOROUGH

30mL (1 oz) Sherry
30mL (1 oz) Cinzano Rosso Vermouth
30mL (1 oz) lime juice
2 dashes raspberry cordial

Method
Shake and pour over ice. Garnish with a red cherry and a swizzle stick.

DUNK

30mL (1 oz) dry vermouth
5mL (0.17 oz) curaçao
30mL (1 oz) gin
garnish:
1 maraschino cherry
15mL (0.5 oz) Galliano Liverno

Method
Stir and strain into a 3 oz cocktail glass, garnish with cherry and serve.

DYEVTCHKA

30mL (1 oz) Smirnoff Vodka
30mL (1 oz) Cointreau
20mL (0.66 oz) fresh lime juice
20mL (0.66 oz) fresh lemon juice
15mL (0.5 oz) pineapple juice

Method
Shake with ice and pour. Garnish with a pineapple wedge & cherry. Comments: Open up to the hidden secrets of the Eastern block of Europe.

EL BURRO

15mL (0.5 oz) Kahlúa
30mL (1 oz) cream
15mL (0.5 oz) rum
1/2 banana
30mL (1 oz) coconut cream

Method
Blend ingredients with a Scoop and ice. Pour into a 9 oz cocktail glass. Garnish with a banana slice, mint leaves and serve.

ELDORADO

30mL (1 oz) white rum
30mL (1 oz) advocaat
30mL (1 oz) crème de cacao
garnish:
1 tsp grated coconut

Method
Shake and strain into 4 oz cocktail glass and serve.

EL DIABLO

30mL (1 oz) Jose Cuervo Tequila
15mL (0.5 oz) Creme de Cassis
10mL (0.33 oz) lime juice
top up with ginger ale

Method
Build over ice and top up with ginger ale. Garnish with puréed lime.

ELECTRIC BANANA SHOOTER

15mL (0.5 oz) banana liqueur
15mL (0.5 oz) tequila
15mL (0.5 oz) lime juice

Method
Layer in order in a shot glass and serve.

ELECTRIC BLUE

15mL (0.5 oz) vodka
30mL (1 oz) dry vermouth
15mL (0.5 oz) blue curaçao
lemonade

Method
Pour vodka, vermouth and curaçao over ice in a 10 oz highball glass. Top with lemonade and serve.

EL REVOLTO SHOOTER

15mL (0.5 oz) crème de menthe
15mL (0.5 oz) Cointreau
15mL (0.5 oz) Bailey's Irish cream

Method
Layer in order in a shot glass and serve.

EDITOR'S CURSE

30mL (1 oz) scotch whiskey
30mL (1 oz) orange juice
30mL (1 oz) Van der Hum

Method
Stir in 4 oz cocktail glass and serve.

EDWARD VIII

45mL (1.5 oz) Canadian whiskey
2 tbsp water
1 dash Pernod
garnish:
1 strip orange peel
2 tbsp Italian vermouth
cracked ice

Method
Stir and strain into and Old Fashioned glass and serve.

EGG SOUR

30mL (1 oz) brandy
juice 1/4 lemon
30mL (1 oz) white curaçao
1 tbsp castor sugar
1 egg
cracked ice

Method
Shake and strain into sour glass and serve.

EGGNOG

30mL (1 oz) brandy
1 egg
1 tbsp sugar
ice
milk
garnish:
nutmeg

Method
Shake brandy, egg and sugar with ice and strain into an Old Fashioned glass. Fill with milk, sprinkle with nutmeg and serve.

EH-BOMB SHOOTER

10mL (0.33 oz) crème de menthe
10mL (0.33 oz) ouzo
10mL (0.33 oz) Bailey's Irish cream
15mL (0.5 oz) tequila

Method
Layer in order in a shot glass and serve.

E

EARLY SUMMER

30mL (1 oz) gin

30mL (1 oz) orange juice

30mL (1 oz) apricot brandy

garnish:

1 slice apple

30mL (1 oz) Calvados

cracked ice

Method
Shake and strain into a 5 oz cocktail glass, garnish with apple slice and serve.

EARTHQUAKE

30mL (1 oz) rye whiskey

30mL (1 oz) gin

30mL (1 oz) Pernod

cracked ice

Method
Half fill shaker with ice and add ingredients. Shake and strain into a 5 oz cocktail glass and serve.

EAST INDIA

40mL (1.33 oz) white rum

1 tbsp pineapple juice

1 tbsp Cointreau

garnish:

1 maraschino cherry

1 dash Angostura bitters

cracked ice

Method
Shake ingredients and strain into a 3 oz cocktail glass. Garnish with cherry and serve.

EAST WIND

25mL (0.83 oz) vodka

2-3 dashes white rum

15mL (0.5 oz) dry vermouth

cracked ice

15mL (0.5 oz) sweet vermouth

Method
Shake and strain into a 3 oz cocktail glass and serve.

EDGEMOORE

30mL (1 oz) white rum

90mL (3 oz) pineapple juice

30mL (1 oz) dark rum

soda water

30mL (1 oz) Irish mint

garnish:

2 maraschino Cherries

Method
Shake all ingredients except soda. Pour into a 10 oz highball glass, top with soda, garnish with Cherries and serve.

ELECTRIC LEMONADE

30mL (1 oz) triple sec
30mL (1 oz) vodka
30mL (1 oz) tequila
30mL (1 oz) gin
30mL (1 oz) white rum
lemonade

Method
Shake all ingredients except
lemonade and strain into a 10 oz
highball glass. Top with lemonade
and serve.

ELEPHANT WALK

30mL (1 oz) gin
1 dash Angostura bitters
15mL (0.5 oz) tequila
garnish:
1/2 orange slice
1 dash grenadine
1/2 lemon slice
15mL (0.5 oz) orange juice
1 Stick Cucumber

Method
Fill an Old Fashioned glass with
cracked ice, add ingredients and
garnish with fruit and cucumber.
Add swizzle stick and serve.

EMERALD QUEEN

60mL (2 oz) vodka
10mL (0.33 oz) blue curaçao
40mL (1.33 oz) dry vermouth
garnish:
1 maraschino cherry
20mL (0.66oz) Galliano Liverno
cracked ice

Method
Half fill mixing glass with cracked
ice, add ingredients and stir. Strain
into 5 oz champagne glass, garnish
with cherry and serve.

EMPIRE

25mL (0.83 oz) gin
garnish:
2 maraschino Cherries
15mL (0.5 oz) Calvados
cracked ice
15mL (0.5 oz) apricot brandy

Method
Shake and strain into 3 oz cocktail
glass, garnish with Cherries and
serve.

E

ESME'S PERIL

190mL (6.33 oz) Bacardi rum
60mL (2 oz) lemon juice
30mL (1 oz) dark rum
30mL (1 oz) orange juice
2 tbsp banana liqueur
3 tbsp cream
1/2 banana
2 tsp sugar
4 strawberries
ice

Method
Blend all ingredients until smooth, pour into a Tankard and serve.

EVERGREEN

15mL (0.5 oz) dry vermouth
15mL (0.5 oz) Midori
30mL (1 oz) dry gin
7mL (0.23 oz) blue curaçao

Method
Shake ingredients and strain into a 3 oz cocktail glass. Garnish with a cherry and serve.

ETON BLAZER

25mL (0.83 oz) gin
15mL (0.5 oz) lemon juice
25mL (0.83 oz) kirsch
soda water
2 tsp sugar syrup
garnish:
2 maraschino Cherries

Method
Place ingredients except soda and Cherries in a 10 oz highball glass, top with soda, garnish with cherries and serve.

EXXON VALDESE SHOOTER

30mL (1 oz) sambuca
30mL (1 oz) Opal Nera

Method
Layer in shot glass an serve.

FACE-OFF SHOOTER

10mL (0.33 oz) grenadine
10mL (0.33 oz) parfait amour
15mL (0.5 oz) crème de menthe
10mL (0.33 oz) sambuca

Method
Layer in order in a shot glass and
serve.

FAIR LADY

60mL (2 oz) gin
270mL (9 oz) grapefruit juice
1 dash Cointreau
Powdered sugar
1 egg white
ice

Method
Rim two 5 oz cocktail glass with
egg white and sugar. Shake
remaining ingredients and strain
into glasses and serve.

FALCON'S DELIGHT SHOOTER

30mL (1 oz) sambuca
30mL (1 oz) tequila
30mL (1 oz) crème de cacao

Method
Layer in shot glass and serve.

FALLEN ANGEL

30mL (1 oz) gin
juice 1/2 lemon
2 dash crème de menthe
cracked ice
1 dash Angostura bitters

Method
Shake and strain into a 3 oz
cocktail glass and serve.

FERNET-BRANCA

45mL (1.5 oz) Fernet Branca
45mL (1.5 oz) Pernod

Method
Mix with ice in an Old Fashioned
glass and serve.

FIGHTING BOB

60mL (2 oz) gin
1 dash Angostura bitters
15mL (0.5 oz) cherry brandy
1 tsp lemon juice
15mL (0.5 oz) Chartreuse
soda water

Method
Shake ingredients except soda.
pour into highball glass. Top with
soda water and serve.

FIRE AND ICE

20mL (0.66 oz) tequila
10mL (0.33 oz) crème de menthe

Method
Layer in shot glass and serve.

FIREMAN'S SOUR

80mL (2.66 oz) white rum
garnish:
6 small lemon triangles
1 tsp grenadine
3 maraschino Cherries
15mL (0.5 oz) lemon juice
3 ice cubes
soda water

Method
Shake ice, rum, lemon juice and grenadine. Strain into a Tumble glass and add lemon triangles. Top with soda and serve.

FJORD

30mL (1 oz) Milne Brandy
10mL (0.33 oz) Aquavit
10mL (0.33 oz) orange juice
10mL (0.33 oz) lime juice
5mL (0.17 oz) Grenadine

Method
Shake over ice and strain then add Grenadine. Garnish with an orange slice.

FIZZ

Bacardi

60mL (2 oz) Bacardi rum
soda water
60mL (2 oz) lemon juice
cracked ice

Method
Shake all ingredients except soda water and strain over ice in a 10 oz highball glass. Top with soda water, add straws and serve.

Banana

30mL (1 oz) banana liqueur
1/2 banana
30mL (1 oz) lemon juice
soda water
15mL (0.5 oz) sugar syrup
ice
1 egg white

Method
Blend all ingredients except soda water, pour into a 10 oz highball glass. Top with soda water, add straws and serve.

FLAME THROWER SHOOTER

20mL (0.66 oz) crème de cacao
25mL (0.83 oz) B & B

Method
Layer in shot glass and serve.

FLAMING DIAMOND SHOOTER

10mL (0.33 oz) strawberry liqueur
10mL (0.33 oz) Grand Marnier
10mL (0.33 oz) vodka

Method
Layer in shot glass and serve.

FLAMING ORGY SHOOTER

10mL (0.33 oz) grenadine
15mL (0.5 oz) brandy
10mL (0.33 oz) crème de menthe
10mL (0.33 oz) tequila

Method
Layer in order in a shot glass
and serve.

FLAMING SAMBUCA

30mL (1 oz) Romana Sambuca
3 coffee beans

Method
Pour Romana Sambuca, float coffee
beans and light. Shoot after flame
extinguished.

FLIRT WITH DIRT

30mL (1 oz) Kahlúa
30mL (1 oz) Malibu
15mL (0.5 oz) Vandermint
1 float cream

Method
Shake Kahlúa, Vandermint and
Malibu and strain into a 3 oz
cocktail glass. Float cream
and serve.

FLOWER

30mL (1 oz) tequila
15mL (0.5 oz) mango liqueur
15mL (0.5 oz) white curaçao
75mL (2.5 oz) orange juice

Method
Blend for two seconds, pour into a
highball glass over ice and serve.

FLORIDA

30mL (1 oz) Bacardi rum
soda water
1 tbsp crème de menthe
cracked ice
1 tbsp lime juice
1 sprig mint
1 tbsp pineapple juice

Method
Shake all ingredients except soda
water, Strain over ice in a 10 oz
highball glass. Top with soda water,
garnish with mint, straws and
serve.

FLUFFY DUCK

30mL (1 oz) advocaat
15mL (0.5 oz) gin
Galleon Liverno
lemonade

Method
Mix advocaat in a 10 oz highball
glass with ice. Top with lemonade
and float Galleon Liverno on top
and serve.

Fluffy Duck
(Recipe page 96)

Fluffy Duck No.2
(Recipe page 97)

Grasshopper
(Recipe page 112)

G.R.B.
(Recipe page 104)

Green with Envy
(Recipe page 115)

Harvey Wallbanger
(Recipe page 119)

FLUFFY DUCK (INTERNATIONAL)

30mL (1 oz) advocaat

15mL (0.5 oz) gin

15mL (0.5 oz) vodka

30mL (1 oz) cream

15mL (0.5 oz) Cointreau

lemonade

Method
Place all ingredients except lemonade in a 10 oz highball glass and stir. Top with lemonade and serve.

FLUFFY DUCK NO. 2

15mL (0.5 oz) vodka

15mL (0.5 oz) orange curaçao

30mL (1 oz) advocaat

30mL (1 oz) cream

lemonade

Method
Mix all ingredients except lemonade in a 10 oz highball glass. Top with lemonade and serve.

FLUFFY DUCK NO. 3

30mL (1 oz) gin

30mL (1 oz) orange juice

30mL (1 oz) advocaat

soda water

15mL (0.5 oz) Cointreau

ice

Method
Place all ingredients except soda in a 10 oz highball glass and stir. Top with soda and serve.

FLYING CARPET

30mL (1 oz) vodka

15mL (0.5 oz) banana liqueur

15mL (0.5 oz) advocaat

30mL (1 oz) cream

Method
Shake and strain into a 3 oz cocktail glass and serve.

FLYING DUTCHMAN

10mL (0.33 oz) Cointreau

30mL (1 oz) Gilbey's Gin

Method
Coat glass with Cointreau then pour Gilbey's Gin over ice. Garnish with a lemon twist.

FLYING HIGH

30mL (1 oz) Bailey's Irish cream

15mL (0.5 oz) Drambuie

30mL (1 oz) Cointreau

ice

Method
Shake and strain into a 3 oz cocktail glass and serve.

FOG CUTTER

15mL (0.5 oz) Coruba Rum
10mL (0.33 oz) Milne Brandy
15mL (0.5 oz) Orgeat
25mL (0.83 oz) lemon juice
150mL (5 oz) orange juice

Method
Shake over ice and pour. Garnish with a strawberry.

FOREIGN AFFAIR

15mL (0.5 oz) Cointreau
30mL (1 oz) Rubis
30mL (1 oz) vodka
orange juice

Method
Shake and strain ingredients into a 10 oz highball glass. Top with orange juice and serve.

FORTY WINKS

1 teaspoon honey
15mL (0.5 oz) Peach Liqueur
15mL (0.5 oz) Orange Curacao
4-5 drops Grenadine

Method
Pour Peach Liqueur onto honey, layer Orange Curacao, then drop Grenadine.

FORWARD PASS

30mL (1 oz) vodka
30mL (1 oz) Cointreau
30mL (1 oz) dry vermouth
30mL (1 oz) pure lemon juice

Method
Shake ingredients and strain into a 5 oz cocktail glass and serve.

FOURTH OF JULY

30mL (1 oz) bourbon
orange juice
30mL (1 oz) Kahlúa
cream
Galleon Liverno

Method
Place bourbon and Kahlúa in a 10 oz highball glass. Fill to 2.5 cm (1/2 inch) from top with orange juice and add cream. Float Galleon Liverno on top and serve.

401 SHOOTER

10mL (0.33 oz) Kahlúa
5mL (0.17 oz) Bailey's Irish cream
10mL (0.33 oz) banana liqueur
5mL (0.17 oz) Jack Daniel's

Method
Layer in order in a shot glass and serve.

FRAISE ANNÉE

30mL (1 oz) strawberry liqueur
45mL (1.5 oz) cream
30mL (1 oz) white cream de cacao
garnish:
4 strawberries
15mL (0.5 oz) brandy

Method
Blend ingredients and pour into a colada glass. Garnish with a strawberry and serve.

FRANGELICO LUAU

45mL (1.5 oz) Frangelico
200mL (6.66 oz) pineapple juice
dash of Grenadine

Method
Blend with ice and pour. Garnish with a pineapple slice and leaves.

FRAPPÉ

Byrrh

60mL (2 oz) Byrrh
garnish:
1 twist lemon
cracked ice

Method
Fill 3 oz cocktail glass with ice and pour Byrrh over ice. Garnish with lemon and serve.

Crème de menthe

60mL (2 oz) crème de menthe
garnish:
1 twist lemon
cracked ice

Method
Fill 3 oz cocktail glass with ice and pour crème de menthe over ice. Garnish with lemon and serve.

Grand Marnier

60mL (2 oz) Grand Marnier
garnish:
grated chocolate
cracked ice

Method
Fill 3 oz cocktail glass with cracked ice and pour Grand Marnier over top. Garnish with grated chocolate and serve.

Midori & Cointreau

15mL (0.5 oz) Midori
crushed ice
15mL (0.5 oz) Cointreau

Method
Fill a 5 oz cocktail glass with crushed ice. Build ingredients over ice, garnish with cherry, 2 Short straws and serve.

Southern peach

30mL (1 oz) strawberry liqueur
crushed ice
30mL (1 oz) Southern Comfort

Method
Build ingredients over crushed ice in a 140 mL cocktail glass and serve.

FREDDY FUDPUCKER

60mL (2 oz) tequila
garnish:
1 slice orange
Galliano
1 maraschino cherry
orange juice
ice

Method
Fill a 10 oz highball glass with ice, add tequila and fill 1/2 inch from top with orange juice. Float Galleon Liverno, garnish with orange slice and cherry and serve.

FRENCH

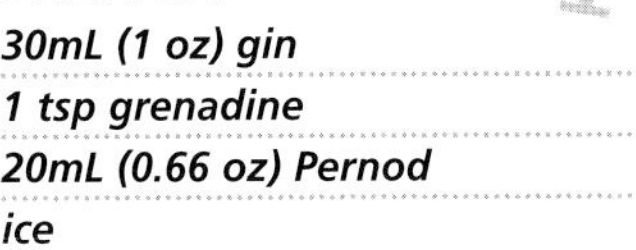

30mL (1 oz) gin
1 tsp grenadine
20mL (0.66 oz) Pernod
ice

Method
Shake and strain into 3 oz cocktail glass and serve.

FRENCH 69

15mL (0.5 oz) gin
5mL (0.17 oz) lemon juice
10mL (0.33 oz) Pernod
5mL (0.17 oz) sugar syrup
champagne

Method
Pour ingredients into champagne glass, top with champagne and serve.

FRENCH 75

45mL (1.5 oz) gin
juice 1/2 lemon
90mL (3 oz) champagne
1 tsp Powered sugar
cracked ice
garnish:
1 twist lemon peel

Method
Combine gin, sugar, lemon juice and ice in a mixing glass. Strain into a 10 oz highball glass and fill with champagne. Garnish with lemon peel and serve.

FRENCH 95

45mL (0.66 oz) bourbon
juice 1/2 lemon
90mL (3 oz) champagne
1 tsp Powdered sugar
cracked ice
garnish:
1 twist lemon peel

Method
Combine bourbon, sugar, lemon juice and ice in a mixing glass. Strain into a 10 oz highball glass and fill with champagne. Garnish with lemon peel and serve.

FRENCH CONNECTION

45mL (1.5 oz) brandy
20mL (0.66 oz) amaretto

Method
Shake and strain into an Old Fashioned glass and serve.

F

FRENCH FANTASY

30mL (1 oz) vodka
30mL (1 oz) crème de Grand Marnier
15mL (0.5 oz) Tia Maria
30mL (1 oz) orange juice
30mL (1 oz) pineapple juice
garnish:
1 slice banana

Method
Blend and pour into a 5 oz cocktail glass, garnish with a slice of banana and a maraschino cherry and serve.

FRENCH GREENERY

30mL (1 oz) Pernod
3 ice cubes
30mL (1 oz) crème de menthe
garnish:
1 sprig mint

Method
Pour ingredients over ice in a Old Fashioned glass. Garnish with the sprig of mint and serve.

FRENCH KISS

30mL (1 oz) gin
garnish:
1 maraschino cherry
30mL (1 oz) dry vermouth
crushed ice
30mL (1 oz) Dubonnet

Method
Stir in mixing glass. Pour into a 5 oz cocktail glass and serve.

FRENCH SAFARI

30mL (1 oz) Rubis
15mL (0.5 oz) Afrikoko
15mL (0.5 oz) Cointreau
30mL (1 oz) cream

Method
Shake and strain into a 3 oz cocktail glass and serve.

FRISCO SOUR

60mL (2 oz) scotch whisky
10mL (0.33 oz) lemon juice
10mL (0.33 oz) lime juice
10mL (0.33 oz) Grenadine
top up with soda

Method
Shake with ice and pour then top up with soda. Garnish with a lime slice.

FROTH AND BUBBLE

60mL (2 oz) (1 oz) vodka
15mL (0.5 oz) orange juice
15mL (0.5 oz) blue curaçao
1/2 egg white
15mL (0.5 oz) Galleon Liverno
garnish:
1 maraschino cherry

Method
Shake and strain into a 5 oz cocktail glass, garnish with cherry and serve.

FROZEN AQUAVIT

45mL (1.5 oz) Aquavit
10mL (0.33 oz) Kirsch
10mL (0.33 oz) lime juice
10mL (0.33 oz) sugar syrup
10mL (0.33 oz) egg white

Method
Blend over ice and pour. Garnish with one cocktail onion.

FROZEN LEANGO

30mL (1 oz) gin
60mL (2 oz) orange juice
30mL (1 oz) banana liqueur
2 scoops ice
30mL (1 oz) mango liqueur

Method
Blend and pour into a 12 oz tulip glass and serve with straws.

FROZEN MUDSLIDE

30mL (1 oz) Smirnoff Vodka
20mL (0.66 oz) Baileys Irish Cream
20mL (0.66 oz) Kahlúa
top up with milk
whipped cream
hundreds and thousands,
confectionary balls
thickened chocolate

Method
Blend with ice, pour into glass. top up with milk then add whipped cream in a swirling motion. With a teaspoon slide the thickened chocolate (or Ice Magic), thereby creating a Mud Slide. Place strawberry on side of glass with hundreds and thousands.

FRUIT CUP

10mL (0.33 oz) Mango Liqueur
10mL (0.33 oz) passionfruit pulp
10mL (0.33 oz) guava juice

Method
Layer passionfruit pulp onto Mango Liqueur, then pour in order.

FRUIT PASSION

30mL (1 oz) vodka
15mL (0.5 oz) passionfruit pulp
30mL (1 oz) rum
pineapple juice

Method
One third fill a 10 oz highball glass with cracked ice, add vodka, rum and passionfruit pulp. Stir and top with pineapple juice, garnish with a pineapple wedge, straws and serve.

F

FRUIT SALAD

10mL (0.33 oz) Banana Liqueur
10mL (0.33 oz) Strawberry Liqueur
10mL (0.33 oz) Malibu

Method
Layer in order, then float vanilla
ice cream.

FRUIT SOUR

30mL (1 oz) scotch whiskey
garnish:
1 maraschino cherry
30mL (1 oz) lemon juice
1 orange slice
30mL (1 oz) fruit liqueur
cracked ice

Method
Shake and strain into a 5 oz
cocktail glass, garnish and serve.

FRUIT TINGLE

30mL (1 oz) vodka
lemonade
15mL (0.5 oz) parfait amour
1 dash grenadine
15mL (0.5 oz) blue curaçao

Method
Build ingredients over ice in a
colada glass, top with lemonade,
add grenadine. Serve with straws.

FULL MOON

30mL (1 oz) vodka
20mL (0.66 oz) coconut cream
15mL (0.5 oz) blue curaçao
cracked ice
20mL (0.66 oz) cream
garnish:
Shaved chocolate

Method
Shake and strain into a 3 oz
cocktail glass, garnish with
chocolate and serve.

G.R.B.

30mL (1 oz) Galleon Liverno

30mL (1 oz) Bacardi rum

10mL (0.33 oz) grenadine

garnish:

1 mint leaf

Method
Build over ice in a 3 oz cocktail glass, garnish with mint leaf floating on top and serve.

GALLIANO HOT SHOT

15mL (0.5 oz) Galleon Liverno

5mL (0.17 oz) cream (float)

25mL (0.83 oz) hot black coffee

Method
Top Galliano with black coffee in a 3 oz shot glass. Float cream and serve.

GARDEN CITY

60mL (2 oz) brandy

30mL (1 oz) orange juice

30mL (1 oz) sweet vermouth

garnish:

1 maraschino cherry

15mL (0.5 oz) Pernod

ice

Method
Shake and strain into a 5 oz cocktail glass, garnish with cherry and serve.

GARIBALDI

45mL (1.5 oz) Campari

ice

orange juice

Method
Half fill a 10 oz highball glass with ice and build Campari. Top with orange juice, add straws and serve.

GASLIGHT

30mL (1 oz) Metaxa brandy

1 dash Galleon Liverno

15mL (0.5 oz) apricot brandy

Method
Shake and strain into a 3 oz cocktail glass and serve.

GEISHA

30mL Jim Beam Bourbon

30mL Gekkeikan Sake

10mL (0.33 oz) lemon juice

10mL (0.33 oz) sugar syrup

Method
Shake over ice and strain. Garnish with a red cherry.

G

GEISHA DELIGHT

30mL (1 oz) Midori
5mL (0.66 oz) coconut rum
15mL (0.5 oz) Galliano
60mL (2 oz) pineapple juice
15mL (0.5 oz) Cointreau
garnish:
1 pineapple wedge

Method
Blend and pour into a 10 oz colada glass, garnish with pineapple wedge and serve.

GEORGIA PEACH

30mL (1 oz) Bacardi
30mL (1 oz) Peach Liqueur
90mL (3 oz) cranberry juice

Method
Build over ice and pour. Garnish with a peach slice.

GERMAN CHOCOLATE CAKE

30mL (1 oz) Kahlúa
30mL (1 oz) Malibu
30mL (1 oz) chocolate syrup
2 chopped pecan nuts
2 scoops vanilla ice cream

Method
Blend without ice and pour over crushed ice. Garnish with shredded pecans.

GET GOING

45mL (1.5 oz) gin
30mL (1 oz) Cola Tonic
30mL (1 oz) lemon juice
1 dash sugar syrup
1 dash grenadine
lemonade

Method
Half fill a 10 oz highball glass with cracked ice. Add ingredients, top with lemonade, add straws and serve.

GHETTO BLASTER SHOOTER

10mL (0.33 oz) Kahlúa
10mL (0.33 oz) rye whiskey
25mL (0.83 oz) tequila

Method
Layer in a shot glass and serve.

GIBSON DRY

20mL (0.66 oz) gin
garnish:
1 Pickled Onion
20mL (0.66 oz) French vermouth
cracked ice

Method
Stir ingredients and strain into a 3 oz cocktail glass. Garnish with Onion and serve.

GIBSON SWEET

20mL (0.66 oz) gin
garnish:
1 Pickled Onion
20mL (0.66 oz) sweet vermouth
cracked ice

Method
Stir ingredients and strain into a
3 oz cocktail glass. Garnish with
Onion and serve.

GIGOLO'S DELIGHT

30mL (1 oz) gin
garnish:
2 strips orange peel
60mL (2 oz) sweet vermouth
1 maraschino cherry
2 tbsp orange juice
cracked ice

Method
Shake and strain over ice in a rocks
glass. Garnish with orange peel,
cherry and serve.

GILROY

15mL (0.5 oz) cherry brandy
10mL (0.33 oz) lemon juice
15mL (0.5 oz) gin
1 dash orange bitters
10mL (0.33 oz) sweet vermouth
cracked ice

Method
Shake and strain into a 3 oz
cocktail glass and serve.

GIMLET

20mL (0.66 oz) gin
garnish:
1 twist lemon
10mL (0.33 oz) lime juice
cracked ice

Method
Shake and strain into a 3 oz
cocktail glass, garnish with twist of
lemon and serve.

GIN

45mL (0.66 oz) gin
1 dash egg white
15mL (0.5 oz) sugar syrup
soda water
15mL (0.5 oz) lemon juice
cracked ice

Method
Half fill a 10 oz highball glass with
cracked ice, add gin, sugar syrup,
lemon juice and egg white. Top
with soda, add straws and serve.

GIN AND IT

30mL (1 oz) sweet vermouth
ice
45mL (1.5 oz) gin

Method
Shake and strain into a 5 oz
cocktail glass and serve.

GIN AND SIN

60mL (2 oz) gin
soda water
30mL (1 oz) lime juice
cracked ice

Method
Shake ingredients except soda
water and strain into an Old
Fashioned glass. Top with soda
water and serve.

GIN COOLER

60mL (2 oz) gin
ginger beer
60mL (2 oz) lemon juice
cracked ice
1/2 tbsp sugar

Method
Shake ingredients except ginger
beer and strain into a 10 oz
highball glass. Top with ginger
beer, add straws and serve.

GIN FIX

30mL (1 oz) gin
30mL (1 oz) lemon juice
30mL (1 oz) Galleon Liverno
30mL (1 oz) cold water
30mL (1 oz) grenadine
Shaved ice

Method
Fill a 10 oz highball glass with
Shaved ice, add ingredients and stir.
Garnish with fruit and serve.

GIN SLING

60mL (2 oz) gin
soda water
1 dash grenadine
cracked ice
30mL (1 oz) lemon juice
garnish:
1 lemon slice

Method
Pour ingredients over ice in a 5 oz
cocktail glass. Garnish with lemon
slice and serve.

GIN SQUASH

30mL (1 oz) gin
lemonade or soda water
15mL (0.5 oz) lemon cordial
ice

Method
Half fill a 10 oz highball glass with
ice. Add gin and almost top with
lemonade or soda. Finally add
cordial and stir. Serve with straws.

GIN TROPICAL

30mL (1 oz) gin
soda water
30mL (1 oz) passionfruit
1 maraschino cherry
15mL (0.5 oz) blue curaçao
1 slice orange

Method
Shake ingredients except soda
water, orange slice and cherry.
Strain into a 10 oz highball glass,
garnish with orange and cherry
and serve.

GIN TWIST

30mL (1 oz) gin
1 dash orange bitters
30mL (1 oz) Dubonnet
garnish:
1 slice orange
10mL (0.33 oz) Pernod
cracked ice

Method
Shake and strain into a 5 oz
cocktail glass. Garnish with slice
of orange and serve.

GIN WALL BANGER

30mL (1 oz) gin
garnish:
1/2 slice orange
15mL (0.5 oz) Galleon Liverno
cracked ice
180mL (6 oz) orange juice

Method
Half fill a 10 oz highball glass with
ice. Add ingredients and stir.
Garnish with orange slice and serve.

GINGER SIN

30mL (1 oz) gin
30mL (1 oz) lime juice
ginger beer
cracked ice

Method
Stir ingredients and strain into a
10 oz highball glass. Top with
ginger beer and serve.

GIRL TALK

45mL (1.5 oz) While rum
1 dash Angostura bitters
15mL (0.5 oz) sweet vermouth
15mL (0.5 oz) orange juice
15mL (0.5 oz) dry vermouth
garnish:
1 maraschino cherry
cracked ice

Method
Half fill mixing glass with cracked
ice. Add ingredients and stir. Strain
into a 5 oz cocktail glass. Garnish
with cherry and serve.

GLOBE GLADNESS

30mL (1 oz) Grand Marnier
1 dash Galleon Liverno
15mL (0.5 oz) Schnapps
lemonade
15mL (0.5 oz) Tia Maria

Method
Shake Grand Marnier, Tia Maria
and Schnapps. Strain into a 10 oz
highball glass. Top with lemonade.
Float Galleon Liverno and serve.

GLASGOW

30mL (0.33 oz) scotch whisky
10mL (0.33 oz) lemon juice
5mL (0.17 oz) dry vermouth
5mL (0.17 oz) almond extract

Method
Shake over ice and pour then add
cubed ice. Garnish with shredded
almonds and a dried flower.

G

GODDAUGHTER

30mL (1 oz) sambuca
30mL (1 oz) cream
30mL (1 oz) amaretto
5mL (0.17 oz) grenadine

Method
Shake ingredients and strain into a champagne saucer. Garnish with Flake chocolate, strawberry and a sprig of mint.

GODFATHER

45mL (1.5 oz) scotch whiskey
20mL (0.66 oz) Galleon amaretto
ice

Method
Build into a 5 oz Old Fashioned glass filled with ice and serve.

GODMOTHER

45mL (1.5 oz) vodka
ice
20mL (0.66 oz) Galleon amaretto

Method
Build into a 5 oz Old Fashioned glass filled with ice and serve.

GOLD PASSION

30mL (1 oz) Bacardi rum
chilled pineapple juice
30mL (1 oz) vodka
30mL (1 oz) passionfruit

Method
Pour ingredients over ice in a large Tumbler glass and top with pineapple juice. Garnish with a slice of pineapple, pineapple leaves, cherry and serve.

GOLDEN

60mL (2 oz) Bacardi rum
1 egg yolk
1 tsp sugar
soda water
60mL (2 oz) lemon juice
cracked ice

Method
Shake ingredients except soda water and strain over ice in a 10 oz highball glass. Top with soda water, add straws and serve.

GOLDEN CADILLAC NO. 1

30mL (1 oz) Galleon Liverno
30mL (1 oz) cream
30mL (1 oz) white crème de menthe
cracked ice

Method
Shake and strain into a 3 oz cocktail glass and serve.

GOLDEN CADILLAC NO. 2

30mL (1 oz) Galleon Liverno
30mL (1 oz) cream
30mL (1 oz) white crème de cacao
ice

Method
Shake and strain into a 5 oz cocktail glass and serve.

GOLDEN DRAGON

30mL (1 oz) Galleon Liverno
15mL (0.5 oz) white curaçao
20mL (0.66 oz) cream
1 dash egg white

Method
Shake and strain into a 3 oz
cocktail and serve.

GOLDEN DREAM NO. 1

20mL (0.66 oz) Galleon
15mL (0.5 oz) orange juice
15mL (0.5 oz) Cointreau
15mL (0.5 oz) cream

Method
Shake and strain into a 3 oz
cocktail glass and serve.

GOLDEN DREAM NO. 2

30mL (1 oz) brandy
15mL (0.5 oz) lemon juice
30mL (1 oz) Grand Marnier
60mL (2 oz) orange juice

Method
Shake and strain into 5 oz cocktail
glass and serve.

GOLDEN DREAM NO. 3

15mL (0.5 oz) Galliano Liverno
60mL (2 oz) cream
15mL (0.5 oz) Cointreau
ice
15mL (0.5 oz) orange juice
garnish:
frosted strawberry
60mL (2 oz) cream
chocolate Flakes

Method
Shake and strain into a 6 oz
tulip glass, garnish with frosted
strawberry, chocolate flakes
and serve.

GOLDEN FLEECE

30mL (1 oz) advocaat
60mL (2 oz) milk
20mL (0.66 oz) Galleon Liverno
30mL (1 oz) cream

Method
Shake and strain into a champagne
saucer and serve.

GOLDEN LOVER

30mL (1 oz) Midori
75mL (2.5oz) milk
20mL (0.66 oz) Galleon Liverno
30mL (1 oz) cream

Method
Blend and pour into a 10 oz
highball glass and serve.

GOLDEN NEST

30mL (1 oz) Galleon Liverno
45mL (1.5 oz) orange juice
30mL (1 oz) rum
garnish:
1 slice orange

Method
Shake and strain into a 5 oz
cocktail glass, garnish with orange
slice and serve.

GOLDEN ORCHID

30mL (1 oz) scotch whiskey
15mL (0.5 oz) maraschino
30mL (1 oz) advocaat
ice

Method
Shake and strain into a 5 oz
cocktail glass and serve.

GOLDEN SHOT

30mL (1 oz) scotch whiskey
90mL (3 oz) orange juice
1 egg yolk
ice

Method
Blend and pour into a rocks glass
and serve.

GOLDEN SLIPPER

30mL Yellow Chartreuse
10mL (0.33 oz) Apricot Brandy
1 egg yolk

Method
Shake over ice and strain.

GONE TROPPO

45mL (1.5 oz) peach liqueur
3 strawberries
35mL (1.17 oz) banana liqueur
1 scoop ice
30mL (1 oz) pineapple juice
garnish:
pineapple wedge
2 pineapple leaves

Method
Blend ingredients except pineapple
juice and pour into a 6 oz tulip
glass. Float pineapple juice on top.
Garnish with a pineapple wedge,
cherry and two pineapple leaves
and serve.

GOOD MORNING

20mL (0.66 oz) rum
1 egg white
20mL (0.66 oz) port
15mL (0.5 oz) lemon juice
1 tsp sugar
3 ice cubes

Method
Shake and strain into a small
Tumbler glass and serve.

GORGEOUS GRACE

30mL (1 oz) brandy
1 slice orange
15mL (0.5 oz) Cointreau
cracked ice
champagne

Method
Stir ail ingredients except champagne. Strain into a champagne saucer and top with champagne. Garnish with orange slice and serve.

GRAND BAILEY'S SHOOTER

20mL (0.66 oz) Bailey's Irish cream
10mL (0.33 oz) Grand Marnier

Method
Layer in a shot glass and serve.

GRAND SLAM SHOOTER

10mL (0.33 oz) banana liqueur
10mL (0.33 oz) Grand Marnier
10mL (0.33 oz) Bailey's Irish cream

Method
Layer in order in a shot glass and serve.

GRASSHOPPER

45mL (1.5 oz) crème de menthe
60mL (2 oz) cream
30mL (1 oz) crème de cacao
cracked ice

Method
Shake and strain into a champagne saucer and serve.

GRAVE DIGGER

40mL (1.33 oz) dry vermouth
1 dash Angostura bitters
20mL (0.66 oz) brandy
40mL (1.33 oz) orange juice
20mL (0.66 oz) Cointreau

Method
Shake and strain into a 5 oz cocktail glass and serve.

GREAT WHITE NORTH SHOOTER

15mL (0.5 oz) Kahlúa
15mL (0.5 oz) ouzo
15mL (0.5 oz) Bailey's Irish cream

Method
Layer in order in a shot glass and serve.

GREEDY

45mL (1.5 oz) Midori
2 scoops crushed ice
30mL (1 oz) Framboise
1 tsp raspberry syrup
5mL (0.17 oz) grenadine
30mL (1 oz) lime juice

Method
Blend Midori, lime juice and one scoop of ice until frozen and place in a champagne saucer. Blend other ingredients until semi frozen, add to other mixture and serve.

GREEN

15mL (0.5 oz) crème de menthe
25mL (0.83 oz) lemon juice
50mL (2.66 oz) gin
1 egg white
10mL (0.33 oz) sugar syrup
cracked ice
soda water

Method
Shake all ingredients except soda water and strain over ice in a 10 oz highball glass. Top with soda water, add straws and serve.

GREEK BUCK

30mL (1 oz) Milne Brandy
10mL (0.33 oz) lemon juice
top up with ginger ale
10mL (0.33 oz) Aphrodite Ouzo

Method
Shake Brandy with lemon juice and top up with ginger ale then float Aphrodite Ouzo. Garnish with a lemon slice.

GREEN BACK

30mL (1 oz) Beefeater Gin
10mL (0.33 oz) lime juice
10mL (0.33 oz) Green Creme de Menthe

Method
Stir over ice and pour. Garnish with a lime slice (optional).

GREEK GOD

15mL (0.5 oz) Aphrodite Ouzo
15mL (0.5 oz) Pernod

Method
Pour in order then shoot.

GREEN DEVIL

3 tbsp vodka
2 tbsp crushed ice
1 1/2 tbsp crème de menthe
garnish:
1 strip lemon peel
juice 1/2 lemon

Method
Mix and strain into a 3 oz cocktail glass, garnish with lemon peel and serve.

GREEN DRAGON

40mL (1.33 oz) Midori
8mL (0.27 oz) lemon juice
15mL (0.5 oz) Galleon Liverno
30mL (1 oz) cream

Method
Place Midori in a champagne
saucer, shake Galleon Liverno
and cream. Strain over Midori
and serve.

GREEN DRAGON NO. 2

45mL (1.5 oz) vodka
cracked ice
45mL (1.5 oz) crème de menthe

Method
Shake and strain into a small
Goblet glass and serve.

GREEN DRAGON NO. 3

30mL (1 oz) light rum
30mL (1 oz) vodka
30mL (1 oz) Midori
lemonade

Method
Shake all ingredients except
lemonade, strain over ice into
a Goblet glass. Top with lemonade,
garnish with watermelon wedge,
cherry and serve.

GREEN EYES

30mL (1 oz) Midori
15mL (0.5 oz) coconut milk
30mL (1 oz) Gold rum
15mL (0.5 oz) lime juice
45mL (1.5 oz) pineapple juice

Method
Blend ingredients and pour into a
10 oz colada glass. Garnish with
pineapple wedge, straws and serve.

GREEN HAT

30mL (1 oz) gin
soda water
30mL (1 oz) crème de menthe
cracked ice

Method
Half fill a large Tumbler glass with
cracked ice, add gin and crème de
menthe. Top with soda water, add
straws and serve.

GREEN LAND

30mL (1 oz) Midori
Tonic water
30mL (1 oz) white wine

Method
Build ingredients in a 10 ?/.
highball glass over ice and serve.

GREEN PARADISE

45mL (1.5 oz) Midori
15mL (0.5 oz) orange juice
20mL (0.66 oz) Cointreau
15mL (0.5 oz) pineapple juice
10mL (0.33 oz) lemon juice
1 scoop crushed ice
grenadine

Method
Blend all ingredients except grenadine until frozen. Place a tbsp grenadine in the bottom of a 5 oz cocktail glass. Pour in frozen ingredients and serve.

GREEN SEA

30mL (1 oz) vodka
20mL (0.66 oz) crème de menthe
20mL (0.66 oz) dry vermouth
cracked ice

Method
Shake and strain into a small Goblet glass and serve.

GREEN SILKS

30mL (1 oz) Midori
60mL (2 oz) cream
15mL (0.5 oz) Grand Marnier
60g Rockmelon
30mL (1 oz) pineapple juice

Method
Blend with ice and pour into a 10 oz colada glass. Garnish with pineapple leaves, straws and serve.

GREEN SLAMMER

45mL (1.5 oz) vodka
30mL (1 oz) Midori
15mL (0.5 oz) Galleon Liverno
30mL (1 oz) lemon juice

Method
Shake and strain into an Old Fashioned glass and serve.

GREEN SOLDIERS

30mL (1 oz) lemon juice
1 egg white
15mL (0.5 oz) lemon juice
cracked ice

Method
Shake and strain into a 3 oz cocktail glass, garnish with a lemon wheel and serve.

GREEN WITH ENVY

30mL (1 oz) ouzo
120mL (4 oz) pineapple juice
15mL (0.5 oz) blue curaçao
garnish:
1 maraschino cherry

Method
Shake and strain into a 10 oz highball glass, garnish with cherry, straws and serve.

GREENHORN

60mL (2 oz) crème de menthe
soda water
20mL (0.66 oz) lemon juice
cracked ice

Method
Shake all ingredients except soda
water over ice into a 10 oz highball
glass. Top with soda water, add
straws and serve.

GREENPEACE SORBET

30mL (1 oz) Cointreau
1 kiwifruit (peeled)
60mL (2 oz) Riesling
2 scoops crushed ice

Method
Blend until smooth and pour into a
5 oz cocktail glass and serve.

GRINGO

30mL (1 oz) tequila
30mL (1 oz) vodka
30mL (1 oz) Midori
10mL (0.33 oz) lemon juice

Method
Shake and strain into a 5 oz
cocktail glass and serve.

GYPSY

30mL (1 oz) vodka
1 dash Angostura bitters
15mL (0.5 oz) Benedictine
cracked ice
garnish: 1 strip lemon peel

Method
Shake and strain into a 3 oz
cocktail glass, garnish with lemon
peel and serve.

GYPSY KING

7mL (0.23 oz) lime cordial
10mL (0.33 oz) Parfait Amour
10mL (0.33 oz) Green Creme de
Menthe
10mL (0.33 oz) Yellow Chartreuse

Method
Pour in order, then layer Yellow
Chartreuse.

G

HAIR OF THE DOG

60mL (2 oz) scotch whiskey
30mL (1 oz) honey
60mL (2 oz) cream
ice

Method
Fill an Old Fashioned glass with ice, shake other ingredients and strain over ice and serve.

HAIRLESS DUCK

30mL (1 oz) advocaat
15mL (0.5 oz) Bacardi rum
30mL (1 oz) vodka
orange juice

Method
Shake advocaat, vodka and rum together and strain over ice in a 10 oz highball glass. Top with orange juice, add straws and serve.

HALF NELSON

10mL (0.33 oz) Green Creme de Menthe
10mL (0.33 oz) Strawberry Liqueur
10mL (0.33 oz) Grand Marnier

Method
Layer in order then shoot.

HALO

30mL (1 oz) sambuca
lemonade
30mL (1 oz) gin

Method
Place sambuca and gin in a 5 oz Tumbler. Slowly top with lemonade and serve.

HARBOUR LIGHTS

15mL (0.5 oz) Kahlúa
15mL (0.5 oz) green Chartreuse
15mL (0.5 oz) sambuca

Method
Layer in order in a 45 mL cordial glass, add a Straw and serve.

HARBOUR MIST

30mL (1 oz) banana liqueur
15mL (0.5 oz) blue curaçao
20mL (0.66 oz) Grand Marnier
30mL (1 oz) cream

Method
Shake and strain into a 5 oz cocktail glass and serve.

HARD ON

30mL (1 oz) Bailey's Irish cream
30mL (1 oz) Kahlúa
30mL (1 oz) banana liqueur

Method
Float ingredients in a 3 oz cocktail glass and serve.

HARD ON (TROPICAL)

30mL (1 oz) Kahlúa
30mL (1 oz) mango liqueur
30mL (1 oz) Bailey's Irish cream

Method
Layer ingredients in a 3 oz cocktail glass and serve.

HARD ON (BLACK)

30mL (1 oz) Opal Nera
30mL (1 oz) banana liqueur
30mL (1 oz) Bailey's Irish cream

Method
Layer ingredients in a 3 oz cocktail glass and serve.

HARLEQUIN

30mL (1 oz) cognac
ice
15mL (0.5 oz) Grand Marnier

Method
frost a 5 oz cocktail glass with harlequin frosting. coffee and sugar. Stir and strain liquid ingredients into glass and serve.

HARD ON (BLOODY)

30mL (1 oz) Kahlúa
30mL (1 oz) strawberry liqueur
30mL (1 oz) Bailey's Irish cream

Method
Layer ingredients in a 3 oz cocktail glass and serve.

HARVEY COWPUNCHER

45mL (1.5 oz) Galleon Liverno
cracked ice
120mL (4 oz) milk

Method
Half fill a 10 oz highball glass with cracked ice. Pour Galleon Liverno over ice and top with milk.

HARVEY WALLBANGER

30mL (1 oz) vodka
garnish:
1 maraschino cherry
30mL (1 oz) Galleon Liverno
1 slice orange
orange juice

Method
Place Galleon Liverno and vodka over ice in a 10 oz highball glass. Top with orange juice, garnish with cherry, orange slice , straws and serve.

HARVEY WALLBANGER NO. 2

40mL (1.33 oz) vodka
2 tsp Galleon Liverno
60mL (2 oz) orange juice
ice

Method
Build vodka and orange juice over ice in a 6 oz Old Fashioned glass. Float Galleon Liverno over top and serve.

HARVEY WALLBANGER NO. 3

30mL (1 oz) vodka
orange juice
15mL (0.5 oz) Galleon Liverno
ice

Method
Three-quarters fill a 10 oz highball glass with ice. Pour in vodka and top with orange juice and stir. Float Galliano Liverno on top, add straws and serve.

HAVANA CLUB

40mL (1.33 oz) Bacardi rum
garnish:
1 maraschino cherry
20mL (0.66 oz) sweet vermouth
cracked ice

Method
Shake and strain into a 3 oz cocktail glass and serve.

HAWAIIAN HONEYMOON

45mL (1.5 oz) Bacardi rum
1 dash grenadine
60mL (2 oz) orange juice
garnish:
1 maraschino cherry
30mL (1 oz) pineapple juice
1 pineapple wedge
1 dash lemon juice
1 orange slice
Pernod (float)

Method
Mix liquid ingredients except Pernod. Pour into a 5 oz cocktail glass. Float Pernod, garnish with fruit and serve.

HAWAIIAN PUNCH

20mL (0.66 oz) Southern Comfort

20mL (0.66 oz) Amaretto di Galliano

15mL (0.5oz) Smirnoff Vodka

40mL (1.33 oz) pineapple juice

40mL (1.33 oz) orange juice

20mL (0.66 oz) lime juice

20mL (0.66 oz) Grenadine

Method
Shake over ice and pour then add Grenadine. Garnish with lime squeeze, lemon squeeze, orange slice and a red cherry.

HAZY CUBAN

30mL (1 oz) Bacardi rum

30mL (1 oz) coconut cream

30mL (1 oz) milk

60mL (2 oz) pineapple juice

garnish: 1 slice pineapple

Method
Blend and pour into an Old Fashioned glass and serve.

HEAD STUD

30mL (1 oz) Galleon Liverno

30mL (1 oz) Afrikoko

60mL (2 oz) cream

Method
Layer in a 5 oz cocktail glass and serve.

HEARTBREAKER

30mL (1 oz) strawberry liqueur

60mL (2 oz) cream

15mL (0.5 oz) Tia Maria

4 strawberries

15mL (0.5 oz) Cointreau

Method
Blend until smooth and pour into a 8 oz colada glass and serve.

HEAVENLY CLOUD

45mL (1.5 oz) Kahlúa

60mL (2 oz) cream

45mL (1.5 oz) Rubis

1/2 banana

4 strawberries

Method
Blend until smooth, pour into a champagne saucer and serve.

HELEN'S HANGOVER

30mL (1 oz) advocaat

pineapple juice

30mL (1 oz) Galleon Liverno

Method
Pour advocaat and Galleon Liverno over ice in a 10 oz highball glass. Top with orange juice, add straws and serve.

HELL RAISER SHOOTER

30mL (1 oz) Midori
30mL (1 oz) strawberry liqueur
30mL (1 oz) sambuca

Method
Layer in a 3 oz shot glass and serve.

HEMMINGWAY

40mL (1.33 oz) Cointreau
40mL (1.33 oz) grapefruit juice
40mL (1.33 oz) Bacardi rum
cracked ice
Sparkling white wine

Method
Shake all ingredients except white
wine, strain into a 5 oz champagne
saucer. Top with white wine and
serve.

HIGHBALL BACARDI

30mL (1 oz) Bacardi rum
soda water
30mL (1 oz) Cointreau
3 ice cubes
1 tsp lemon juice

Method
Shake ingredients except soda
water. Pour into a 10 oz highball
glass and top with soda water.
Serve with straws.

Bourbon

60mL (2 oz) bourbon
soda water
2 dashes Angostura bitters
ice
1 dash lemon juice

Method
Place ingredients except soda water
in a 10 oz highball glass, stir rapidly
and top with soda water and serve.

Brandy

30mL (1 oz) brandy
2 dash Angostura bitters
1 tsp sugar syrup
soda water
1 tsp lemon juice
3 ice cubes

Method
Shake ingredients except soda
water, pour into a 10 oz highball
glass, top with soda water
and serve.

Crystal

20mL (0.66 oz) sweet vermouth
soda water
1 tsp sugar syrup
1 spiral orange juice
20mL (0.66 oz) Bianco vermouth
2 ice cubes

Method
Place all ingredients in a 10 oz
highball glass and stir. Top with
soda water and serve.

Ginger

30mL (1 oz) scotch whiskey

dry ginger ale

1 strip lemon peel

ice

Method

Place ingredients in a 10 oz highball glass and stir. Top with dry ginger ale and serve.

Island

15mL (0.5 oz) brandy

1 dash orange bitters

15mL (0.5 oz) sweet vermouth

soda water

2 ice cubes

Method

Place ingredients in a 10 oz highball glass, top with soda and serve.

Saki

90mL (3 oz) saki

soda water

1/4 lemon, squeezed

garnish:

1 slice lemon

1 tsp castor sugar

ice

Method

Stir ingredients except soda water and lemon slice. Pour into a 10 oz highball glass, top with soda water, garnish with lemon slice and serve.

Whiskey

30mL (1 oz) rye whiskey

dry ginger ale

3 drops Angostura bitters

ice

Method

Half fill a 10 oz highball glass with ice. Add whiskey and Angostura bitters, top with ginger ale and serve.

HIGHLAND FLING

30mL (1 oz) scotch whiskey

30mL (1 oz) orange juice

30mL (1 oz) Kahlúa

30mL (1 oz) cream

Method

Blend until smooth, pour over ice in a 10 oz highball glass. Add straws and serve.

HITLER'S GRENADE

15mL (0.5 oz) crème de cacao

15mL (0.5 oz) vodka

15mL (0.5 oz) advocaat

15mL (0.5 oz) B & B

15mL (0.5 oz) tequila

15mL (0.5 oz) sambuca

15mL (0.5 oz) gin

Coca-Cola

Method

Shake ingredients except Coca-Cola. Pour over ice in a 10 oz highball glass. Top with Coca-Cola, add straws and serve.

HOLLYWOOD NIGHTS

30mL (1 oz) vodka

soda water

15mL (0.5 oz) peach liqueur

Midori (float)

30mL (1 oz) pineapple juice

Method
Three-quarters fill a 10 oz highball glass with ice, add vodka, peach liqueur and pineapple juice. Top with soda water, float Midori, add straws and serve.

HOME MAID

15mL (0.5 oz) Bailey's Irish cream

30mL (1 oz) cream

30mL (1 oz) banana liqueur

90mL (3 oz) milk

Method
Shake and strain into a champagne saucer and serve.

HONEY BEE

30mL (1 oz) brandy

15mL (0.5 oz) honey

15mL (0.5 oz) Galliano Liverno

60mL (2 oz) cream

15mL (0.5 oz) grenadine

cracked ice

Method
Shake and strain into a 5 oz cocktail glass and serve.

HONEY FLOW

30mL (1 oz) white rum

45mL (1.5 oz) cream

15mL (0.5 oz) Galliano Liverno

garnish:

1 maraschino cherry

15mL (0.5 oz) honey

cracked ice

Method
Shake and strain into a champagne saucer, garnish with cherry and serve.

HONEYED NUTS

30mL (1 oz) Frangelico

30mL (1 oz) honey

15mL (0.5 oz) Kahlúa

120mL (4 oz) cream

15mL (0.5 oz) advocaat

ice

Method
Blend ingredients and pour into a brandy Balloon rimmed with crushed Hazelnuts and honey and serve.

HONEY TEA

1 orange spice tea bag

30mL (1 oz) Drambuie

top up with hot water

Method
Pour in order then top up with hot water. Garnish with a lemon twist.

HONEYMOON

30mL (1 oz) Benedictine

1/2 orange, squeezed

30mL (1 oz) Calvados

cracked ice

Method
Shake and strain into a 3 oz
cocktail glass and serve.

HONEYMOON PARADISE

30mL (1 oz) blue curaçao

25mL (0.83 oz) lemon juice

15mL (0.5 oz) Cointreau

1 scoop ice cream

champagne

Method
Blend all ingredients except
champagne until frozen. Pour into
a champagne saucer, top with
champagne and serve.

HORANGI

45mL (1.5 oz) vodka

30mL (1 oz) passionfruit juice

30mL (1 oz) advocaat

cracked ice

Method
Shake and strain into a champagne
saucer and serve.

HORNY BULL SHOOTER

10mL (0.33 oz) vodka

10mL (0.33 oz) tequila

10mL (0.33 oz) rum

Method
Layer in a shot glass and serve.

HORSE GUARDS

20mL (0.66 oz) rum

1 egg yolk

20mL (0.66 oz) Cointreau

garnish:

1 spiral lemon peel

Sparkling white wine

3 ice cubes

Method
Shake ingredients except wine and
lemon peel. Strain into Tumbler
glass, top with wine and garnish
with lemon peel and serve.

HORSE'S NECK

30mL (1 oz) brandy

ginger ale

4 drops Angostura bitters

ice

Method
Hang a lemon spiral in a 10 oz
highball glass. Fill the glass with ice
and build brandy and bitters. Top
with ginger ale and serve.

H

HOT BUTTERED RUM

30mL (1 oz) dark rum
1 tsp sugar
1 tbsp Butter
boiling water
1 pinch nutmeg

Method
Mix ingredients in a mixing glass. Strain into a 10 oz highball glass and top with tomato juice serve with straws.

HOT DANISH CIDER

180mL (6 oz) apple cider, heated
15mL (0.5 oz) Orgeat

Method
Build. Garnish with a cinnamon stick.

HOT MILK PUNCH

30mL (1 oz) Bacardi
30mL (1 oz) Milne Brandy
sugar to taste
top up with hot milk

Method
Build and top up with hot milk. Garnish with sprinkle of cinnamon stick.

HOT TODDIES

45mL (1.5 oz) any Spirit
garnish:
slice lemon
1 tsp sugar
sprinkle cinnamon
2 cloves
boiling water

Method
Mix ingredients in a 10 oz Tankard, fill with boiling water poured over a spoon. Garnish with lemon and cinnamon and serve.

HURRICANE

30mL (1 oz) Bacardi rum
30mL (1 oz) passoa
15mL (0.5 oz) lemon cordial
45mL (1.5 oz) lemon juice
45mL (1.5 oz) sugar syrup
15mL (0.5 oz) Bacardi Gold(float)

Method
Shake ingredients and pour into a Hurricane glass. Garnish with slice of orange and a cherry, float Bacardi Gold and serve.

HURRICANE GREG SHOOTER

20mL (0.66 oz) Opal Nera
20mL (0.66 oz) cherry advocaat
20mL (0.66 oz) blue curaçao
20mL (0.66 oz) advocaat

Method
Layer in Test tube or shot glass and serve.

HUSH HONEY

30mL (1 oz) gin
30mL (1 oz) fresh cream
15mL (0.5 oz) Galliano Liverno
15mL (0.5 oz) honey
garnish: 1 maraschino cherry
ice

Method
Shake and strain into a champagne glass. Place cherry on lip of glass and serve.

I LOVE YOU

30mL (1 oz) Kahlúa
30mL (1 oz) Galliano Liverno
30mL (1 oz) Bailey's Irish cream

Method
Float ingredients in a 3 oz cocktail glass and serve.

ICE KACHANG

30mL (1 oz) Smirnoff Vodka
15mL (0.5 oz) Peach Liqueur
30mL (1 oz) cranberry juice
30mL (1 oz) orange juice
top up with lemonade
diced fruit pieces

Method
Mix ingredients and pour over crushed ice. Serve with two straws and a long spoon.
Comments: Known as a dessert delight from the old Portuguese trading port of Malacca, East Malaysia, this cocktail will add another dimension to how you can consume alcohol.

ICE WINGS

75mL (2.5 oz) vodka
ice
30mL (1 oz) white crème de menthe

Method
Shake and strain into a 3 oz cocktail glass and serve.

ICHIGO

30mL (1 oz) strawberry liqueur
20mL (0.66 oz) pineapple juice
15mL (0.5 oz) Galliano Liverno
20mL (0.66 oz) orange juice

Method
Shake and strain into a cocktail glass and serve.

ILLUSION

45mL (1.5 oz) vodka
90mL (3 oz) lemon juice
15mL (0.5 oz) Cointreau
splash lime cordial

Method
Shake and strain into a 5 oz
cocktail glass and serve.

INDEPENDENCE

30mL (1 oz) bourbon
1 tbsp lemon juice
1 tbsp brandy
1 sprig mint
60mL (2 oz) orange juice

Method
Shake ingredients and strain into a
4 oz cocktail glass, garnish with
sprig of mint and serve.

INDEPENDENCE DAY PUNCH

30mL Jim Beam Bourbon
100mL (3.30 oz) pineapple juice
20mL (0.66 oz) lime juice
15mL (0.5 oz) lime juice
top up with soda

Method
Stir over ice and pour then top up
with soda. Garnish with a
pineapple slice and American
'Independence Day' Flag.

INDO SHINER

1 teaspoon of sugar
120mL (4 oz) pineapple juice
30mL (1 oz) lemon juice
15mL (0.5 oz) lime juice
1 dash Angostura Bitters
5mL (0.17 oz) blue vegetable
colouring

Method
Blend over ice and pour. Garnish
with a lemon and lime slice.

INKAHLÚARABLE

10mL (0.33 oz) Kahlúa
10mL (0.33 oz) Cointreau
10mL (0.33 oz) Grand Marnier

Method
Layer in order then shoot.

INK STREET

30mL (1 oz) scotch whiskey
30mL (1 oz) lemon juice
30mL (1 oz) orange juice
cracked ice

Method
Shake and strain into a champagne
glass, garnish with a twist of
orange peel and serve.

INSPIRATION

45mL (1.5 oz) Frangelico
60mL (2 oz) pineapple juice
15mL (0.5 oz) banana liqueur
30mL (1 oz) cream

Method
Shake and strain into a 150 mL
cocktail glass. Garnish with a
strawberry and mint leaf on rim
and serve.

INTERNATIONAL

20mL (0.66 oz) brandy
garnish:
1 lemon wedge
20mL (0.66 oz) green Chartreuse
3 ice cubes
15mL (0.5 oz) pineapple juice

Method
Shake and strain into a 3 oz
cocktail glass and serve.

INTIMATE

20mL (0.66 oz) vodka
garnish:
1 black olive
20mL (0.66 oz) apricot brandy
1 twist lemon peel
20mL (0.66 oz) dry vermouth
ice
2 dashes orange bitters

Method
Mix liquid ingredients and strain
into a 3 oz cocktail glass. Garnish
with olive, lemon peel and serve.

IRISH BANANA

30mL (1 oz) Bailey's Irish cream
50mL (1.66 oz) cream
30mL (1 oz) banana liqueur
1/2 banana
15mL (0.5 oz) advocaat
ice

Method
Blend until smooth, pour into a
5 oz champagne saucer and serve.

IRISH CHEER

30mL (1 oz) Midori
30mL (1 oz) lime juice
45mL (1.5 oz) dry gin
garnish:
1 maraschino cherry

Method
Shake and strain into a 5 oz
cocktail glass, garnish with cherry
and serve.

IRISH COFFEE

30mL (1 oz) Irish whiskey
sugar (to taste)
hot coffee
cream (lightly wrapped)

Method
Mix whiskey and sugar in an Irish
coffee Mug. Pour in hot coffee,
top with cream and serve.

I

IRISH EYES

45mL (1.5 oz) Irish whiskey
60mL (2 oz) fresh cream
60mL (2 oz) crème de menthe
garnish:
1 maraschino cherry

Method
Shake and strain into a 5 oz champagne glass. Garnish with cherry and serve.

IRISH FLAG

15mL (0.5 oz) crème de menthe
15mL (0.5 oz) brandy
15mL (0.5 oz) Bailey's Irish cream

Method
Layer in order in a 2 oz port glass and serve.

IRISH MONKEY SHOOTER

20mL (0.66 oz) banana liqueur
25mL (0.87 oz) Bailey's Irish cream

Method
Layer in a shot glass and serve.

IRON LADY

15mL (0.5 oz) Malibu
45mL (1.5 oz) cream
20mL (0.66 oz) Rubis
5mL (0.17 oz) vanilla Essence
15mL (0.5 oz) white crème de cacao
1 Scoop ice cream

Method
Blend until smooth, pour into a 4 oz cocktail glass serve.

ISLAND COOLER

15mL (0.5 oz) vodka
2 scoops crushed ice
30mL (1 oz) orange juice
2 drops grenadine
30mL (1 oz) Midori
1/4 kiwifruit
8mL (0.27 oz) lemon juice

Method
Blend vodka, orange juice and ice until frozen and place in a 5 oz champagne saucer, add grenadine. Blend Midori, kiwifruit and lemon juice and add to glass, serve.

ISLAND OF CAPRI

30mL (1 oz) Bailey's Irish cream
30mL (1 oz) cream
30mL (1 oz) Galleon Liverno

Method
Float ingredients in a 3 oz cocktail glass and serve.

ITALIAN STALLION

30mL (1 oz) Galleon Liverno
50mL (1.66 oz) cream
30mL (1 oz) sambuca

Method
Shake and strain into a champagne saucer and serve.

J.F. KENNEDY

30mL (1 oz) red crème de menthe
light beer
30mL (1 oz) vodka

Method
Place crème de menthe and vodka
in a Middy glass and stir. Top with
light beer and serve.

JACK IN THE BOX

60mL (2 oz) brandy
1 dash Angostura bitters
60mL (2 oz) pineapple juice
ice

Method
Shake an strain into a 5 oz cocktail
glass and serve.

JACK ROSE

45mL (1.5 oz) brandy
1/2 lemon, squeezed
1 tsp grenadine

Method
Shake and strain into a 3 oz cocktail
glass and serve.

JANE'S TOUCH SHOOTER

10mL (0.33 oz) Kahlúa
10mL (0.33 oz) Bailey's Irish cream
10mL (0.33 oz) Frangelico

Method
Layer in order in a shot glass
and serve.

JAPANESE EGGNOG

45mL (1.5 oz) Cointreau
90mL (3 oz) milk
45mL (1.5 oz) Midori
1 dash egg white

Method
Shake and strain into an Old
Fashioned glass and serve.

JAPANESE SLIPPER

30mL (1 oz) Cointreau
30mL (1 oz) Midori
30mL (1 oz) Margimix

Method
Float ingredients in a 3 oz cocktail
glass and serve.

JAPANESE SLIPPER NO. 2

30mL (1 oz) Midori
30mL (1 oz) lemon juice
30mL (1 oz) Cointreau
ice

Method
Shake and strain into a 3 oz cocktail
glass and serve.

JAPANESE SUNRISE

30mL (1 oz) Midori
30mL (1 oz) lemon juice
10mL (0.33 oz) Galleon Liverno
garnish:
3-4 strawberries
10mL (0.33 oz) orange curaçao

Method
Blend and pour into a 5 oz cocktail
glass, garnish with a slice of
rockmelon, 1/2 strawberry and serve.

J

JAPANESE TRAFFIC LIGHTS

30mL (1 oz) Midori
30mL (1 oz) Rubis
30mL (1 oz) banana liqueur

Method
Float ingredients in a 3 oz cocktail glass and serve.

JAW BREAKER

30mL (1 oz) Kahlúa
30mL (1 oz) sambuca
30mL (1 oz) banana liqueur

Method
Float ingredients over ice in a 4 oz cocktail glass and serve.

JEALOUS JUNE

30mL (1 oz) Midori
15mL (0.5 oz) Cointreau
20mL (0.66 oz) white rum
90mL (3 oz) pineapple juice

Method
Shake and strain into a highball glass and serve.

JELLYBEAN

30mL (1 oz) ouzo
lemonade
15mL (0.5 oz) raspberry cordial
ice

Method
Place ouzo and cordial in a 5 oz cocktail glass with ice and stir. Top with lemonade and serve.

JELLYBEAN (GARBO'S)

45mL (1.5 oz) ouzo
1 dash grenadine
15mL (0.5 oz) gin
lemonade
15mL (0.5 oz) vodka
ice

Method
Place ice in a 10 oz highball glass, add ingredients. Top with lemonade and serve.

JELLYBEAN NO. 2

30mL (1 oz) vodka
1 splash grenadine
30mL (1 oz) Pernod
lemonade

Method
Pour ingredients over ice in a 10 oz highball glass, top with lemonade and serve.

JELLYFISH SHOOTER

30mL (1 oz) Bailey's Irish cream
15mL (0.5 oz) amaretto
30mL (1 oz) vodka
1 dash grenadine

Method
Layer amaretto, vodka and Bailey's in a Test Tube or shot glass, add grenadine and serve.

JEUNE HOMME

30mL (1 oz) dry vermouth
15mL (0.5 oz) Benedictine
15mL (0.5 oz) gin
1 dash Angostura bitters
15mL (0.5 oz) Cointreau
3 ice Cubes

Method
Shake ingredients and strain into
a 3 oz cocktail glass and serve.

JOGGERS

30mL (1 oz) Benedictine
1 spiral lemon peel
45mL (1.5 oz) cognac
soda water
15mL (0.5 oz) lemon juice

Method
Half fill a 10 oz highball glass with
ice, drop in lemon peel and add
lemon juice. Top with soda water
and serve with straws.

JOHN COLLINS

30mL (1 oz) gin
1 tsp sugar
1 lemon, squeezed
1 slice lemon
1 dash Angostura bitters
ice
soda water

Method
Place all ingredients except soda
water and lemon in a 10 oz
highball glass and stir until sugar
is dissolved. Add soda water,
garnish with lemon slice and straws
and serve.

JUNGER STERN

30mL (1 oz) Midori
4 pineapple pieces
15mL (0.5 oz) banana liqueur
pulp 1/2 passionfruit
3 pureed strawberries
Scoop crushed ice

Method
Pour pureed strawberries down the
side of a 10 oz highball glass. Blend
other ingredients and carefully add
to the glass. Garnish with a cherry
and pineapple leaves and serve.

JUNGLE JUICE

45mL (1.5 oz) white rum
30mL (1 oz) pineapple juice
45mL (1.5 oz) Drambuie
30mL (1 oz) cream
45mL (1.5 oz) coconut cream
1/2 banana

Method
Blend until smooth, place in a
champagne glass and serve.

K.G.B.

30mL (1 oz) Bailey's Irish cream
30mL (1 oz) Kahlúa
30mL (1 oz) Grand Marnier

Method
Layer in a 3 oz cocktail glass and
serve.

KAHLÚA CREAM

30mL (1 oz) vodka
15mL (0.5 oz) cream
15mL (0.5 oz) Kahlúa
ice

Method
Shake and strain into a 3 oz
cocktail glass and serve.

KAHLÚA JAFFA

15mL (0.5 oz) Kahlúa
15mL (0.5 oz) orange juice
15mL (0.5 oz) scotch whiskey
30mL (1 oz) cream

Method
Shake and strain into a champagne
saucer, top with mixture of cream
and Grand Marnier and serve.

KAKURI

30mL (1 oz) Pimm's no. 1 cup
5mL (0.17 oz) lemon juice
15mL (0.5 oz) mango liqueur
ice
15mL (0.5 oz) Bianco vermouth

Method
Shake and strain into a 3 oz
cocktail glass and serve.

KAMIKAZE

30mL (1 oz) vodka
15mL (0.5 oz) lemon juice
30mL (1 oz) tequila
1 slice lime juice

Method
Mix ingredients and strain into a
champagne saucer. Garnish with
slice of lime and serve.

KANGAROO

60mL (2 oz) brandy
1 egg
30mL (1 oz) Galliano Liverno
ice

Method
Shake and strain into a champagne
saucer and serve.

KATANGA

45mL (1.5 oz) vodka
garnish:
1 sprig mint
30mL (1 oz) apricot brandy
ice
2 tsp lime juice

Method
Shake and strain into a 3 oz
cocktail glass, garnish with mint
and serve.

KEEP GOING

30mL (1 oz) white rum
15mL (0.5 oz) grapefruit juice
15mL (0.5 oz) anisette liqueur
lemonade
30mL (1 oz) Cola Tonic
1/2 slice lemon
15mL (0.5 oz) lime juice
cracked ice

Method
Half fill a 10 oz highball glass with
cracked ice, shake ingredients and
strain into glass. Garnish with slice
of lemon, straws and serve.

KELLY'S COMFORT

30mL (1 oz) Southern Comfort
15mL (0.5 oz) sugar syrup
30mL (1 oz) Bailey's Irish cream
4 strawberries (1 for garnish)
60mL (2 oz) milk
crushed ice

Method
Blend until smooth, pour into a
10 oz highball glass, garnish with
strawberry, straws and serve.

KEY WEST COOLER

15mL (0.5 oz) Smirnoff Vodka
15mL (0.5 oz) Peach Liqueur
15mL (0.5 oz) Midori
15mL (0.5 oz) Malibu
100mL (3.33 oz) cranberry juice
100mL (3.33 oz) orange juice

Method
Stir over ice and pour. Garnish with
an orange slice.

KICK IN THE BALLS

30mL (1 oz) rum
30mL (1 oz) orange juice
30mL (1 oz) Midori
30mL (1 oz) cream
15mL (0.5 oz) coconut cream
garnish:
2 melon Balls

Method
Shake and strain into a champagne
saucer, garnish with melon Balls
marinated in rum and serve.

KIM'S KLANGER

30mL (1 oz) gin
1/4 lemon, squeezed
1 dash Coca-Cola
ice

Method
Mix and strain into a 3 oz cocktail
glass and serve.

K

KING ALFONSO

30mL (1 oz) Kahlúa
ice
whipped cream

Method
Fill a 6 oz cocktail glass with
cracked ice, build Kahlúa over ice.
Top with whipped cream and serve.

KINGS CROSS NUT

60mL (2 oz) brandy
garnish:
nutmeg
30mL (1 oz) Tia Maria
3 ice cubes
1 coconut

Method
Remove the top from the coconut
and remove milk. Place half the milk,
brandy and Tia Maria in a shaker.
Shake, pour into coconut, dust with
nutmeg and serve with straws.

KIR

15mL (0.5 oz) crème de cassis
dry white wine

Method
Place crème de cassis in a flute glass,
top with white wine and serve.

KIR IMPERIAL

15mL (0.5 oz) crème de Framboise
chilled champagne

Method
Place crème de Framboise in a flute
glass, top with champagne and serve.

KIR ROYALE

15mL (0.5 oz) crème de Cassis
Sparkling white wine

Method
Place crème de cassis in a flute glass,
top with Sparkling wine and serve.

KISS MY ASTEROID

30mL (1 oz) Midori
pineapple juice
30mL (1 oz) blue curaçao
crushed ice
15mL (0.5 oz) Cointreau

Method
Build Midori, Cointreau and
pineapple juice in a 13 oz
Hurricane glass. Add blue curaçao
to one large scoop crushed ice and
float it on top of the pineapple
juice, add straws and serve.

KIWI

30mL (1 oz) Bacardi rum
1 dash sugar
30mL (1 oz) Midori
ice
15mL (0.5 oz) Cointreau
1 kiwifruit
45mL (1.5 oz) lemon juice

Method
Blend and pour into a 10 oz
highball glass, add straws
and serve.

KLONDYKE

40mL (1.33 oz) Calvados

garnish:

1 olive

15mL (0.5 oz) dry vermouth

1 strip lemon peel

1 dash Angostura bitters

ice

Method

Mix ingredients and strain into a 3 oz cocktail glass. Garnish with olive, lemon peel and serve.

KNEE BREAKER

30mL (1 oz) Cointreau

15mL (0.5 oz) Peter Heering

30mL (1 oz) parfait amour

1 dash Frangelico

Method

Shake and strain into a 3 oz cocktail glass and serve.

KNOCKOUT

30mL (1 oz) scotch whiskey

1 egg yolk

2 tsp sugar syrup

cracked ice

Sparkling white wine

Method

Shake all ingredients except wine and strain into a flute glass. Top with wine and serve.

KOTUKA (THE FLYER)

30mL (1 oz) vodka

1 dash lime juice

15mL (0.5 oz) Benedictine

garnish:

1 maraschino cherry

3 drops grenadine

cracked ice

Method

Shake and strain into a 5 oz cocktail glass, garnish with cherry and serve.

KRAZY KAT SHOOTER

30mL (1 oz) Malibu

30mL (1 oz) Kahlúa

30mL (1 oz) banana liqueur

Method

Layer in a shot glass and serve.

KU KLUX KLANGER

30mL (1 oz) white rum

30mL (1 oz) vodka

30mL (1 oz) Southern Comfort

lemonade

Method

Pour ingredients over crushed ice in a 5 oz cocktail glass and serve

L.I.I.T

15mL (0.5 oz) gin
15mL (0.5 oz) Bacardi rum
15mL (0.5 oz) vodka
15mL (0.5 oz) tequila
15mL (0.5 oz) Margimix
Coca-Cola (top up)

Method
Place ingredients into a 10 oz
highball glass with two ice cubes.

LADY BROWN

40mL (1.33 oz) gin
20mL (0.66 oz) orange juice
20mL (0.66 oz) Grand Marnier
garnish:
2 orange Segments
15mL (0.5 oz) lemon juice
cracked ice

Method
Shake and strain into a 5 oz
cocktail glass. Garnish with orange
Segments and serve.

LADY IN RED

30mL (1 oz) vodka
10mL (0.33 oz) lemon juice
30mL (1 oz) Rubis
1 dash egg white
10mL (0.33 oz) grenadine
4 strawberries

Method
Blend and pour into a champagne
saucer and serve.

LADY KILLER SHOOTER

15mL (0.5 oz) Kahlúa
5mL (0.17 oz) Frangelico
10mL (0.33 oz) Midori

Method
Layer in a shot glass and serve.

LADY LEON

30mL (1 oz) gin
30mL (1 oz) Galleon Liverno
30mL (1 oz) dry vermouth
garnish:
1 twist lemon peel
30mL (1 oz) orange curaçao
cracked ice

Method
Shake and strain into a champagne
saucer, garnish with lemon peel
and serve.

LADY LION

20mL (0.66 oz) Kahlúa
15mL (0.5 oz) brandy
20mL (0.66 oz) Bailey's Irish cream
60mL (2 oz) cream

Method
Shake and strain into a champagne
saucer and serve.

LADY LOO

60mL (2 oz) vodka
30mL (1 oz) Galleon Liverno
30mL (1 oz) sweet vermouth
garnish:
1 maraschino cherry
30mL (1 oz) dry vermouth
cracked ice

Method
Shake and strain into a champagne saucer, garnish with cherry and serve.

LADY LOVE

30mL (1 oz) vodka
30mL (1 oz) Galleon Liverno
30mL (1 oz) dry vermouth
garnish:
1 twist orange peel
30mL (1 oz) orange curaçao
cracked ice

Method
Shake and strain into a champagne glass, garnish with orange peel and serve.

LADY LYNNE

45mL (1.5 oz) gin
10mL (0.33 oz) lime juice
30mL (1 oz) parfait amour
ice
1 dash egg white
garnish:
1 strawberry

Method
Shake and strain into a 3 oz cocktail glass. Garnish with strawberry and serve.

LADY M

45mL (1.5 oz) Frangelico
2 scoops vanilla ice cream
45mL (1.5 oz) Midori
garnish:
grated chocolate

Method
Blend for twenty seconds and pour into a 10 oz Hurricane glass. Garnish with a sprinkle of grated chocolate and serve.

LADY'S PLEASURE

60mL (2 oz) vodka
1 dash egg white
30mL (1 oz) Galliano Liverno
cracked ice

Method
Shake and strain into a champagne glass and serve.

LADY THROAT KILLER

20mL (0.66 oz) Kahlúa
15mL (0.5 oz) Midori
10mL (0.33 oz) Frangelico

Method
Layer in order then shoot.
Comments: This superb mixture offers an exquisite after-taste.

LAMBORGHINI

30mL (1 oz) Kahlúa
15mL (0.5 oz) cream
30mL (1 oz) sambuca
nutmeg

Method
Layer the Kahlúa and sambuca in a 3 oz Martini glass and ignite with a match. Sprinkle a small amount of nutmeg over flame to produce sparks. After a few seconds, spoon the cream over the top.

LAMBORGHINI (INTERNATIONAL)

15mL (0.5 oz) Galliano Liverno
30mL (1 oz) Kahlúa
20mL (0.66 oz) sambuca
15mL (0.5 oz) cream

Method
Float ingredients in a port glass and serve.

LAMBORGHINI NO. 2

20mL (0.66 oz) Kahlúa
20mL (0.66 oz) sambuca
20mL (0.66 oz) Cointreau
20mL (0.66 oz) cream

Method
Layer Kahlúa, Cointreau and sambuca in a 5 oz cocktail glass and ignite with a match. Pour cream over the top to extinguish the flame.

LAMBORGHINI NO. 3

15mL (0.5 oz) Galliano Liverno
30mL (1 oz) Kahlúa
15mL (0.5 oz) green Chartreuse
15mL (0.5 oz) cream

Method
Float ingredients in a port glass and serve.

LAMBORGHINI NO. 4

30mL (1 oz) sambuca
30mL (1 oz) Bailey's Irish cream
15mL (0.5 oz) cream

Method
Layer sambuca and Bailey's in a port glass, ignite with a match. Sprinkle a small amount of nutmeg over the flame to produce sparks. Pour cream over the top and serve.

LANDSLIDER SHOOTER

10mL (0.33 oz) amaretto
10mL (0.33 oz) Grand Mariner
10mL (0.33 oz) Bailey's Irish cream

Method
Layer in order in a shot glass and serve.

LASER BEAM SHOOTER

25mL (0.83 oz) Galliano Liverno
20mL (0.66 oz) tequila

Method
Layer in shot glass and serve.

LAST EMPEROR

30mL (1 oz) Canadian whiskey
30mL (1 oz) Bianco vermouth
15mL (0.5 oz) Grand Mariner
30mL (1 oz) orange juice
1 dash Angostura bitters
garnish:
1 strip orange peel

Method
Place ingredients in a 5 oz
cocktail glass. Add strip of orange
peel and serve.

LAST STRAW

30mL (1 oz) Bailey's Irish cream
30mL (1 oz) Cointreau
15mL (0.5 oz) Rubis
30mL (1 oz) cream
6 strawberries (2 for garnish)

Method
Shake ingredients except
strawberries and strain into a 5 oz
cocktail glass. Garnish with
strawberries and serve.

LE PARIS

15mL (0.5 oz) Cointreau
8mL (0.27 oz) Campari
40mL (1.33 oz) Bacardi rum
20mL (0.66 oz) lemon juice
30mL (1 oz) Rubis
5 strawberries

Method
Blend until smooth and pour into a
champagne saucer and serve.

LEATHER AND LACE SHOOTER

10mL (0.33 oz) Kahlúa
10mL (0.33 oz) Bailey's Irish cream
10mL (0.33 oz) vodka

Method
Layer in order in a shot glass
and serve.

LENA

60mL (2 oz) bourbon
15mL (0.5 oz) Campari
30mL (1 oz) sweet vermouth
15mL (0.5 oz) Galleon Liverno
15mL (0.5 oz) dry vermouth
garnish:
1 maraschino cherry

Method
Stir ingredients and strain into a
5 oz cocktail glass. Garnish with
cherry and serve.

LEONARDO DE MANGO

30mL (1 oz) Midori
70mL (2.33 oz) apple juice
15mL (0.5 oz) Bailey's Irish cream
30 g mango
30mL (1 oz) mango liqueur

Method
Blend and Pour into a colada glass and serve.

LEPRECHAUN DANCER

60mL (2 oz) Irish whiskey
soda water
60mL (2 oz) lemon juice
garnish:
lemon peel
dry ginger ale
ice

Method
Place whiskey, lemon juice and ice in a 10 oz highball glass. Top with equal parts of soda water and dry ginger ale. Place lemon peel in top of glass and serve with straws.

LEVIATHAN

60mL (2 oz) brandy
30mL (1 oz) orange juice
30mL (1 oz) sweet vermouth
ice

Method
Shake and strain into a 3 oz cocktail glass and serve.

LICK SIP SUCK

30mL (1 oz) Jose Cuervo Tequila
lemon in quarters or slices
salt

Method
Pour Tequila into glass. On the flat piece of skin between the base of your thumb and index finger, place a pinch of salt. Place a quarter of the lemon by you on the bar. Lick the salt off your hand, shoot the Tequila and then suck the lemon in quick succession.

LIEUTENANT

15mL (0.5 oz) apricot brandy
1 tsp sugar
30mL (1 oz) bourbon
15mL (0.5 oz) grapefruit juice
3 ice Cubes
garnish:
1 maraschino cherry

Method
Shake and strain into a 3 oz cocktail glass. Garnish with cherry and serve.

LIGHT FINGERS

60mL (2 oz) white rum
cracked ice
30mL (1 oz) parfait amour
1 dash grenadine (add last)
30mL (1 oz) anisette liqueur

Method
Pour ingredients over half a mixing glass of cracked ice. Stir gently and strain into a 5 oz cocktail glass. Add dash grenadine and serve.

LIGHTHOUSE SHOOTER

15mL (0.5 oz) Kahlúa
15mL (0.5 oz) tequila
15mL (0.5 oz) Grand Marnier

Method
Layer in order in a shot glass and serve.

LIGHTS OF HAVANA

60mL (2 oz) soda water
40mL (1.33 oz) Malibu
25mL (0.87 oz) Midori
60mL (2 oz) orange juice
60mL (2 oz) pineapple juice

Method
Shake over ice and pour. Garnish with a straw and a lime wheel.

LIME SPIDER

45mL (1.5 oz) lime milk shake syrup
1 tablespoon of sugar
1 small scoop vanilla ice cream
top up with lemonade

Method
Pour over ice and top up with lemonade. Garnish with a banana slice and whipped cream. Serve with spoons and straws.

LION D'OR

30mL (1 oz) gin
cracked ice
60mL (2 oz) Grand Marnier
garnish:
1 strip orange peel
30mL (1 oz) orange juice

Method
Shake and strain into a 5 oz cocktail glass, garnish with orange peel and serve.

LONDON FOG

10mL (0.33 oz) White Creme de Menthe
5mL (0.17 oz) Anisette
2 dashes of Angostura Bitters

Method
Stir over ice and strain. Garnish with a mint sprig.

LONE STAR SHOOTER

15mL (0.5 oz) cherry brandy

5mL (0.17 oz) Bacardi rum

l0mL (0.33 oz) parfait amour

Method
Layer in order in a shot glass and
serve.

LONG BAY BREAKOUT SHOOTER

15mL (0.5 oz) strawberry liqueur

10mL (0.33 oz) Opal Nera

10mL (0.33 oz) Midori

10mL (0.33 oz) gin

Method
Layer ingredients in a 2 oz shot
glass and serve.

LONG GREEN

40mL (1.33 oz) Midori

soda water

20mL (0.66 oz) lemon juice

garnish:

1 lemon wheel

soda water

1 maraschino cherry

Method
Build ingredients over ice in a 10 oz
highball glass. Garnish with lemon
wheel, cherry and serve.

LONG ISLAND ICED TEA

15mL (0.5 oz) tequila

15mL (0.5 oz) Cointreau

15mL (0.5 oz) Bacardi rum

30mL (1 oz) lemon juice

15mL (0.5 oz) vodka

Coca-Cola (top up)

15mL (0.5 oz) gin

cracked ice

Method
Pour ingredients over ice in a 10 oz
highball glass. Top with Cocoa Cola
and serve with straws

LONG NECK

45mL (1.5 oz) vodka

1 dash grenadine (Last)

30mL (1 oz) Midori

1 scoop crushed ice

30mL (1 oz) lemon juice

Method
Blend until frozen, place in an Old
Fashioned glass. Add grenadine
and serve.

LONG SLOE COMFORTABLE SCREW UP AGAINST THE WALL

30mL (1 oz) vodka
orange juice (top up)
15mL (0.5 oz) Southern Comfort
ice
15mL (0.5 oz) sloe gin
garnish:
1 orange wheel
15mL (0.5 oz) Galliano Liverno

Method
Build ingredients over ice in a 10 oz highball glass. Top with orange juice, garnish with orange wheel, straws and serve.

LOUISIANA LULLABY

30mL (1 oz) Coruba Rum
10mL (0.33 oz) Dubonnet
5mL (0.17 oz) Grand Marnier

Method
Shake over ice and strain. Garnish with a twist of lemon.

LOVE BITE

10mL (0.33 oz) Cherry Brandy
10mL (0.33 oz) Parfait Amour
10mL (0.33 oz) cream

Method
Layer in order.

LOVE DORI

30mL (1 oz) Midori
60mL (2 oz) cream
20mL (0.66 oz) vodka
nutmeg (Garnish)
15mL (0.5 oz) Galliano Liverno (float)

Method
Shake Midori, vodka and cream, strain into a champagne saucer. Float Galliano Liverno, sprinkle with nutmeg and serve.

LOVE POTION NUMBER 9

60mL (2 oz) Bacardi rum
1/2 egg white
30mL (1 oz) Cointreau
garnish:
1 maraschino cherry
15mL (0.5 oz) lemon juice
cracked ice

Method
Shake and strain into a champagne saucer, garnish with cherry and serve.

LOVER

60mL (2 oz) scotch whiskey
cracked ice
30mL (1 oz) Campari
garnish:
1 twist orange peel
30mL (1 oz) Bianco vermouth

Method
Shake and strain into a champagne saucer, garnish with orange peel and serve.

Kir
(Recipe page135)

Lady M
(Recipe page 138)

Lamborgini
(Recipe page 139)

Long Island Ice Tea
(Recipe page 143)

Jellybean
(Recipe page 131)

Madam Butterfly
(Recipe page 146)

L

LOVING EYES

30mL (1 oz) Bailey's Irish cream
60mL (2 oz) cream
30mL (1 oz) Cointreau
garnish:
nutmeg
15mL (0.5 oz) Galliano Liverno
(float)

Method
Shake and strain into a champagne saucer, Ignite and sprinkle with nutmeg. Serve while flaming.

LOW FLYER

20mL (0.66 oz) Kahlúa
1/2 banana
20mL (0.66 oz) Malibu
30mL (1 oz) cream
20mL (0.66 oz) banana liqueur

Method
Blend until smooth and pour into a champagne saucer and serve.

LUCKY DIP

60mL (2 oz) vodka
1/2 egg white
30mL (1 oz) crème de banana
cracked ice
30mL (1 oz) lemon Squash

Method
Shake and strain into a champagne saucer and serve.

LUCY'S LAMENT

30mL (1 oz) brandy
30mL (1 oz) cream
30mL (1 oz) Tia Maria
cracked ice
15mL (0.5 oz) Cointreau
3 maraschino Cherries (Garnish)

Method
Shake and strain into a flute glass, drop Cherries in and serve.

LUPY'S LUNCHTIME PICK-ME-UP

45mL (1.5 oz) brandy
150mL (5 oz) chilled milk
15mL (0.5 oz) white curaçao
1 egg

Method
Blend and pour into a 10 oz highball glass and serve with straws.

LYNCHBURG LEMONADE

20mL (0.66 oz) Jack Daniel's
20mL (0.66 oz) Cointreau
20mL (0.66 oz) fresh lime juice
top up with lemonade or soda

Method
Pour in order then top up with lemonade or soda. Garnish with twisted lemon rind.

M

MACAULEY

30mL (1 oz) brandy
1 orange wedge
60mL (2 oz) curaçao
cracked ice
30mL (1 oz) dry vermouth

Method
Shake and strain into a 10 oz
highball glass over ice and serve.

MACHINE GUN KELLY

45mL (1.5 oz) scotch whiskey
1 dash orange bitters
30mL (1 oz) sweet vermouth
cracked ice
30mL (1 oz) dry vermouth
garnish:
1 twist lemon peel

Method
Shake and strain into a champagne
saucer, garnish with lemon peel
and serve.

MACLEAY STREET

30mL (1 oz) bourbon
1 dash grenadine
15mL (0.5 oz) Galliano Liverno
orange juice (top up)

Method
Shake and strain into a 10 oz
highball glass, top with orange
juice, stir and serve.

MADAM BUTTERFLY

30mL (1 oz) passoa
30mL (1 oz) cream
15mL (0.5 oz) Midori
15mL (0.5 oz) Midori
15mL (0.5 oz) white crème de cacao
30mL (1 oz) pineapple juice

Method
Shake passoa, 15mL (0.5 oz) Midori,
white crème de cacao, pineapple
juice and pour into a margarita
glass. Shake cream and
15mL (0.5 oz) Midori, layer over top
and serve.

MADRAS

30mL (1 oz) Smirnoff Vodka
80mL (2.66 oz) cranberry juice
30mL (1 oz) orange juice

Method
Build over ice then top up float
orange juice. Garnish with an
orange slice.

MAGNOLIA BLOSSOM

30mL (1 oz) bourbon
2 tsp cream
2 tsp lemon juice
cracked ice
2 dashes grenadine

Method
Shake and strain into a 3 oz
cocktail glass and serve.

M

MAI TAI

20mL (0.66 oz) dark rum
20mL (0.66 oz) lime juice
20mL (0.66 oz) white rum
crushed ice
20mL (0.66 oz) Cointreau
garnish:
1 pineapple wedge
10mL (0.33 oz) orange syrup
2 maraschino Cherries
10mL (0.33 oz) grenadine

Method
Fill a 10 oz highball glass with crushed ice and build ingredients. Garnish with pineapple wedge, Cherries, straws and serve.

MAI TAI NO. 2

15mL (0.5 oz) white rum
15mL (0.5 oz) pineapple juice
15mL (0.5 oz) Golden rum
15mL (0.5 oz) orange juice
15mL (0.5 oz) tequila
5mL (0.17 oz) grenadine
15mL (0.5 oz) triple sec
cracked ice
15mL (0.5 oz) apricot brandy
garnish:
1 pineapple wedge
15mL (0.5 oz) lemon juice
2 maraschino Cherries

Method
Blend all ingredients except grenadine and pour into a brandy Balloon. Add grenadine, garnish with pineapple wedge, Cherries, straws and serve.

MAIDEN'S BLUSH

60mL (2 oz) gin
ice
30mL (1 oz) grenadine

Method
Shake and strain into a 3 oz cocktail glass and serve.

MAIDEN'S BLUSH NO. 2

60mL (2 oz) vodka
30mL (1 oz) lemon juice
15mL (0.5 oz) Galliano Liverno
garnish:
1 maraschino cherry
1/2 eggwhite
cracked ice
30mL (1 oz) grenadine

Method
Shake and strain into a 5 oz cocktail glass and serve.

MALIBU MAGIC

30mL (1 oz) Malibu
5 strawberries
30mL (1 oz) strawberry liqueur
60mL (2 oz) cream
30mL (1 oz) orange juice
garnish:
1 twist orange peel

Method
Blend and pour into a 10 oz Hurricane glass, garnish with 1 strawberry, orange peel, straws and serve.

MALIBU STING

25mL (0.83 oz) Malibu
30mL (1 oz) lemonade
25mL (0.83 oz) gin
garnish:
1 strawberry, slit
25mL (0.83 oz) blue curaçao
crushed ice
60mL (2 oz) pineapple juice

Method
Shake all ingredients except
lemonade and pour into a flute
glass. Add lemonade, garnish with
strawberry on lip of glass and serve.

MAMA ROSA

30mL (1 oz) Romana Sambuca
30mL (1 oz) Cherry Advocaat
top up with soda water

Method
Build over ice then top up with
soda. Garnish with a maraschino
cherry and pineapple leaves.

MANDARIN SLING

20mL (0.66 oz) Kahlúa
20mL (0.66 oz) Dark Creme de
Cacao
10mL (0.33 oz) chocolate syrup
2 scoops orange sherbert
1/2 a mandarin

Method
Blend without ice. Garnish with a
mandarin or orange slice.

MANGO

60mL (2 oz) mango liqueur
1 dash sugar syrup
15mL (0.5 oz) lemon juice
soda water
30g mango

Method
Blend ail ingredients except soda
water and pour into a 10 oz
highball glass. Top with soda water,
add straws and serve.

MANGO COLADA

30mL (1 oz) white rum
30mL (1 oz) cream
30mL (1 oz) coconut cream
2 slices mango
30mL (1 oz) mango liqueur
1 scoop crushed ice
90mL (3 oz) pineapple juice

Method
Blend and pour into a 13 oz tulip
glass and serve.

MANGO DELICIOUS

30mL (1 oz) Bacardi rum
80mL (2.66 oz) pineapple juice
30mL (1 oz) mango liqueur
1/2 mango
30mL (1 oz) coconut cream
1 small scoop crushed ice
30mL (1 oz) cream

Method
Blend and pour into a white wine
glass and serve.

M

MANGO LANTIS

30mL (1 oz) mango liqueur
1 dash grenadine (Last)
45mL (1.5 oz) orange juice
1 scoop crushed ice
5mL (0.17 oz) lemon juice

Method
Blend until frozen and scoop into a 5 oz cocktail glass. Add grenadine and serve.

MANGO TANGO

20mL (0.66 oz) mango liqueur
30mL (1 oz) orange juice
15mL (0.5 oz) rum
30mL (1 oz) cream
15mL (0.5 oz) white crème de cacao

Method
Shake and strain into a 5 oz cocktail glass and serve.

MANGOTISM

30mL (1 oz) mango liqueur
60mL (2 oz) cream
25mL (0.83 oz) Frangelico
20mL (0.66 oz) advocaat

Method
Blend and pour into a 10 oz highball glass, add straws and serve.

MANHATTAN BRANDY

90mL (3 oz) brandy
cracked ice
30mL (1 oz) sweet vermouth
garnish:
1 maraschino cherry
1 dash Angostura bitters

Method
Place ingredients in a mixing glass and stir gently. Strain into a 5 oz cocktail glass, garnish with cherry and serve.

MANHATTAN DRY

45mL (1.5 oz) rye whiskey
1 dash Angostura bitters
20mL (0.66 oz) dry vermouth
cracked ice

Method
Stir gently in a mixing glass and strain into a 3 oz cocktail glass and serve.

MANHATTAN SWEET

45mL (1.5 oz) rye whiskey
20mL (0.66 oz) sweet vermouth
cracked ice

Method
Stir gently in a mixing glass and strain into a 3 oz cocktail glass and serve.

MAPLES

45mL (1.5 oz) gin
60mL (2 oz) pineapple juice
20mL (0.66 oz) white crème de cacao
cracked ice
1 dash cream

Method
Shake and strain into an Old Fashioned glass and serve.

MARCONI

30mL (1 oz) sweet vermouth
cracked ice
60mL (2 oz) Pernod

Method
Shake and strain into a 3 oz cocktail glass and serve.

MARDI GRAS

20mL (0.66 oz) Cointreau
30mL (1 oz) banana liqueur
20mL (0.66 oz) Tia Maria
cracked ice

Method
Shake and strain into a 3 oz cocktail glass and serve.

MARGARET'S MADNESS SHOOTER

20mL (0.66 oz) Tia Maria
20mL (0.66 oz) cherry advocaat
20mL (0.66 oz) blue curaçao
20mL (0.66 oz) advocaat

Method
Layer in shot glass and serve.

MARGARITA

45mL (1.5 oz) tequila
1 dash egg white
30mL (1 oz) Cointreau
1 slice lime
30mL (1 oz) lime juice
cracked ice

Method
Rim the lip of a margarita glass with salt. Shake liquid ingredients and strain into glass. Garnish with slice of lime and serve.

MARTIN LUTHER KING

30mL (1 oz) vodka
Coca-Cola
30mL (1 oz) gin
cracked ice

Method
Shake all ingredients except Coca-Cola. Strain into a 10 oz highball glass over ice. Top with Cocoa Cola and serve.

MARTINI (DRY)

60mL (2 oz) dry gin

ice

30mL (1 oz) dry vermouth

garnish:

1 green olive

Method
Shake or stir and strain into a 5 oz cocktail glass and serve with olive in glass.

MARTINI (EXTRA DRY)

120mL (4 oz) dry gin

ice

1 dash dry vermouth

garnish:

1 green olive

Method
Shake or stir and strain into a 5 oz cocktail glass and serve.

MARTINI (SWEET)

60mL (2 oz) gin

garnish:

1 maraschino cherry

30mL (1 oz) sweet vermouth

ice

Method
Mix and strain into a 3 oz cocktail glass with cherry and serve.

MARY QUEEN OF SCOTS

30mL (1 oz) scotch whiskey

garnish:

1 maraschino cherry

15mL (0.5 oz) Drambuie

1 tbsp castor sugar

15mL (0.5 oz) green Chartreuse

3 ice cubes

15mL (0.5 oz) lemon juice

Method
Dip the rim of a 3 oz cocktail glass in lemon juice then in sugar. Shake scotch whiskey, Drambuie and Chartreuse with ice and strain into rimmed glass. Garnish with cherry and serve.

MEDITERRANEAN

60mL (2 oz) water

60mL (2 oz) plain yoghurt

10mL (0.33 oz) dried mint

pinch of salt

Method
Blend with ice. Garnish with mint leaves.

MELON BALL

30mL (1 oz) Midori

30mL (1 oz) strawberry liqueur

30mL (1 oz) banana liqueur

1 strawberry

Method
Float liquid ingredients in a 3 oz cocktail glass, place strawberry on lip of glass and serve.

MELON ROCK

60mL (2 oz) Midori
60g honeydew melon
30mL (1 oz) lemon juice
garnish:
1 slice honeydew melon
10mL (0.33 oz) sugar syrup

Method
Blend and pour into a colada
glass, garnish with melon slice,
straws and serve.

MELON TREE

30mL (1 oz) Midori
120mL (4 oz) milk
30mL (1 oz) peach tree
1 dash cream
20mL (0.66 oz) Galliano Liverno
1 scoop ice cream

Method
Blend and pour into a 10 oz
highball glass and serve with
straws.

MÉNAGE À TROIS

30mL (1 oz) Pernod
30mL (1 oz) Malibu
60mL (2 oz) pineapple juice
15mL (0.5 oz) coconut cream
1 scoop orange sherbert
1 scoop vanilla ice cream

Method
Blend with ice. Garnish with
a plastic swizzle stick with three
straws.

MERRY WIDOW

60mL (2 oz) cherry brandy
garnish:
1 maraschino cherry
60mL (2 oz) maraschino liqueur
cracked ice

Method
Shake and strain into a 5 oz
cocktail glass, garnish with cherry
on lip of glass and serve.

METROPOLIS

30mL (1 oz) Midori
30mL (1 oz) Bailey's Irish cream

Method
Fill an Old Fashioned glass
with cracked ice, build ingredients
and serve.

MEXICAN BERRY SHOOTER

10mL (0.33 oz) Kahlúa
10mL (0.33 oz) tequila
10mL (0.33 oz) strawberry liqueur

Method
Layer in order in a shot glass
and serve.

MEXICAN FLAG SHOOTER

15mL (0.5 oz) grenadine
15mL (0.5 oz) tequila
15mL (0.5 oz) crème de menthe

Method
Layer in order in a shot glass and serve.

MEXICAN PUMPER SHOOTER

15mL (0.5 oz) grenadine
15mL (0.5 oz) tequila
15mL (0.5 oz) Kahlúa

Method
Layer in order in a shot glass and serve.

MEXICAN MADNESS

30mL (1 oz) tequila
1/2 banana
30mL (1 oz) Bailey's Irish cream
60mL (2 oz) pineapple juice
15mL (0.5 oz) Malibu
crushed ice

Method
Blend until smooth and pour into a Fancy glass and serve.

MEXICAN RUNNER

30mL (1 oz) Jose Cuervo Tequila
15mL (0.5 oz) Tia Maria
15mL (0.5 oz) Grand Marnier
15mL (0.5 oz) Blackberry Liqueur
30mL (1 oz) lemon juice
half a banana
2 strawberries

Method
Blend over ice and pour. Garnish with a strawberry with umbrella parasol.

MEXICAN MANGO

30mL (1 oz) tequila
15mL (0.5 oz) white curaçao
30mL (1 oz) mango liqueur
60mL (2 oz) orange juice

Method
Blend with ice and pour into a colada glass. Add straws and serve.

MIAMI ADVICE

30mL (1 oz) Malibu
garnish:
1 slice banana
30mL (1 oz) banana liqueur
cream

Method
Layer in a 3 oz cocktail glass, place banana slice on lip of glass and serve.

MICHAELANGELO

90g zucchini
90mL (3 oz) tomato juice
1 thinly sliced onion
1 dash Italian seasoning

Method
Blend with ice then pour. Garnish with a zucchini slice.

MIDNIGHT ROSE

30mL (1 oz) advocaat
30mL (1 oz)cream
15mL (0.5 oz) strawberry liqueur
1/2 strawberry (Garnish)
15mL (0.5 oz) kirsch
cracked ice

Method
Shake and strain into 5 oz cocktail glass, garnish with strawberry and serve.

MIDNIGHT SAX

30mL (1 oz) Midori
30mL (1 oz) Southern Comfort
30mL (1 oz) orange and mango
fruit juices
top up with ginger ale

Method
Pour over ice and stir, then top up with ginger ale. Garnish with slices of oranges in the glass and orange rind on the side.

MIDNIGHT SLIDE

30mL (1 oz) Opal Nero
7mL (0.23 oz) lemon juice

Method
Pour Opal Nero, then float lemon juice.

MIDORI ALEXANDER

30mL (1 oz) Midori
cracked ice
30mL (1 oz) white curaçao
garnish:
nutmeg
60mL (2 oz) cream

Method
Shake and strain into a 5 oz cocktail glass, sprinkle with nutmeg and serve.

MIDORI AND MILK

60mL (2 oz) Midori
90mL (3 oz) milk

Method
Half fill a 10 oz highball glass with ice. Pour ingredients into glass and serve with straws.

M

MIDORI AVALANCHE

30mL (1 oz) blue curaçao
60mL (2 oz) pineapple juice
30mL (1 oz) Midori
garnish:
1 pineapple wedge
15mL (0.5 oz) triple sec

Method
Pour curaçao into a 10 oz Hurricane glass. Blend remaining ingredients with ice and add to glass, garnish with pineapple wedge. straws and serve.

MIDORI COLADA

30mL (1 oz) Midori
90mL (3 oz) pineapple juice
30mL (1 oz) white rum
1 slice pineapple
30mL (1 oz) coconut cream
1 scoop crushed ice
30mL (1 oz) cream
garnish:
1 pineapple wedge

Method
Blend until smooth and pour into a 10 oz tulip glass, garnish with pineapple wedge, straws and serve.

MIDORI COOLER

30mL (1 oz) Midori
60mL (2 oz) soda water

Method
Pour Midori over ice an a 10 oz highball glass, top with soda water. Add straws and serve.

MIDORI MARGARITA

30mL (1 oz) Midori
20mL (0.66 oz) Cointreau
30mL (1 oz) tequila
5mL (0.17 oz) sugar syrup
30mL (1 oz) lemon juice

Method
Shake and strain into a Salt Rimmed margarita glass and serve.

MIDORI MELTDOWN

45mL (1.5 oz) Midori
Angostura bitters
15mL (0.5 oz) lime juice
soda water

Method
Blend ingredients except soda and pour into a sugar rimmed Hurricane glass. Top with soda and add a dash of Angostura bitters and serve.

MIDORI MIST

30mL (1 oz) Midori
champagne

Method
Build ingredients into a flute glass and serve.

MIDORI SOUR

30mL (1 oz) Midori
60mL (2 oz) lemon juice
1 tsp sugar

Method
Blend and strain into a 3 oz cocktail
glass and serve.

MIDORI SPLICE

45mL (1.5 oz) Midori
15mL (0.5 oz) cream (float)
30mL (1 oz) Malibu
cracked ice
120mL (4 oz) pineapple juice

Method
Build ingredients in a 9 oz brandy
Balloon, float cream and serve.

MIKADO

60mL (2 oz) Midori
1 slice pineapple
15mL (0.5 oz) vodka
60mL (2 oz) pineapple juice
15mL (0.5 oz) banana liqueur
crushed ice

Method
Blend until smooth and pour into
a 10 oz highball glass and .serve
with straws.

MILES OF SMILES SHOOTER

15mL (0.5 oz) crème de menthe
15mL (0.5 oz) rye whiskey
15mL (0.5 oz) amaretto

Method
Layer in order in a shot glass
and serve.

MIMOSA

chilled champagne
chilled orange juice

Method
Half fill a champagne flute with
orange juice, top with champagne
and serve.

MINT JULEP

60mL (2 oz) bourbon
1 tbsp water
1 tbsp Chopped mint
crushed ice
1 tsp sugar
garnish:
mint leaves

Method
Muddle sugar, mint and water in
a 5 oz cocktail glass. Half fill glass
with crushed ice and add bourbon.
Garnish with mint leaves and serve.

Bourbon

60mL (2 oz) bourbon
garnish:
1 slice lemon
1 dash dark rum
mint leaves
1/2 tsp sugar
cracked ice

Method
Muddle bourbon, sugar and mint leaves in a 10 oz highball glass. Half fill a 10 oz highball glass with ice and add rum. Garnish with mint leaves. lemon slice and serve with straws.

Mod's

80mL (2.66 oz) bourbon
2 tsp sugar
2 tsp white crème de menthe
garnish:
1 sprig mint
2 pieces pineapple
Finely crushed ice

Method
Muddle mint and sugar in a 10 oz highball glass. Half fill glass with crushed ice, add bourbon and pineapple Pieces. Float crème de menthe and serve with straws.

MISS AILEEN

30mL (1 oz) advocaat
30mL (1 oz) Galliano Liverno
30mL (1 oz) Vandermint
ice

Method
Shake and strain into a 3 oz cocktail glass and serve.

MISS ANDREA

20mL (0.66 oz) crème de menthe
15mL (0.5 oz) Midori
15mL (0.5 oz) parfait amour
soda water

Method
Shake ingredients except soda water. Strain into a 10 oz highball glass. Top with soda water and float Galliano Liverno and serve.

MISSION IMPOSSIBLE

30mL (1 oz) Cointreau
30mL (1 oz) Midori
30mL (1 oz) strawberry liqueur
30mL (1 oz) banana liqueur

Method
Layer in a 4 oz cocktail glass and serve.

MISSISSIPPI MUD

30mL (1 oz) Kahlúa
Coca-Cola
30mL (1 oz) Southern Comfort
garnish:
sprinkle grated chocolate
1 small scoop ice cream
cracked ice

Method
Place Kahlúa, Southern Comfort
and ice cream in a 10 oz highball
glass. Top with Coca-Cola.
Sprinkle grated chocolate over the
top. Add two straws and serve.

MOCHA MINT

20mL (0.66 oz) Kahlúa
20mL (0.66 oz) White Creme de
Menthe
20mL (0.66 oz) White Creme de
Cacao

Method
Shake with ice and strain. Garnish
with peppermint chocolate flakes.

MODEL "T" SHOOTER

15mL (0.5 oz) tequila
15mL (0.5 oz) Tia Maria
15mL (0.5 oz) banana liqueur

Method
Layer in order in a shot glass and
serve.

MOLFETTA MADNESS

30mL (1 oz) sambuca
20mL (0.66 oz) cream
30mL (0.66 oz) Mandarin liqueur
garnish:
1 slice orange
30mL (1 oz) orange juice
cracked ice

Method
Shake and strain into a 4 oz
cocktail glass. Garnish with orange
slice and serve.

MONK'S MADNESS

20mL (0.66 oz) strawberry liqueur
60mL (2 oz) cream
30mL (1 oz) crème de cacao
cracked ice
50mL (1.66oz) Benedictine
garnish:
shaved chocolate

Method
Shake and strain into a 5 oz
cocktail glass frosted with shaved
chocolate.

MONKEY GLAND

60mL (2 oz) dry gin
30mL (1 oz) orange juice
15mL (0.5 oz) Pernod
cracked ice
15mL (0.5 oz) grenadine

Method
Shake and strain into a 5 oz
cocktail glass and serve.

MONKEY'S HABITS

60mL (2 oz) vodka
30mL (1 oz) lemon juice
15mL (0.5 oz) Pernod
cracked ice
15mL (0.5 oz) grenadine

Method
Shake and strain into a champagne
glass and serve.

MONKEY'S PUNCH SHOOTER

10mL (0.33 oz) Kahlua
15mL (0.5 oz) Bailey's Irish cream
15mL (0.5 oz) crème de menthe

Method
Layer in order in a shot glass and
serve.

MONKEY'S TAIL

30mL (1 oz) Cointreau
30mL (1 oz) lemon vodka
20mL (0.66 oz) apricot nectar
30mL (1 oz) cream

Method
Shake and strain into a 5 oz
cocktail glass and serve.

MONTE CARLO

30mL (1 oz) rye rhisky
10mL (0.33 oz) Benedictine
2 dashes of Angostura Bitters

Method
Shake with ice and strain.

MONTMARTRE

10mL (0.33 oz) Cointreau
30mL (1 oz) Gilbey's Gin
10mL (0.33 oz) Cinzano Sweet
Vermouth

Method.
Coat glass with Cointreau then
pour Gilbey's Gin and Cinzano
Sweet Vermouth over ice. Garnish
with a red cherry.

MOOMBA

30mL (1 oz) Bacardi rum
1 dash grenadine
30mL (1 oz) Grand Marnier
cracked ice
15mL (0.5 oz) orange juice
garnish:
1 twist orange peel
10mL (0.33 oz) lemon juice

Method
Shake and strain into a 5 oz
cocktail glass, garnish with orange
peel and serve.

MOON BEAM

30mL (1 oz) Midori
30mL (1 oz) cream
20mL (0.66 oz) vodka
20mL (0.66 oz) orange juice
15mL (0.5 oz) Grand Marnier
garnish:
1 slice kiwifruit

Method
Shake and strain into 5 oz cocktail glass, garnish with kiwifruit and serve.

MOON CRATER

30mL (1 oz) vodka
garnish:
nutmeg
30mL (1 oz) advocaat
1 maraschino cherry
orange soda
cracked ice
fresh cream (float)

Method
Place vodka and advocaat in a 10 oz highball glass, top with orange soda. Float cream, dust with nutmeg and garnish with cherry and serve.

MOON'S ECLIPSE

30mL (1 oz) Campari
30mL (1 oz) fresh cream
30mL (1 oz) Drambuie
garnish:
nutmeg
30mL (1 oz) Amsterdam
1 maraschino cherry
30mL (1 oz) orange juice

Method
Shake and strain into a champagne saucer, sprinkle with nutmeg. Garnish with cherry and serve.

MORNING GLORY

30mL (1 oz) J&B scotch whisky
30mL (1 oz) Milne Brandy
5mL (0.17 oz) Pernod
5mL (0.17 oz) White Curacao
dashes Angostura Bitters
top up with soda

Method
Shake with ice and pour then top up with soda. Garnish with an orange twist.

Mai Tai
(Recipe page 147)

Margarita
(Recipe page 150)

Martini
(Recipe page 151)

Pretty Woman
(Recipe page 184)

Pina Colada
(Recipe page 178)

Ready, Set, Go!
(Recipe page 190)

MORNING STAR

30mL (1 oz) Bacardi rum
lemonade (top up)
20mL (0.66 oz) Galliano Liverno
cracked ice
45mL (1.5 oz) advocaat

Method
Shake and strain into a 10 oz highball glass, top with lemonade. Add straws and serve.

MOROCCAN COCKTAIL

30mL (1 oz) Gilbey's Gin
30mL (1 oz) Cointreau
5mL (0.17 oz) Orange Curacao

Method
Shake with ice and strain. Garnish with a lemon wheel.

MOSCOW MULE

60mL (2 oz) vodka
cracked ice
30mL (1 oz) lemon juice
garnish:
1 sprig mint
ginger beer (top up)

Method
Shake and strain into a 10 oz highball glass, top with ginger beer. Garnish with sprig of mint, straws and serve.

MOULIN ROUGE

30mL (1 oz) gin
Sparkling white wine (top up)
20mL (0.66 oz) apricot brandy
garnish:
1 orange slice
20mL (0.66 oz) lemon juice
cracked ice
1 tsp grenadine

Method
Shake and strain into a champagne saucer, top with Sparkling white wine. Garnish with orange slice and serve.

MOUNT COOK SUNSET

45mL (1.5 oz) vodka
15mL (0.5 oz) lemon juice
15mL (0.5 oz) maraschino liqueur
15mL (0.5 oz) orange juice
1 dash grenadine
cracked ice

Method
Shake and strain into a champagne saucer and serve.

MOUNT FUJI

30mL (1 oz) Gilbey's Gin
15mL (0.5 oz) lemon juice
10mL (0.33 oz) heavy cream
1 egg white

Method
Shake with ice and strain. Garnish with a red cherry.

MOUNT TEMPLE

30mL (1 oz) Kahlúa
30mL (1 oz) coconut liqueur
30mL (1 oz) tequila

Method
Build over ice in a 3 oz cocktail
glass and serve.

MOUNTAIN

45mL scotch whiskey
30mL (1 oz) Galleon Liverno
30mL (1 oz) green ginger wine
45mL (1.5 oz) pineapple juice

Method
Shake and strain into a champagne
saucer and serve.

MUCHO MARGARITA

30mL (1 oz) tequila
30mL (1 oz) Cointreau
30mL (1 oz) Margimix

Method
Shake and strain into a Salt rimmed
3 oz cocktail glass and serve.

MULE'S HIND LEG

15mL (0.5 oz) Calvados
15mL (0.5 oz) Benedictine
15mL (0.5 oz) apricot liqueur
10mL (0.33 oz) Maple syrup
15mL (0.5 oz) gin
cracked ice

Method
Place ingredients in a mixing glass
and stir gently. Strain into a 3 oz
cocktail glass and serve.

MYRA

15mL (0.5 oz) vodka
30mL (1 oz) dry red wine
15mL (0.5 oz) sweet vermouth
cracked ice

Method
Place ingredients in a mixing glass
and stir gently. Strain into a 3 oz
cocktail glass and serve.

NAPOLEON

45mL (1.5 oz) gin
1 dash white curaçao
1 dash Fernet Branca
cracked ice

Method
Stir and strain into a 3 oz cocktail glass and serve.

NAPOLEON SEDUCTION

15mL (0.5 oz) mango liqueur
30mL (1 oz) cream
30mL (1 oz) Mandarin Napoleon
20g mango
15mL (0.5 oz) Sabra
garnish:
1 maraschino cherry

Method
Blend until smooth and pour into a colada glass, garnish with cherry and serve.

NATASHA

15mL (0.5 oz) Pear brandy
1 dash orange bitters
15mL (0.5 oz) apricot brandy
garnish:
1 maraschino cherry
15mL (0.5 oz) sweet vermouth
cracked ice

Method
Shake and strain into a 3 oz cocktail glass, garnish with cherry and serve.

NAUGHTY NUPTIAL

30mL (1 oz) Tia Maria
1/2 banana
15mL (0.5 oz) Jamaican rum
cracked ice
60mL (2 oz) orange juice
garnish:
1 pineapple wedge
60mL (2 oz) pineapple juice

Method
Blend until smooth and pour into a champagne saucer, garnish with pineapple wedge and serve.

NEGRONI

30mL (1 oz) gin
soda water
15mL (0.5 oz) Campari
garnish:
1 twist lemon peel
30mL (1 oz) sweet vermouth
cracked ice

Method
Stir gin, Campari, vermouth and ice in a mixing glass and strain into a 6 oz Old Fashioned glass. Add a splash of soda water, garnish with lemon peel and serve.

NEGRONI NO. 2

30mL (1 oz) Campari
4 ice cubes
30mL (1 oz) sweet vermouth
1 dash Angostura bitters
30mL (1 oz) gin
garnish:
1 slice orange

Method
Place ice cubes in a 5 oz cocktail glass and add ingredients. Garnish with orange slice and serve.

NEUTRON BOMB SHOOTER

15mL (0.5 oz) Kahlúa
I5mL (0.5 oz) tequila
15mL (0.5 oz) Bundaberg rum

Method
Layer in order in a shot glass and serve.

NEW ICED TEA

30mL (1 oz) vodka
30mL (1 oz) grapefruit juice
30mL (1 oz) Cointreau
Coca-Cola
30mL (1 oz) tequila
cracked ice
30mL (1 oz) white rum
garnish:
1 sprig mint

Method
Fill a 10 oz highball glass with ice and add ingredients. Garnish with mint and Serve with straws.

NEW ORLEANS

60mL (2 oz) gin
2 dashes orange flower water
30mL (1 oz) lemon juice
1 dash vanilla Essence
1 tsp sugar
cracked ice
30mL (1 oz) cream
soda water
1 egg white

Method
Shake al! ingredients except soda water and strain over ice in a 10 oz highball glass. Top with soda water, add straws and serve.

NEW YORK

60mL (2 oz) Canadian whiskey
garnish:
1 twist orange peel
4 dashes grenadine
cracked ice

Method
Shake and strain into a 3 oz cocktail glass, garnish with orange peel and serve.

NEW YORKER

15mL (0.5 oz) gin
1 dash Cointreau
45mL (1.5 oz) French vermouth
cracked ice
15mL (0.5 oz) sweet sherry

Method
Stir and strain into a 3 oz cocktail glass and serve.

N

NICKEL FEVER

1 tsp Southern Comfort
2 tbsp cream
1 tsp Galliano Liverno
2 tbsp orange juice
10mL (0.33 oz) blue curaçao
cracked ice

Method
Shake and strain into a 3 oz cocktail glass and serve.

NIGHT OF PASSION

60mL (2 oz) gin
1 tbsp lemon juice
30mL (1 oz) Cointreau
60mL (2 oz) passionfruit juice
60mL (2 oz) peach nectar
cracked ice

Method
Shake and strain into a rocks glass and serve.

NIGHT STAR

45mL (1.5 oz) vodka
20mL (0.66 oz) goldwasser
45mL (1.5 oz) dry vermouth
10mL (0.33 oz) blue curaçao

Method
Stir and strain into a 5 oz cocktail glass and serve.

19 DUKE DRIVE SHOOTER

15mL (0.5 oz) Vandermint
15mL (0.5 oz) banana liqueur
15mL (0.5 oz) cherry brandy

Method
Layer in order in a shot glass and serve.

NOAH'S ARK

10mL (0.33 oz) Blue Curacao
10mL (0.33 oz) cream
10mL (0.33 oz) lemonade

Method
Shake Blue Curacao with cream, then layer lemonade. Optionally, place half a lychee nut in glass before pouring.

NORMAN CONQUEST

60mL (2 oz) Calvados
1 tsp grenadine
2 tbsp lemon juice
cracked ice

Method
Shake and strain into a 3 oz cocktail glass and serve.

NUDE BOMB SHOOTER

10mL (0.33 oz) Kahlúa
10mL (0.33 oz) banana liqueur
10mL (0.33 oz) amaretto

Method
Layer in order in a shot glass and serve.

NUTTY IRISHMAN

30mL (1 oz) Frangelico
30mL (1 oz) Baileys Irish Cream
15mL (0.5 oz) fresh lime juice
top up with fresh milk

Method
Build over ice. Garnish with sprinkled nutmeg or chocolate flakes.

NUTTY BUDDY SHOOTER

15mL (0.5 oz) Kahlúa
15mL (0.5 oz) Frangelico
15mL (0.5 oz) crème de menthe

Method
Layer in order in a shot glass and serve.

OCEANIC

45mL (1.5 oz) scotch whiskey
garnish:
1 spiral orange peel
15mL (0.5 oz) Bianco vermouth
cracked ice
30mL (1 oz) Kahlúa

Method
Mix in a mixing glass and strain into a champagne glass. Garnish with a spiral of orange peel and serve.

OFF THE LEASH

90mL (3 oz) brandy
cracked ice
30mL (1 oz) sweet vermouth
garnish:
1 maraschino cherry

Method
Mix in a mixing glass and strain into a champagne glass. Garnish with a maraschino cherry and serve.

OLD FASHIONED APPETISER

1 cube of ice
20mL (0.66 oz) Jim Beam Bourbon
20mL (0.66 oz) Dubonnet
5mL (0.17 oz) Cointreau
5mL (0.17 oz) Pernod
1 dash Angostura Bitters

Method
Build over ice. Garnish with lemon and orange peel.

OLD FASHIONED SCOTCH

30mL(1 oz) scotch whisky
dash Angostura Bitters
sugar cube
soda water

Method
Build over ice. Garnish with 1/2 slice of orange and lemon and a cherry. A swizzle stick may be used.

OIL FEVER

60mL (2 oz) dark rum
cracked ice
60mL (2 oz) Kahlúa
garnish:
1 spiral orange peel

OLD PAL

30mL (1 oz) bourbon
garnish:
1 Piece lemon peel
15mL (0.5 oz) dry vermouth
3 ice cubes
15mL (0.5 oz) Campari

Method
Mix in a mixing glass and strain into a 3 oz cocktail glass. Garnish with lemon peel and serve.

OLD SAN FRANCISCO

30mL (1 oz) kirsch
2 dashes grenadine
30mL (1 oz) Knock
fresh cream
2 dashes lime cordial
1/2 tsp Instant coffee

Method
Mix kirsch, Kueck and grenadine with ice and strain into a 5 oz cocktail glass and add cordial. Mix coffee with cream and float on top and serve.

OPAL ROYALE

30mL (1 oz) Opal Nera
30mL (1 oz) cream
30mL (1 oz) brandy
garnish:
1 maraschino cherry
15mL (0.5 oz) white crème de menthe

Method
Shake and strain all ingredients except cream. Strain into a 5 oz cocktail glass and float cream. Garnish with cherry and serve.

OLÉ

45mL (1.5 oz) tequila
5mL (0.17 oz) blue curaçao
30mL (1 oz) banana liqueur
cracked ice

Method
Stir tequila and banana liqueur and strain over ice in a 5 oz cocktail glass. Add blue curaçao and serve.

OPPENHEIM COCKTAIL

30mL (1 oz) Jim Beam Bourbon
20mL (0.66 oz) Grenadine
20mL (0.66 oz) Cinzano Rosso Vermouth
5mL (0.17 oz) Pernod

Method
Stir over ice and strain. Garnish with lemon and orange peel and a parasol.

OPAL MAGIC SHOOTER

30mL (1 oz) Midori
30mL (1 oz) Opal Nera
30mL (1 oz) Cointreau

Method
Layer in a shot glass and serve.

ORANGE BLOSSOM

30mL (1 oz) gin
cracked ice
60mL (2 oz) orange juice

Method
Shake and strain into a 3 oz cocktail glass and serve.

O

ORANGE BOMB

45mL (1.5 oz) scotch whiskey
10mL (0.33 oz) Pernod
30mL (1 oz) orange juice
5mL (0.17 oz) sugar syrup
soda water
cracked ice

Method
Shake all ingredients except soda water and strain into a 10 oz highball glass. Top with soda water and serve with straws.

ORANGE BUS

30mL (1 oz) mango liqueur
30mL (1 oz) banana liqueur
90mL (3 oz) orange juice
cracked ice

Method
Shake and strain into an Old Fashioned glass and serve.

ORANGE NOG

1 egg
120mL (4 oz) milk
130mL (4.33 oz) orange juice
10mL (0.33 oz) sugar syrup

Method
Blend over ice and pour. Garnish with a sprinkle of ground nutmeg and twisted orange peel.

ORANGUTANG

30mL (1 oz) Midori
90mL (3 oz) orange juice
30mL (1 oz) Mandarin Napoleon
garnish:
2 orange slices
90mL (3 oz) pineapple juice
pineapple leaves

Method
Half fill a 10 oz highball glass with ice, add ingredients and garnish with orange slices, pineapple leaves. straws and serve.

ORGASM (MULTIPLE)

30mL (1 oz) Bailey's Irish cream
30mL (1 oz) Cointreau
30mL (1 oz) Galleon Liverno

Method
Layer in order in a 3 oz cocktail glass and serve.

ORGASM (MULTIPLE NO. 2)

30mL (1 oz) Bailey's Irish cream
30mL (1 oz) cream
30mL (1 oz) Cointreau
cracked ice

Method
Build in a 9 oz brandy Balloon and serve.

ORGASM (SCREAMING MULTIPLE)

30mL (1 oz) Bailey's Irish cream
30mL (1 oz) cream
30mL (1 oz) Cointreau
cracked ice
15mL (0.5 oz) Galliano Liverno

Method
Build in a 9 oz brandy Balloon
and serve.

ORGASM (SCREAMING)

30mL (1 oz) Bailey's Irish cream
30mL (1 oz) Cointreau
30mL (1 oz) cherry brandy

Method
Layer in a 3 oz cocktail glass
and serve.

ORGASM SHOOTER

30mL (1 oz) Bailey's Irish cream
cracked ice
30mL (1 oz) Cointreau

Method
Layer in order in a shot glass
and serve.

ORGASM SHOOTER (SCREAMING NO. 2)

30mL (1 oz) Bailey's Irish cream
30mL (1 oz) Cointreau
30mL (1 oz) Kahlúa

Method
Layer in order in a shot glass
and serve.

ORIENTAL BLOSSOM

30mL (1 oz) banana liqueur
90mL (3 oz) apple juice
30mL (1 oz) Southern Comfort
30mL (1 oz) cream
15mL (0.5 oz) red curaçao
2 apple slices

Method
Shake and strain into a colada
glass, garnish with apple slices
and serve.

ORIENTAL PEARL

20mL (0.66 oz) white rum
15mL (0.5 oz) fresh cream
10mL (0.33 oz) crème de cassis
cracked ice
15mL (0.5 oz) Cola syrup

Method
Shake and strain into a champagne
glass and serve.

O

OUTER SPACE

45mL (1.5 oz) vodka
10mL (0.33 oz) lime juice.
45mL (1.5 oz) Bacardi rum
garnish:
1 maraschino cherry
20mL (0.66 oz) Galliano Liverno

Method
Shake and strain into a 5 oz
cocktail glass, garnish and serve.

OYSTER SHOOTER (HEARTSTARTER)

10mL (0.33 oz) Smirnoff Vodka
10mL (0.33 oz) tomato juice
5mL (0.17 oz) cocktail sauce
Worcestershire sauce to taste
Tabasco sauce to taste
1 fresh oyster

Method
Pour tomato juice onto the
Smirnoff Vodka, float the cocktail
sauce, dash sauces to taste and
drop in oyster. Shoot.

PABLO

30mL (1 oz) Bacardi rum
garnish:
1 slice pineapple
15mL (0.5 oz) Cointreau
1 maraschino cherry
15mL (0.5 oz) advocaat
cracked ice

Method
Shake and strain into a 5 oz
cocktail glass, garnish with
pineapple, cherry and serve.

PADDY'S PERIL

60mL (2 oz) Bailey's Irish cream
1 dash grenadine
30mL (1 oz) vodka
crushed ice
coconut milk

Method
Shake and strain into a 5 oz
cocktail glass and serve.

PAGO PAGO

30mL (1 oz) Bacardi Gold Rum
10mL (0.33 oz) lime juice
10mL (0.33 oz) pineapple juice
5mL (0.17 oz) Green Chartreuse
5mL (0.17 oz) Cointreau

Method
Shake with ice and strain over 3
cube of ice. Garnish with a
pineapple wedge and a cherry.

PAINT BOX

30mL (1 oz) cherry advocaat
30mL (1 oz) advocaat
30mL (1 oz) blue curaçao

Method
Layer in a 3 oz cocktail glass
and serve.

PALM SUNDAE

45mL (1.5 oz) peach liqueur
3 strawberries
30mL (1 oz) coconut liqueur
garnish:
1 orange wheel
15mL (0.5 oz) banana liqueur
pineapple leaves
60mL (2 oz) Tropical fruit juice
1 maraschino cherry

Method
Blend with ice and pour into a
10 oz Hurricane glass. Garnish and
serve with straws.

PALM TREE

15mL (0.5 oz) Grand Marnier
15mL (0.5 oz) mango liqueur
15mL (0.5 oz) cognac
30mL (1 oz) cream
15mL (0.5 oz) Bacardi rum
garnish:
1 maraschino cherry
15mL (0.5 oz) Malibu
pineapple leaves
15mL (0.5 oz) peach liqueur

Method
Shake and strain into a 5 oz
margarita glass, garnish with
cherry, pineapple leaves and serve.

PALOMINO

20mL (0.66 oz) Galliano Liverno
30mL (1 oz) Kahlúa
45mL (1.5 oz) cream

Method
Shake and strain into a 5 oz
cocktail glass and serve.

PANTY DROPPER
SHOOTER

20mL (0.66 oz) Frangelico
10mL (0.33 oz) gin

Method
Layer in a shot glass and serve.

PAPAYA SLING

30mL (1 oz) Gilbey's Gin
15mL (0.5 oz) lime juice
20mL (0.66 oz) papaya juice or
syrup
2 dashes of Angostura Bitters

Method
Shake with ice and pour then
top up with soda. Garnish with
lime juice.

PARADISE

45mL (1.5 oz) Midori
1/2 kiwifruit
120mL (4 oz) pineapple juice

Method
Blend until smooth, pour into an
Old Fashioned glass and serve.

PARADISE NO. 2

30mL (1 oz) gin
5mL (0.17 oz) orange juice
15mL (0.5 oz) apricot brandy
ice

Method
Shake and strain into a 3 ox
cocktail glass and serve.

PARIS BY NIGHT

30mL (1 oz) Pernod
lemonade (top up)
30mL (1 oz) Strega
garnish:
1 slice orange
15mL (0.5 oz) Amsterdam
1 maraschino cherry

Method
Place all ingredients except
lemonade in a 10 oz highball glass,
top with lemonade. Garnish with
lemonade, add straws and serve.

PARIS PEACH

60mL (2 oz) peach liqueur
10mL (0.33 oz) Pernod

Method
Pour over ice in a 3 oz cocktail
glass and serve.

PASSION OFF

30mL (1 oz) vodka
45mL (1.5 oz) fresh cream
15mL (0.5 oz) Grand Marnier
garnish:
1 maraschino cherry
pulp 1 passionfruit

Method
Shake and pour into a champagne
saucer, garnish with cherry and
serve.

PASSIONATE SCENE

45mL (1.5 oz) strawberry liqueur
1 tsp passionfruit pulp
60mL (2 oz) orange juice
5mL (0.17 oz) lemon juice

Method
Pour ingredients into 10 oz highball glass, float passionfruit pulp **(Do not stir)** and serve.

PASSIONATE SCENE NO. 2

45mL (1.5 oz) strawberry liqueur
1 tsp passionfruit pulp
60mL (2 oz) orange juice
1 tsp passionfruit juice
60mL (2 oz) lemonade
1 scoop crushed ice

Method
Pour all ingredients except passionfruit fruit pulp, lemon juice and lemonade into a 10 oz highball glass. Add other ingredient except passionfruit pulp and stir. Add passionfruit pulp, add straws and serve.

PAULA STAFFORD

30mL (1 oz) gin
60mL (2 oz) Cleopatra
60mL (2 oz) Pimm's no. 1

Method
Shake and strain into a 5 oz cocktail glass and serve.

PEACH ALMOND SHAKE

60mL (2 oz) Peach Liqueur
1 whole peeled peach
30mL (1 oz) Amaretto di Galliano
2 scoops of vanilla ice cream
top up with lemonade

Method
Blend with ice and pour then top up with lemonade. Garnish with a peach slice and shredded almonds and a straw.

PEACH BOMB

45mL (1.5 oz) peach liqueur
5mL (0.17 oz) lemon juice
15mL (0.5 oz) vodka

Method
Stir ingredients and pour over ice in a 3 oz cocktail glass and serve.

PEACH EXPLOSION

45mL (1.5 oz) peach liqueur
45mL (1.5 oz) vodka

Method
Pour over ice in a 5 oz cocktail glass and serve.

P

PEACH LANTIS

45mL (1.5 oz) peach liqueur
1 dash grenadine
15mL (0.5 oz) lemon juice
1 scoop cracked ice
45mL (1.5 oz) orange juice

Method
Blend until frozen, scoop into a 10 oz highball glass and serve.

PEACH MARNIER

30mL (1 oz) Grand Marnier
2 peaches (Skinned and sliced)
30mL (1 oz) white rum
crushed ice
20mL (0.66 oz) sugar syrup
garnish:
pineapple slice
30mL (1 oz) pineapple juice

Method
Blend with crushed ice until smooth, pour into a l0 oz highball glass. Garnish with a pineapple slice, straws and serve.

PEACH ME

30mL (1 oz) Southern Comfort
30mL (1 oz) cream
30mL (1 oz) white crème de Calvados
1 dash grenadine
60mL (2 oz) orange juice
2 peach halves

Method
Blend until smooth and pour into a 7 oz brandy Balloon and serve.

PEACH SURPRISE

30mL (1 oz) peach liqueur
1 dash grenadine
15mL (0.5 oz) Malibu
4 strawberries

Method
Blend until smooth and pour into a champagne saucer and serve.

PEACHY BUM

30mL (1 oz) mango liqueur
30mL (1 oz) cream
30mL (1 oz) peach liqueur
30mL (1 oz) orange juice

Method
Shake and strain into a 5 oz cocktail glass and serve.

PEARL HARBOUR

30mL (1 oz) saki
lemonade
30mL (1 oz) blue curaçao
cracked ice

Method
In a 7 oz brandy Balloon place 1 scoop of cracked ice. Pour in saki and curaçao, top with lemonade and serve with straws.

PENALTY SHOT SHOOTER

15mL (0.5 oz) crème de menthe
15mL (0.5 oz) vodka
15mL (0.5 oz) Tia Maria

Method
Layer in order in a shot glass and serve.

PEPPERMINT

60mL (2 oz) Vandermint
15mL (0.5 oz) crème de menthe
30mL (1 oz) fresh cream
garnish:
1 maraschino cherry
ginger beer
grated chocolate

Method
Shake all ingredients except ginger beer and strain over ice in a 10 oz highball glass. Top with ginger beer, garnish with cherry, chocolate, straws and serve.

PEPPER 2000

40mL (1.33 oz) crème de menthe
15mL (0.5 oz) Cointreau
40mL (1.33 oz) white curaçao
30mL (1 oz) cream

Method
Shake crème de menthe and curaçao and strain into a 5 oz champagne saucer. Mix Cointreau and cream and float on top and serve.

PERFECT

45mL (1.5 oz) dry gin
30mL (1 oz) sweet vermouth
30mL (1 oz) dry vermouth

Method
Stir and strain into a 3 oz cocktail glass and serve.

PERNOD POLYNESIAN

15mL (0.5 oz) Pernod
30mL (1 oz) cream
30mL (1 oz) Southern Comfort
60mL (2 oz) orange & mango juice
15mL (0.5 oz) blue curaçao
2 ice cubes

Method
Place ice cubes in a 10 oz highball glass, pour liquid ingredients over ice and serve with straws.

PETER'S PRIDE

30mL (1 oz) Galliano Liverno
60mL (2 oz) pineapple juice
20mL (0.66 oz) tequila
60mL (2 oz) orange juice
30mL (1 oz) Bacardi rum

Method
Shake and strain into a 10 oz highball glass and serve with straws.

PETITE FLEUR

60mL (2 oz) Bacardi rum
cracked ice
30mL (1 oz) Cointreau
garnish:
1 maraschino cherry
30mL (1 oz) grapefruit juice

Method
Shake and strain into a 5 oz champagne glass, garnish with cherry and serve.

P

PHOTO FINISH

45mL (1.5 oz) Bacardi rum
10mL (0.33 oz) lime juice
45mL (1.5 oz) apricot brandy
cracked ice
30mL (1 oz) dry vermouth
garnish:
1 twist lemon peel

Method
Shake and strain into a 5 oz cocktail glass, garnish with twist of lemon peel and serve.

PIAFF

30mL (1 oz) brandy
1 tbsp sugar
30mL (1 oz) white curaçao
1 egg
15mL (0.5 oz) lemon juice
cracked ice

Method
Shake and strain into a 5 oz cocktail glass and serve.

PICADILLY PUNCH

30mL (1 oz) Courvoisier Cognac
10mL (0.33 oz) sugar
15mL (0.5 oz) lemon juice
1 clove
cinnamon stick
ground nutmeg

Method
Simmer all ingredients except for Courvoisier Cognac. Pour Cognac into ladle and ignite before infusing the punch mix. Stir and serve. Garnish with an orange slice and a red cherry.

PICASSO

30mL (1 oz) Courvoisier Cognac
10mL (0.33 oz) Dubonnet
10mL (0.33 oz) lime juice
15mL (0.5 oz) sugar syrup

Method
Shake over ice and strain. Garnish with an orange twist.

PICKLED BRAIN SHOOTER

30mL (1 oz) Kahlúa
30mL (1 oz) sweet vermouth
30mL (1 oz) dry vermouth

Method
Layer in order in a shot glass and serve.

PICK-ME-UP

30mL (1 oz) cognac
30mL (1 oz) sweet vermouth
30mL (1 oz) dry vermouth

Method
Stir and strain into a 3 o/. cocktail glass and serve.

PICK-ME-UP NO. 2

60mL (2 oz) brandy
milk
1 dash Angostura bitters
soda water
1 tsp sugar

Method
In a 10 oz highball glass place
Angostura bitters, sugar and
brandy. Fill glass with milk and add
a dash of soda water and serve
with straws.

PIMM'S

45mL (1.5 oz) Pimm's No. 1
garnish:
1 slice Cucumber
ginger ale
1 slice orange
3 ice cubes
1 maraschino cherry

Method
Place 3 ice cubes in a 10 oz highball
glass and pour Pimm's over and top
with ginger ale. Garnish with
Cucumber, orange slice, cherry,
straws and serve.

PIMM'S NO. 1 CUP

45mL (1.5 oz) Pimm's No. 1
ice
lemonade
garnish:
1 lemon slice
ginger ale

Method
Build over ice using equal pans of
ginger ale and lemonade in a 10 oz
highball glass. Garnish with a slice
of lemon, straws and serve.

PIÑA COLADA

30mL (1 oz) white rum
crushed ice
30mL (1 oz) coconut milk
1 maraschino cherry
75mL (2.5 oz) pineapple juice
garnish:
1 pineapple wedge
1 piece pineapple
1 maraschino cherry

Method
Blend until smooth and pour into a
large colada glass. Garnish with
pineapple wedge, cherry, straws
and serve.

PIÑA COLADA NO. 2

30mL (1 oz) white rum
30mL (1 oz) cream
30mL (1 oz) coconut cream
pineapple Pieces
90mL (3 oz) pineapple juice
garnish:
1 maraschino cherry

Method
Blend until smooth and pour into a
large colada glass. Garnish with
cherry, straws and serve.

PINCHGUT PERIL

30mL (1 oz) scotch whiskey
ice cubes
15mL (0.5 oz) gin
Shaved ice
15mL (0.5 oz) lime juice
1 pineapple wedge
pineapple Pieces
1 orange slice
1 dash grenadine

Method
Blend whiskey, gin, lime juice, grenadine and pineapple Pieces until smooth. Pour over Shaved ice into a 10 oz highball glass. Garnish with pineapple wedge, orange slice, straws and serve.

PINEAPPLE BOMBER

45mL (1.5 oz) Southern Comfort
15mL (0.5 oz) Galleon amaretto
90mL (3 oz) pineapple juice
garnish:
1 pineapple wedge

Method
Shake and strain into a 5 oz cocktail glass, garnish with pineapple wedge and serve.

PINEAPPLE PLANTATION

30mL (1 oz) Amaretto di Galliano
30mL (1 oz) Southern Comfort
90mL (3 oz) pineapple juice
top up with lemonade

Method
Blend with ice and pour then top up with lemonade. Garnish with a pineapple wedge and a cherry.

PINK ANGEL

30mL (1 oz) Bacardi rum
1 egg white
15mL (0.5 oz) advocaat
30mL (1 oz) fresh cream
15mL (0.5 oz) cherry brandy

Method
Shake and strain into a 5 oz champagne glass and serve.

PINK CHEVROLET

30mL (1 oz) strawberry champagne
10mL (0.33 oz) lemon juice

Method
Build ingredients in a flute glass and serve.

PINK ELEPHANT

30mL (1 oz) vodka
30mL (1 oz) fresh cream
30mL (1 oz) Galliano Liverno
1 dash grenadine
30mL (1 oz) almond liqueur
cracked ice
30mL (1 oz) orange juice
garnish:
cinnamon

Method
Shake and strain into a 5 oz champagne saucer, sprinkle with nutmeg and serve.

PINK GIN

45mL (1.5 oz) gin
30mL (1 oz) water
3 dashes grenadine
2 ice cubes

Method
Place ice and Angostura bitters in a Goblet glass and swirl. Discard bitters and add ingredients and serve.

PINK LADY

60mL (2 oz) gin
4 dashes fresh cream
4 dashes grenadine
cracked ice
4 dashes brandy

Method
Shake and strain into 5 oz champagne saucer and serve.

PINK LADY NO. 2

60mL (2 oz) gin
cracked ice
4 dashes grenadine
1 dash egg white

Method
Shake and strain into a 5 oz champagne glass and serve.

PINK MINTY

30mL (1 oz) red crème de menthe
30mL (1 oz) fresh cream
1 dash grenadine
cracked ice

Method
Shake and strain into a 3 oz cocktail glass and serve.

PINK PANTHER

60mL (2 oz) bourbon
45mL (1.5 oz) coconut liqueur
90mL (3 oz) vodka
15mL (0.5 oz) grenadine
120mL (4 oz) fresh cream
cracked ice

Method
Shake and Strain into a 12 oz brandy Balloon and serve.

P

PINK POODLE

30mL (1 oz) Campari
45mL (1.5 oz) cream
30mL (1 oz) gin
4 strawberries

Method
Blend until smooth, pour into a
5 oz cocktail saucer and serve.

PINK PUSSY

30mL (1 oz) Campari
Bitter lemon Soft Drink
1 dash egg white
garnish:
1 slice lemon
15mL (0.5 oz) peach brandy

Method
Shake all ingredients except Soft
Drink and strain into a 10 oz
highball glass. Top with Soft Drink,
garnish with slice of lemon, straws
and serve.

PINK SQUIRREL

30mL (1 oz) amaretto
5mL (0.17 oz) grenadine
30mL (1 oz) white crème de cacao
50mL (1.66 oz) cream

Method
Shake and strain into a 5 oz
champagne saucer and serve.

PINKY

60mL (2 oz) brandy
15mL (0.5 oz) grenadine
15mL (0.5 oz) crème de banana
cracked ice
60mL (2 oz) fresh cream

Method
Shake and strain into a champagne
saucer and serve.

PIPELINE SHOOTER

25mL (0.83 oz) tequila
20mL (0.66 oz) vodka

Method
Layer in a shot glass and serve.

PIRATES PLUNDER

30mL (1 oz) Tia Maria
30mL (1 oz) coconut cream
30mL (1 oz) Bacardi rum
90mL (3 oz) pineapple juice
20mL (0.66 oz) Malibu
1 slice pineapple

Method
Blend until smooth and pour into
a 10 oz highball glass and serve
with straws.

PJ

30mL (1 oz) vodka
1 dash egg white
30mL (1 oz) Campari
garnish:
1 maraschino cherry
30mL (1 oz) orange juice
cracked ice

Method
Shake and strain into a 5 oz
cocktail glass, garnish with cherry
and serve.

PLANTATION NIGHT

45mL (1.5 oz) Kahlúa
4 strawberry liqueur
45mL (1.5 oz) banana liqueur
1 banana
45mL (1.5 oz) cream
1 scoop crushed ice

Method
Blend until smooth and pour into
a flute glass and serve.

PLANTER'S PUNCH

30mL (1 oz) Coruba Rum
30mL (1 oz) lemon or lime juice
60mL (2 oz) orange juice
5mL (0.17 oz) Grenadine

Method
Build over ice then add dash of
grenadine. Garnish with fruit slices.

PLAYGROUND

30mL (1 oz) Bailey's Irish cream
30mL (1 oz) Malibu
30mL (1 oz) banana liqueur

Method
Layer in a 3 oz cocktail glass
and serve.

POLISH SIDECAR

Ingredients
Glass:
140mL Cocktail Glass
Mixers:
20mL (0.66 oz) Gilbey's Gin
20mL (0.66 oz) lemon juice
10mL (0.33 oz) Blackberry Liqueur

Method
Shake with ice and pour then float
blackberries. Garnish with
blackberries or raspberries.

POLYNESIA

30mL (1 oz) Bacardi
30mL (1 oz) Passionfruit Liqueur
10mL (0.33 oz) lime juice
half egg white

Method
Blend with ice and pour. Garnish
with passionfruit.

P

POPSICLE SHOOTER

15mL (0.5 oz) Tia Maria
15mL (0.5 oz) vodka
10mL (0.33 oz) Bailey's Irish cream

Method
Layer in order in a shot glass
and serve.

PORT IN A STORM

45mL (1.5 oz) port
1/3 strip orange peel
60mL (2 oz) red wine
cracked ice
15mL (0.5 oz) brandy
1 sprig mint

Method
Fill a large Goblet glass with ice.
Stir liquid ingredients and pour
over ice. Garnish with sprig of
mint and serve.

PORTO FLIP

45mL (1.5 oz) port
1 egg yolk
10mL (0.33 oz) cognac
cracked ice
10mL (0.33 oz) sugar syrup
garnish:
nutmeg

Method
Shake and strain into a 5 oz
cocktail glass, sprinkle with
nutmeg and serve.

POTTS POINT SPECIAL

30mL (1 oz) vodka
garnish:
1/4 slice pineapple
30mL (1 oz) white curaçao
cracked ice
30mL (1 oz) pineapple juice

Method
Shake and strain into a
champagne glass, garnish with
pineapple and serve.

POUSSE CAFÉ

15mL (0.5 oz) brandy
15mL (0.5 oz) grenadine
15mL (0.5 oz) crème de Menthe
15mL (0.5 oz) maraschino liqueur
15mL (0.5 oz) Yvette liqueur
15mL (0.5 oz) crème de cacao

Method
Layer in a 3 oz cocktail glass
and serve.

PRAIRIE FIRE SHOOTER

45mL (1.5 oz) tequila
10 drops Tabasco Sauce

Method
Layer in order in a shot glass
and serve.

PRAIRIE OYSTER

30mL (1 oz) Milne Brandy
salt and pepper
Worcestershire sauce
Tabasco sauce
1 egg yolk

Method
Build, no ice.

PRETTY WOMAN

30mL (1 oz) Midori
30mL (1 oz) strawberry liqueur
30mL (1 oz) Malibu
4 strawberries
1 Scoop crushed ice
crushed ice

Method
Blend Midori and Malibu with
1 scoop of crushed ice. Separately,
blend strawberry liqueur, fresh
strawberries and crushed ice. Pour the
first mixture into a 10 oz Hurricane
glass, followed by the second mixture.
Garnish with an Umbrella on
strawberry and serve with straws.

PRINCE OF WALES

15mL (0.5 oz) Cointreau
1 dash Angostura bitters
15mL (0.5 oz) brandy
garnish:
1/2 lemon slice
Sparkling white wine
cracked ice

Method
Shake ingredients except Sparkling
wine and strain into a 10 oz highball
glass. Top with wine, garnish with
lemon slice, straws and serve.

PURPLE SHELL

90mL (3 oz) sloe gin
15mL (0.5 oz) parfait amour
15mL (0.5 oz) dry gin
45mL (1.5 oz) fresh cream

Method
Shake and strain into a 5 oz
champagne glass and serve.

PURPLE WATERS

20mL (0.66 oz) Bacardi rum
15mL (0.5 oz) parfait amour
15mL (0.5 oz) orange curaçao
15mL (0.5 oz) yellow Chartreuse

Method
Layer in order in a 3 oz cocktail
glass and serve.

P.S. I LOVE YOU

30mL (1 oz) Amaretto di Galliano
30mL (1 oz) Kahlúa
30mL (1 oz) Baileys Irish Cream
5mL (0.17 oz) Grenadine

Method
Build over ice and stir. Garnish
with sprinkled nutmeg.

P

PUERTO RICAN PINK LADY

30mL (1 oz) Bacardi Gold Rum
10mL (0.33 oz) lemon juice
10mL (0.33 oz) Grenadine
half egg white

Method
Blend with ice and strain. Garnish with a strawberry splashed with Grenadine.

PURPLE PEOPLE EATER

30mL (1 oz) Parfait Amour
30mL (1 oz) Gilbey's Gin
5mL (0.17 oz) lemon juice

Method
Shake over ice and strain. Garnish with a strawberry and pink parasol.

PUSSY FOOT

60mL (2 oz) orange juice
30mL (1 oz) lemon juice
30mL (1 oz) lime juice
5mL (0.17 oz) egg yolk
dash of Grenadine

Method
Shake over ice and pour. Garnish with an orange slice and red cherry.

QUEBEC

30mL (1 oz) Canadian Club Whisky
10mL (0.33 oz) Cinzano Dry Vermouth
10mL (0.33 oz) Amer Picon
10mL (0.33 oz) Maraschino Liqueur

Method
Shake over ice and strain. Garnish with a cocktail onion.

QUEEN BEE

30mL (1 oz) gin
1 dash Pernod
30mL (1 oz) Cointreau
cracked ice

Method
Shake and strain into a 3 oz cocktail glass and serve.

QUEEN ELIZABETH

30mL (1 oz) gin
15mL (0.5 oz) lemon juice
15mL (0.5 oz) Cointreau
garnish:
1 maraschino cherry
1 dash Pernod
crushed ice

Method
Shake and strain into a 3 oz cocktail glass, garnish with cherry and serve.

QUEEN'S PEG

30mL (1 oz) gin
1 large ice cube
Sparkling white wine (top up)

Method
Place ice cube in a Goblet glass, add gin and top with wine before serving.

QUEENS

30mL (1 oz) dry gin
30mL (1 oz) pineapple juice
30mL (1 oz) dry vermouth
garnish:
1 maraschino cherry
30mL (1 oz) sweet vermouth
1 pineapple wedge

Method
Shake and strain into a 5 oz cocktail glass, garnish with cherry, pineapple wedge and serve.

QUICK FUCK SHOOTER

30mL (1 oz) Midori
30mL (1 oz) Kahlúa
30mL (1 oz) Bailey's Irish cream

Method
Layer in order in a shot glass and serve.

QUICKSILVER SHOOTER

10mL (0.33 oz) banana liqueur
10mL (0.33 oz) vodka
10mL (0.33 oz) tequila

Method
Layer in order in a shot glass and serve.

R&R

30mL (1 oz) Cointreau
30mL (1 oz) Midori
30mL (1 oz) tequila

Method
Layer in order in a 3 oz cocktail glass and serve.

RABBIT'S REVENGE

40mL (1.33 oz) bourbon
Tonic water (top up)
3 dashes grenadine
garnish:
1 slice orange
30mL (1 oz) pineapple juice
cracked ice

Method
Shake ingredients except Tonic water and strain into a Tumbler glass. Top with Tonic water, garnish with orange slice and serve with straws

RAFFLES' SINGAPORE SLING

30mL (1 oz) gin
30mL (1 oz) pineapple juice
30mL (1 oz) cherry brandy
garnish:
1 orange wedge
15mL (0.5 oz) triple sec
1 maraschino cherry
15mL (0.5 oz) Benedictine
mint leaves
30mL (1 oz) orange juice
cracked ice
30mL (1 oz) lime juice

Method
Shake and strain into a 10 oz highball glass, garnish with orange wedge, cherry, mint leaves, swizzle stick, straws and serve.

RAGING BULL

30mL (1 oz) Afrikoko
milk (top up)
30mL (1 oz) Sabra
cracked ice

Method
Pour over ice in an Old Fashioned glass, top with milk and serve.

RAIDER SHOOTER

15mL (0.5 oz) Bailey's Irish cream
15mL (0.5 oz) Cointreau
15mL (0.5 oz) Grand Marnier

Method
Layer in order in a shot glass and
serve.

RAINBOW SHERBERT

15mL (0.5 oz) Midori
15mL (0.5 oz) Banana Liqueur
15mL (0.5 oz) Strawberry Liqueur
60mL (2 oz) orange juice
2 dashes Grenadine
2 scoops orange sherbert
blue vegetable dye

Method
Blend without ice. Garnish with
assorted fruit and a dash of blue
vegetable dye.

RAM

30mL (1 oz) Malibu
45mL (1.5 oz) orange juice
15mL (0.5 oz) Galliano Liverno
whipped cream

Method
Shake ingredients except whipped
cream and strain into a 5 oz
champagne saucer. Float whipped
cream and serve.

RAMONA

60mL (2 oz) Bacardi rum
2 tsp castor sugar
30mL (1 oz) Cointreau
cracked ice
60mL (2 oz) lemon juice
garnish:
1 lemon slice
soda water

Method
Shake all ingredients except soda
water and strain over ice in a 10 oz
highball glass. Top with soda water,
garnish with lemon slice. straws
and serve.

Ramoz

60mL (2 oz) gin
2 dashed orange flower water
30mL (1 oz) lemon juice
2 egg Whites
30mL (1 oz) lime juice
1 tsp sugar
30mL (1 oz) heavy cream
cracked ice
soda water

Method
Shake and strain all ingredients
except soda over ice in a 10 oz
highball glass. Top with soda water,
add straws and serve.

Ritz

30mL (1 oz) brandy
chilled champagne
15mL (0.5 oz) Cointreau
cracked ice
15mL (0.5 oz) orange juice

Method
Shake ingredients except champagne. Strain into a 5 oz Epsom glass. Top with champagne and serve.

Silver

60mL (2 oz) Bacardi rum
1 egg yolk
1 tsp sugar
soda water
60mL (2 oz) lemon juice
cracked ice

Method
Shake all ingredients except soda water and strain over ice in a 10 oz highball glass. Top with soda water, add straws and serve.

Strawberry

30mL (1 oz) strawberry liqueur
4 strawberries
30mL (1 oz) lemon juice
soda water
15mL (0.5 oz) sugar syrup
ice
1 egg white

Method
Blend all ingredients except soda water and pour into a 10 oz highball glass. Top with soda water, add straws and serve.

Vodka

30mL (1 oz) vodka
1/2 tsp sugar
2 tsp lemon juice
garnish:
1/2 slice lime
1 egg white
1 strip lemon peel
soda water
cracked ice

Method
Shake all ingredients except soda water, strain over ice in a 10 oz highball glass. Top with soda water, garnish with lime slice. lemon peel, straws and serve.

RASPUTIN'S REVENGE

60mL (2 oz) vodka
30mL (1 oz) orange juice

Method
Shake and strain over ice in a rocks glass and serve.

RAY LONG

30mL (1 oz) Bianco vermouth
1 tsp Pernod
20mL (0.66 oz) brandy
cracked ice
1 dash Angostura bitters

Method
Mix ingredients and strain into a 3 oz cocktail glass and serve.

READY, SET, GO!

30mL (1 oz) Midori
30mL (1 oz) strawberry liqueur
30mL (1 oz) banana liqueur

Method
Layer in a 3 oz cocktail glass and serve.

RED CUCUMBER BOWL

150mL (5 oz) red wine
1 pinch ground Cloves
15mL (0.5 oz) maraschino liqueur
garnish:
2 thin slices Cucumber
1 pinch cinnamon
cracked ice

Method
Shake ingredients except Cucumber. Strain into a 6 oz Tumbler glass, garnish with Cucumber and serve.

RED EYE

150mL (5 oz) cold beer
150mL (5 oz) tomato juice

Method
Place tomato juice in a 10 oz highball glass, add beer and serve.

RED LIGHTS

20mL (0.66 oz) gin
15mL (0.5 oz) Cointreau
15mL (0.5 oz) Galleon Liverno
60mL (2 oz) orange juice

Method
Shake and strain into a 10 oz highball glass and serve.

RED RAY

60mL (2 oz) gin
60mL (2 oz) white crème de menthe
30mL (1 oz) grenadine
cracked ice

Method
Shake and strain into a Old Fashioned glass filled with ice. Garnish with and orange wheel and serve.

RED SHADOW

30mL (1 oz) scotch whiskey
1 tsp lemon juice
15mL (0.5 oz) apricot brandy
cracked ice
15mL (0.5 oz) cherry brandy

Method
Shake and strain into a 3 oz cocktail glass and serve.

REFLECTIONS

30mL (1 oz) Frangelico
cracked ice
2 tbsp white crème de cacao
garnish:
2 maraschino Cherries
1 tbsp Cheri-Suisse
1 red Straw

Method
Shake and strain into a 3 oz Martini glass. Cut 5 mm off a red Straw and use it to join 2 maraschino cherries. Place one of the Cherries in the glass, the other above the liquid creating a reflection effect and serve.

REMARKABLE COW

30mL (1 oz) gin
juice 1 lemon
30mL (1 oz) Van der Hum
1 dash sugar syrup
1 dash grenadine

Method
Shake and strain into a 5 oz champagne saucer and serve.

RENDEZVOUS

30mL (1 oz) Cointreau
30mL (1 oz) vodka
15mL (0.5 oz) Rubis
lemonade (top up)

Method
Shake and strain into a flute glass, top with lemonade and serve.

RHETT BUTLER

30mL (1 oz) Southern Comfort
5mL (0.17 oz) lime cordial
30mL (1 oz) orange curaçao
soda water (top up)
15mL (0.5 oz) lemon juice
garnish:
1 orange wheel

Method
Build ingredients over ice in a 10 oz highball glass, top with soda water. Garnish with orange wheel and serve with straws.

RHYTHM OF LOVE

10mL (0.33 oz) Midori
small piece of kiwifruit
10mL (0.33 oz) Creme de Cassis
float cream

Method
Squeeze kiwifruit onto Midori into glass, then layer in order.

RICK O'SHEA

10mL (0.33 oz) Galliano
10mL (0.33 oz) Bacardi
10mL (0.33 oz) orange juice

Method
Layer in order.
Comments: One shot and you'll be bouncing back over the Irish Sea for more.

RIO LADY

30mL (1 oz) white cream de cacao
50mL (1.66 oz) cream
15mL (0.5 oz) goldwasser

Method
Shake and strain into a 5 oz champagne saucer and serve.

RITZ

30mL (1 oz) brandy
chilled champagne (top up)
15mL (0.5 oz) Cointreau
cracked ice
15mL (0.5 oz) orange juice

Method
Shake and strain into a 5 oz Epsom glass, top with champagne and serve.

ROB ROY

60mL (2 oz) scotch whiskey
garnish:
1 maraschino cherry
15mL (0.5 oz) sweet vermouth
cracked ice
1 dash Angostura bitters

Method
Stir and strain into a 3 oz cocktail glass, garnish with cherry and serve.

ROCK LOBSTER

45mL (1.5 oz) Grand Marnier
30mL (1 oz) cream (float)
15mL (0.5 oz) amaretto
garnish:
cinnamon
milk (top up)

Method
Build over ice in a 10 oz margarita glass, top with milk, float cream. Sprinkle with cinnamon and serve.

ROCKET FUEL (AUSTRALIAN)

15mL (0.5 oz) white rum
15mL (0.5 oz) gin
15mL (0.5 oz) vodka
lemonade (top up)
15mL (0.5 oz) tequila
cracked ice

Method
Build ingredients over ice in a 10 oz highball glass, top with lemonade, add straws and serve.

ROCKET FUEL (BLACK)

10 mL (0.33 oz) each Spirit behind the bar
cracked ice

Method
Shake and strain into a 10 oz highball glass and serve.

R

ROCKET FUEL (MULTICOLOURED)

10mL (0.33 oz) each white Spirit behind the bar
one of the following:
20mL (0.66 oz) crème de menthe for green
20mL (0.66 oz) grenadine for red
20mL (0.66 oz) advocaat for yellow
20mL (0.66 oz) blue curaçao for Blue

Method
Shake and strain into a 10 oz highball glass and serve.

ROCKET FUEL (WHITE)

10mL (0.33 oz) all white Spirits behind the bar

Method
Shake and strain into a 10 oz highball glass and serve.

ROLLS ROYCE

30mL (1 oz) dry gin
10mL (0.33 oz) Benedictine
15mL (0.5 oz) dry vermouth
cracked ice
15mL (0.5 oz) sweet vermouth

Method
Stir and strain into a 3 oz cocktail glass and serve.

ROMAN DRIVER

30mL (1 oz) Galleon Liverno
1 dash grenadine
15mL (0.5 oz) vodka
20mL (0.66 oz) cream
20mL (0.66 oz) almond syrup
cracked ice

Method
Shake and strain into a champagne saucer and serve.

ROMAN THE GLOMAN

60mL (2 oz) scotch whiskey
1 tbsp orange juice
30mL (1 oz) Cointreau
cracked ice

Method
Shake and strain over ice in a rocks glass and serve.

ROMULAN ALE

30mL (1 oz) blue curaçao
15mL (0.5 oz) gin
15mL (0.5 oz) vodka
15mL (0.5 oz) tequila
15mL (0.5 oz) white curaçao
1 splash dry vermouth
15mL (0.5 oz) Bacardi rum
lemonade (top up)

Method
Shake and strain over ice in a 10 oz highball glass, top with lemonade, add straws and serve.

ROSE

30mL (1 oz) gin

15mL (0.5 oz) lemon juice (Glass Rim)

15mL (0.5 oz) dry vermouth

1 tbsp castor sugar

15mL (0.5 oz) apricot brandy

1 maraschino cherry

1 dash grenadine

cracked ice

Method
Rim a 3 oz cocktail glass with sugar. Shake the rest of the ingredients and strain into the Rimmed glass and serve.

ROSE AND FAMMO SPECIAL

30mL (1 oz) Bacardi rum

10mL (0.33 oz) blue curaçao

30mL (1 oz) white crème de cacao

garnish:

1 twist lemon peel

15mL (0.5 oz) dry vermouth

1 maraschino cherry

10mL (0.33 oz) orange gin

cracked ice

Method
Stir and strain into a 5 oz champagne saucer, garnish with lemon peel, cherry and serve.

ROSE NO. 2

15mL (0.5 oz) cherry brandy

cracked ice

15mL (0.5 oz) kirsch

garnish:

1 maraschino cherry

45mL (1.5 oz) dry vermouth

Method
Stir ingredients and strain into a 3 oz cocktail glass, garnish with cherry and serve.

ROSE NO. 3

45mL (1.5 oz) apricot brandy

20mL (0.66 oz) dry vermouth

45mL (1.5 oz) gin

1 dash grenadine

Method
Shake and strain into a 3 oz cocktail glass and serve.

ROYAL FLUSH

30mL (1 oz) brandy

60mL (2 oz) grapefruit juice

60mL (2 oz) Cointreau

10mL (0.33 oz) grenadine

Sparkling white wine (top up)

cracked ice

Method
Shake and strain into a Tumbler glass, top with white wine and serve with straws.

ROYAL SNOWCAP

30mL (1 oz) Bacardi rum
1 egg white
30mL (1 oz) dry vermouth
garnish:
chocolate Flakes
15mL (0.5 oz) parfait amour
cracked ice
1 dash lemon juice

Method
Shake and strain into a 3 oz cocktail glass, garnish with chocolate Flakes and serve.

RUBY SHY

30mL (1 oz) Malibu
lemonade (top up)
30mL (1 oz) raspberry cordial
garnish:
grated coconut

Method
Pour Malibu and raspberry cordial over ice in a 10 oz highball glass. Garnish with grated coconut, straws and serve.

RUM

30mL (1 oz) white rum
cracked ice
1 tsp sugar syrup
garnish:
1 spiral orange peel
3 dash Angostura bitters

Method
Stir and strain over ice into a 3 oz cocktail glass, garnish with spiral of orange peel and serve.

RUM ALEXANDER

30mL (1 oz) crème de cacao
cracked ice
15mL (0.5 oz) white rum
garnish:
nutmeg
15mL (0.5 oz) cream

Method
Shake and strain into a champagne saucer, cross two straws over top and sprinkle with nutmeg. Remove straws and serve.

RUM COOLER

60mL (2 oz) rum
soda water (top up)
60mL (2 oz) lemon juice
cracked ice
4 dashes grenadine
fruit or garnish

Method
Shake and strain over ice into a 10 oz highball glass, top with soda, garnish with fruit. straws and serve.

RUM REBELLION

30mL (1 oz) Bacardi rum
5mL (0.17 oz) cherry brandy
30mL (1 oz) banana liqueur
75mL (2.5 oz) pineapple juice
1 scoop crushed ice

Method
Blend until smooth and pour into an Old Fashioned glass and serve.

RUM THING

30mL (1 oz) Bacardi rum
30mL (1 oz) Galliano Liverno
30mL (1 oz) orange curaçao
1 twist orange peel
30mL (1 oz) dry vermouth

Method
Stir and strain into a champagne
saucer, garnish with twist of orange
peel and serve.

RUMFUSTATION

120mL (4 oz) beer
1 pinch Ground ginger
75mL (2.5 oz) Still white wine
1 pinch cinnamon
1 tsp sugar
1 pinch nutmeg
1 egg yolk

Method
Beat ingredients over a low heat
until warmed. Pour into an Old
Fashioned glass and serve.

RUNNING HOT

45mL (1.5 oz) Bacardi rum
40mL (1.33 oz) pineapple juice
30mL (1 oz) Cointreau
1 dash grenadine

Method
Shake and strain over ice in an Old
Fashioned glass and serve.

RUSSIAN

30mL (1 oz) vodka
30mL (1 oz) crème de cacao
30mL (1 oz) dry gin
cracked ice

Method
Shake and strain into a 3 oz
cocktail glass and serve.

RUSSIAN (AUSTRALIAN)

45mL (1.5 oz) vodka
whipped cream (float)
30mL (1 oz) Tia Maria
cracked ice

Method
Pour vodka and Tia Maria over ice
in an Old Fashioned glass. Float
whipped cream and serve.

RUSSIAN (BLACK NO. 2)

30mL (1 oz) vodka
cracked ice
30mL (1 oz) Kahlúa

Method
Build in an ice filled Old Fashioned
glass and serve.

RUSSIAN (BLACK NO. 3)

30mL (1 oz) vodka
Coca-Cola (top up)
30mL (1 oz) Kahlúa
cracked ice

Method
Build over ice in a 10 oz highball glass, top with Coca-Cola, add straws and serve.

RUSSIAN (BLACK)

30mL (1 oz) vodka
cracked ice
15mL (0.5 oz) Kahlúa

Method
Build in an ice filled 3 oz cocktail glass and serve.

RUSSIAN (BROWN)

45mL (1.5 oz) vodka
cracked ice
30mL (1 oz) amaretto

Method
Shake and strain into a 3 oz cocktail glass and serve.

RUSSIAN (GOLDEN)

45mL (1.5 oz) vodka
cracked ice
30mL (1 oz) Galliano Liverno

Method
Shake and strain into a 3 oz cocktail glass and serve.

RUSSIAN (WHITE)

40mL (1.33 oz) vodka
60mL (2 oz) cream
15mL (0.5 oz) coffee liqueur
cracked ice

Method
Shake and strain into a 5 oz cocktail glass and serve.

RUSSIAN COW

30mL (1 oz) vodka
10mL (0.33 oz) Galliano Liverno
30mL (1 oz) coconut milk
60mL (2 oz) milk

Method
Blend with a scoop of ice until smooth, pour into a 10 oz highball glass and serve.

RUSSIAN HOLIDAY

30mL (1 oz) vodka
60mL (2 oz) pineapple juice
20mL (0.66 oz) Grand Marnier
whipped cream (float)

Method
Pour vodka and pineapple juice over ice in a 10 oz highball glass. Float whipped cream, add Grand Marnier and serve.

RUSSIAN ROULETTE

15mL (0.5 oz) Galliano Liverno

10mL (0.33 oz) sugar syrup

15mL (0.5 oz) banana liqueur

1/2 banana

15mL (0.5 oz) vodka

15mL (0.5 oz) lemon juice

30mL (1 oz) orange juice

1 scoop crushed ice

Method
Blend until smooth and pour into
a brandy Balloon and serve.

RUSTY BUCKET

30mL (1 oz) port wine

Coca-Cola

Method
Pour into a 5 oz cocktail glass
and serve.

RUSTY NAIL

30mL (1 oz) scotch whiskey

cracked ice

30mL (1 oz) Drambuie

Method
Fill an Old fashioned glass with
cracked ice. Add ingredients
and serve.

RUSTY NAIL NO. 2

45mL (1.5 oz) scotch whiskey

garnish:

1 twist lemon peel

45mL (1.5 oz) Drambuie

cracked ice

Method
Pour ingredients over ice in an
Old Fashioned glass, garnish with
lemon peel and serve.

RUSTY SPADE

1 mango

1 dash cream

30mL (1 oz) strawberry liqueur

ice

pulp 1 passionfruit

garnish:

1 strawberry

Method
Blend until Smooth and pour into
a margarita glass, garnish with
strawberry and serve.

RYAN'S RUSH SHOOTER

10mL (0.33 oz) Kahlúa

10mL (0.33 oz) Bacardi rum

10mL (0.33 oz) Bailey's Irish cream

Method
Layer in order in a shot glass
and serve.

S

SAIL AWAY

30mL (1 oz) Midori
30mL (1 oz) lime juice
15mL (0.5 oz) peach liqueur
1 dash lemon juice
30mL (1 oz) vodka
garnish:
1 lime wheel

Method
Shake ingredients and strain into a
5 oz cocktail glass. Garnish with a
lime wheel and serve.

SAINT MORITZ

30mL (1 oz) Schnapps

Method
Build with ice. Garnish with a layer
of heavy cream.

SAINT PETERSBURG

30mL (1 oz) vodka
lemonade (top up)
30mL (1 oz) blue curaçao

Method
Shake vodka and curaçao and
strain into a 5 oz cocktail glass. Top
with lemonade and serve.

SAINT VINCENT

30mL (1 oz) gin
30mL (1 oz) cream
30mL (1 oz) Galliano Liverno
cracked ice
1 dash grenadine

Method
Shake and strain into a champagne
glass and serve.

SAKETINI

30mL (1 oz) Gilbey's Gin
5-10mL (.17-.33 oz) Gekkeikan Sake

Method
Shake over ice and pour. Garnish
with an olive.

SAKI SPECIAL

30mL (1 oz) saki
2 dashes Angostura bitters
60mL (2 oz) gin
cracked ice

Method
Mix ingredients in a mixing glass,
strain into a 3 oz cocktail glass and
serve.

SALTY DOG

45mL (1.5 oz) vodka
cracked ice
grapefruit juice (top up)

Method
Place ingredients in a 10 oz highball glass, top with grapefruit juice and serve with straws.

SALUBRIOUS SALUTATIONS

15mL (0.5 oz) Galliano Liverno
15mL (0.5 oz) Benedictine
15mL (0.5 oz) Drambuie
30mL (1 oz) fresh cream
15mL (0.5 oz) gin
cracked ice

Method
Shake and strain into a 3 oz cocktail glass and serve.

SAMBUCA SHAKER

30mL (1 oz) Romana Sambuca

Method
Pour Sambuca then light. Cup your hand entirely over the rim while it flames, creating suction. Shake the glass, place under your nose, take hand from glass to inhale the fumes, then shoot.

SAN FRANCISCO

45mL (1.5 oz) gin
1 dash Angostura bitters
10mL (0.33 oz) sweet vermouth
cracked ice
10mL (0.33 oz) dry vermouth
garnish:
1 maraschino cherry
1 dash orange bitters

Method
Stir ingredients in a mixing glass, strain into a 5 oz cocktail glass, garnish with cherry and serve.

SANGRIA

150mL (5 oz) Spanish Red Wine
20mL (0.66 oz) Cointreau
20mL (0.66 oz) Milne Brandy
20mL (0.66 oz) Bacardi
orange, lime, lemon and
strawberry pieces
sugar syrup

Method
Pour in order.

SATIN PILLOW

5mL (0.17 oz) strawberry liqueur
15mL (0.5 oz) Tia Maria
10mL (0.33 oz) Cointreau
20mL (0.66 oz) pineapple juice
15mL (0.5 oz) Frangelico
garnish:
1 strawberry
20mL (0.66 oz) cream

Method
Blend with ice and pour into a 5 oz
cocktail glass. Garnish with cut
strawberry and a dash of cream
and serve.

SATURDAY NIGHT

15mL (0.5 oz) banana liqueur
60mL (2 oz) lemon juice
30mL (1 oz) gin
garnish:
1 maraschino cherry
15mL (0.5 oz) blue curaçao
1 lime wheel
60mL (2 oz) cream

Method
Shake and strain into a colada
glass, garnish with lime wheel,
cherry and serve.

SAYONARA

30mL (1 oz) Midori
75mL (2.5 oz) cream
30mL (1 oz) advocaat
cracked ice

Method
Shake well, strain into a 5 oz
cocktail glass and serve.

SCANDINAVIAN GLÖGG

30mL (1 oz) Smirnoff Vodka
60mL (2 oz) red wine
3 blanched almonds
3 raisins
grated orange peel
1 dried fig
4 cardamon seeds
1 cinnamon stick
1 clove
1 sugar cube per serve

Method
Simmer all ingredients in a
saucepan for a few minutes except
for sugar cubes, then pour.

SCARLET O'HARA

45mL (1.5 oz) Southern Comfort
45mL (1.5 oz) cranberry juice
30mL (1 oz) lime juice
garnish:
1 maraschino cherry

Method
Shake and strain into a champagne
glass. Garnish with cherry and serve.

SCORPION

15mL (0.5 oz) Coruba Dark Rum
15mL (0.5 oz) Courvoisier Cognac
15mL (0.5 oz) Romana Sambuca
15mL (0.5 oz) Orgeat
45mL (1.5 oz) orange juice
15mL (0.5 oz) emon juice

Method
Blend with ice. Garnish with a lime wheel with cherry.

SCOTCH FROG

60mL (2 oz) vodka
15mL (0.5 oz) lime cordial
30mL (1 oz) Galliano Liverno
garnish:
1 maraschino cherry
1 dash Angostura bitters

Method
Shake and strain into a champagne saucer, garnish with cherry and serve.

SCOTCH MATE

45mL (1.5 oz) scotch whiskey
30mL (1 oz) sweet vermouth
30mL (1 oz) Galliano Liverno
30mL (1 oz) orange juice
cracked ice
garnish:
1 strip orange peel

Method
Shake and strain into a champagne saucer, garnish with orange peel and serve.

SCOTCH MIST

60mL (2 oz) scotch whiskey
garnish:
1 twist lemon peel
cracked ice

Method
3/4 fill an Old Fashioned glass with ice. Pour scotch whiskey into a shaker with lemon peel and pour unstrained into glass and serve.

SCOTCH SOLACE

30mL (1 oz) scotch whiskey
150mL (5 oz) milk
15mL (0.5 oz) Cointreau
30mL (1 oz) cream
1 tsp honey
1 tsp grated orange peel

Method
Fill a 10 oz highball glass with cracked ice, add whiskey, Cointreau, honey and stir. Add milk, cream, orange peel and serve with straws.

SCREAMING LIZARD

30mL (1 oz) crème de menthe
1 dash soda water
30mL (1 oz) Chartreuse
cracked ice

Method
Pour ingredients over ice in an Old Fashioned glass and serve.

SCREWDRIVER

45mL (1.5 oz) vodka
cracked ice
orange juice (top up)
garnish:
1 orange wheel

Method
Place ice in a 10 oz highball glass
and add vodka, top with orange
juice. Garnish with orange wheel,
straws and serve.

SEA BREEZE

15mL (0.5 oz) Malibu
60mL (2 oz) pineapple juice
15mL (0.5 oz) blue curaçao
cracked ice
30mL (1 oz) gin
garnish:
1 slice kiwifruit
30mL (1 oz) cream

Method
Shake and strain into a 5 oz
cocktail glass, garnish with kiwifruit
and serve.

SEDUCTION

20mL (0.66 oz) Grand Marnier
30mL (1 oz) cream
15mL (0.5 oz) Cointreau
10mL (0.33 oz) orange bitters
20mL (0.66 oz) banana liqueur
1 banana

Method
Blend until smooth and pour into a
margarita glass and serve.

SEE THROUGH

30mL (1 oz) Bacardi rum
1 dash blue curaçao
15mL (0.5 oz) Cointreau
cracked ice
15mL (0.5 oz) orange gin
garnish:
1 cocktail Onion

Method
Stir ingredients in a mixing glass
and strain into a 3 oz cocktail glass.
Garnish with Onion on a Toothpick
in the glass and serve.

SENORITA

20mL (0.66 oz) tequila
20mL (0.66 oz) cream
20mL (0.66 oz) crème de noyaux
20mL (0.66 oz) orange juice
20mL (0.66 oz) Galliano Liverno
garnish:
cinnamon

Method
Shake and strain into a
champagne saucer, sprinkle with
cinnamon and serve.

SENTRY DELIGHT

30mL (1 oz) Midori
15mL (0.5 oz) lemon juice
15mL (0.5 oz) strawberry liqueur
15mL (0.5 oz) lime juice
15mL (0.5 oz) mango liqueur
garnish:
1 strawberry

Method
Blend and pour into a 3 oz cocktail
glass, garnish with Fanned
strawberry and serve.

SERPENTS STING

30mL (1 oz) Bacardi rum
30mL (1 oz) cream
30mL (1 oz) Galliano Liverno
cracked ice
30mL (1 oz) almond liqueur
1 maraschino cherry
30mL (1 oz) orange juice

Method
Shake and strain into a 5 oz
cocktail glass, garnish with cherry
and serve.

77 SUNSET STRIP

15mL (0.5 oz) vodka
1 dash grenadine
15mL (0.5 oz) gin
60mL (2 oz) lemonade
15mL (0.5 oz) triple sec
60mL (2 oz) pineapple juice

Method
Pour ingredients over ice in a 6 oz
tulip glass, add straws and serve.

SEX ON THE BEACH

15mL (0.5 oz) Kahlúa
60mL (2 oz) cream
30mL (1 oz) Malibu
garnish:
1 pineapple wedge
30mL (1 oz) pineapple juice

Method
Shake and strain into a 5 oz
cocktail glass, garnish with
pineapple wedge and serve.

SHADY LADY

30mL (1 oz) Midori
garnish:
1 slice lemon
30mL (1 oz) tequila
1 slice lime
90mL (3 oz) grapefruit juice
1 maraschino cherry

Method
Shake and pour over ice in a 10 oz
highball glass, garnish with lemon,
lime, cherry and serve.

SHAMROCK SHOOTER

10mL (0.33 oz) crème de cacao
10mL (0.33 oz) Bailey's Irish cream
10mL (0.33 oz) crème de Menthe

Method
Layer in order in a shot glass and
serve.

SHANDY

150mL (5 oz) beer
150mL (5 oz) lemonade

Method
Half fill a 300 mL beer glass with
lemonade, top with beer and serve.

S

SHANGHAI PUNCH

30mL (1 oz) Courvoisier Cognac
30mL (1 oz) Coruba Rum
40mL (1.33 oz) orange juice
20mL (0.66 oz) Cointreau
20mL (0.66 oz) lemon juice
almond extract
fresh tea
grated orange and lemon peels
cinnamon sticks

Method
Boil tea and add ingredients then
stir.

SHEEP'S HEAD

15mL (0.5 oz) sweet vermouth
garnish:
1 maraschino cherry
40mL (1.33 oz) bourbon
1 piece lemon peel
1 tsp Benedictine
cracked ice

Method
Stir and strain into a small Tumbler
glass, garnish with lemon peel.
cherry and serve.

SHERIDAN SHOOTER

20mL (0.66 oz) Black Sheridan's
10mL (0.33 oz) White Sheridan's

Method
Layer in order.
Comments: Try this newest shooter
straight from the bottle.

SHERRY

30mL (1 oz) gin
30mL (1 oz) lemon juice
30mL (1 oz) sweet sherry
cracked ice

Method
Shake and strain into a 3 oz
cocktail glass and serve.

SHERRY NO. 2

30mL (1 oz) sweet sherry
1 egg yolk
15mL (0.5 oz) cream
1 tsp sugar

Method
Blend ingredients and pour into a
champagne saucer and serve.

SHIRLEY TEMPLE

15mL (0.5 oz) Grenadine
ginger ale or lemonade to top-up

Method
Build over ice. Garnish with slice of
orange, serve with swizzle stick and
two straws.

SHOCKING BLUE

30mL (1 oz) blue curaçao

30mL (1 oz) lemonade

30mL (1 oz) Midori

garnish:

1 lime wheel

30mL (1 oz) banana liqueur

Method
Fill a 10 oz highball glass with ice and gently layer ingredients. Garnish with lime wheel and serve.

SHOOTING STAR

30mL (1 oz) Midori

30mL (1 oz) cream

30mL (1 oz) peach liqueur

30g Rockmelon

15mL (0.5 oz) orange curaçao

Method
Blend until smooth and pour into a colada glass.

SHY MARIA

30mL (1 oz) Tia Maria

10mL (0.33 oz) Frangelico

15mL (0.5 oz) Cointreau

60mL (2 oz) cream

Method
Shake with ice and strain into a champagne saucer and serve.

SICILIAN KISS

20mL (0.66 oz) Southern Comfort

20mL (0.66 oz) Amaretto di Galliano

Method
Build with ice.

SIDECAR

30mL (1 oz) brandy

garnish:

1 maraschino cherry

15mL (0.5 oz) Cointreau

cracked ice

15mL (0.5 oz) lemon juice

Method
Shake and strain into a 3 oz cocktail glass, garnish with impaled cherry and serve.

SILVER STREAK

30mL (1 oz) kümmel liqueur

cracked ice

30mL (1 oz) gin

Method
Shake and strain into a 3 oz cocktail glass and serve.

SILVER THREAD SHOOTER

15mL (0.5 oz) crème de menthe
15mL (0.5 oz) Tia Maria
15mL (0.5 oz) banana liqueur

Method
Layer in order in a shot glass and serve.

SIMON'S BALL BUSTER SHOOTER

30mL (1 oz) Jack Daniel's whiskey
garnish:
1 coffee Bean
30mL (1 oz) Frangelico

Method
Layer in a shot glass, float coffee Bean and serve.

SIMPLY PEACHES

45mL (1.5 oz) peach liqueur
2 peach halves
30mL (1 oz) Cointreau
2 scoops ice cream
75mL (2.5 oz) peach nectar
1 scoop ice

Method
Blend until smooth and pour into a colada glass. Float a small scoop of ice cream, add straws and serve.

SING SING

60mL (2 oz) scotch whiskey
cracked ice
30mL (1 oz) sweet vermouth
garnish:
1 twist orange peel
30mL (1 oz) orange curaçao

Method
Stir and strain into a 5 oz cocktail glass, garnish with twist of orange peel and serve.

SINGAPORE ISLAND

45mL (1.5 oz) gin
5mL (0.17 oz) sugar syrup
20mL (0.66 oz) Peter Heering
5mL (0.17 oz) lemon juice
5mL (0.17 oz) grenadine
lemonade (top up)
70mL (2.33 oz) pineapple juice

Method
Shake and strain into a 10 ox highball glass.
Top with lemonade, add straws and serve.

SINGAPORE SLING

60mL (2 oz) gin
soda water (top up)
30mL (1 oz) cherry brandy
garnish:
1 strip lemon peel
30mL (1 oz) lemon juice
1 sprig mint

Method
Place ingredients with ice in a 10 oz highball glass, top with soda water. Garnish with lemon peel, mint, straws and serve.

SINKING SUN

80mL (2.66 oz) scotch whiskey
garnish:
1 strip lemon peel
180mL (6 oz) dry apple cider (top up)
cracked ice

Method
Stir ingredients and strain into a rocks glass.
Top with apple cider, garnish with lemon peel and serve.

69ER

15mL (0.5 oz) Kahlúa
90mL (3 oz) cream
15mL (0.5 oz) Malibu
1 banana
15mL (0.5 oz) Tia Maria
crushed ice

Method
Blend until smooth and pour into a brandy Balloon and serve.

SKY WALKER

45mL (1.5 oz) Bacardi rum
20mL (0.66 oz) advocaat
30mL (1 oz) Cointreau
60mL (2 oz) cream

Method
Shake and strain into a champagne saucer and serve.

SLIDE YOUR THIGH

20mL (0.66 oz) banana liqueur
15mL (0.5 oz) white crème de cacao
20mL (0.66 oz) Midori
45mL (1.5 oz) cream

Method
Shake and strain into a 5 oz cocktail glass and serve.

SLIPPERY NIPPLE

60mL (2 oz) sambuca
60mL (2 oz) Bailey's Irish Cream

Method
Float sambuca over Bailey's in a 5 oz cocktail glass and serve.

SLOW COMFORTABLE SCREW No.1

30mL (1 oz) vodka
orange juice (top up)
15mL (0.5 oz) sloe gin
cracked ice
15mL (0.5 oz) Southern Comfort

Method
Build over ice in a 10 oz highball glass, top with orange juice and serve with straws.

Rocket Fuel
(Recipe page 192)

Screwdriver
(Recipe page 203)

South Pacific
(Recipe page 212)

Stars and Stripes
(Recipe page 215)

Strawberry Blonde
(Recipe page 215)

Tequila Sunrise
(Recipe page 224)

SLOW COMFORTABLE SCREW No.2

30mL (1 oz) gin
garnish:
1 orange wheel
60mL (2 oz) Southern Comfort
1 maraschino cherry
120mL (4 oz) orange juice
cracked ice

Method
Shake and strain into a 10 oz highball glass, garnish with orange wheel, cherry, straws and serve.

SMARTIE SHOOTER

15mL (0.5 oz) grenadine
5mL (0.17 oz) tequila
10mL (0.33 oz) Kahlúa

Method
Layer in order in a shot glass and sieve.

SMOG CITY

30mL (1 oz) tequila
60mL (2 oz) (1 oz) cream
30mL (1 oz) crème de cacao
Coca-Cola (top up)

Method
Half fill a highball glass with cracked ice, add liquid ingredients and lop with Coca-Cola. Add straws, swizzle stick and serve.

SMOOTH LADY

30mL (1 oz) Midori
30mL (1 oz) coconut cream
15mL (0.5 oz) Tia Maria
30mL (1 oz) cream
70mL (2.33 oz) pineapple juice
garnish:
Orchids

Method
Shake and strain into two 3 oz cocktail glasses. Garnish with Orchids (if available) and serve.

SMUGGLER'S GOLD

60mL (2 oz) scotch whiskey
1 dash lemon juice
1 dash goldwasser
cracked ice
30mL (1 oz) Forester liqueur

Method
Shake and strain into a 5 oz cocktail glass and serve.

SNAKE IN THE GRASS

30mL (1 oz) gin
30mL (1 oz) lemon juice
30mL (1 oz) sweet vermouth
garnish:
1 twist lemon peel
30mL (1 oz) Cointreau

Method
Shake and strain into a champagne saucer, garnish with lemon peel and serve.

SNAKEBITE

60mL (2 oz) gin
60mL (2 oz) crème de menthe

Method
Shake and strain into a 3 oz
cocktail glass and serve.

SNAKEBITE SHOOTER

45mL (1.5 oz) Galliano Liverno
20mL (0.66 oz) crème de menthe

Method
Layer in a shot glass and serve.

SNOOPY'S GLEAM

30mL (1 oz) bourbon
15mL (0.5 oz) orange soda (float)
10mL (0.33 oz) orange curaçao
garnish:
1 orange wheel
10mL (0.33 oz) grenadine
1 maraschino cherry

Method
Shake and strain into a 3 oz
cocktail glass, garnish with orange
peel, cherry and serve.

SNOWBALL

30mL (1 oz) advocaat
cream (float)
190mL (6.33 oz) lemonade (top up)
garnish:
1 maraschino cherry

Method
Pour advocaat over ice in a 10 oz
highball glass and top with
lemonade. Float cream, garnish
with cherry and serve with straws.

SNOWDROP

60mL (2 oz) scotch whiskey
30mL (1 oz) orange juice
30mL (1 oz) Benedictine
garnish:
1 twist lemon peel
2 dashes green ginger wine

Method
Shake and strain into a champagne
saucer, garnish with lemon peel
and serve.

SNOWFLAKE

30mL (1 oz) vodka
10mL (0.33 oz) advocaat
15mL (0.5 oz) Galliano Liverno
1 dash cream
15mL (0.5 oz) Southern Comfort
lemonade (top up)
20mL (0.66 oz) orange juice

Method
Shake and strain into a 10 oz
highball glass, top with lemonade
and serve with straws.

SOCK IT TO ME, BLUEY

60mL (2 oz) vodka
cracked ice
60mL (2 oz) white crème de menthe
garnish:
1 maraschino cherry
10mL (0.33 oz) blue curaçao

Method
Shake and strain into a champagne saucer, garnish with cherry and serve.

SOMBRERO SPINNER

30mL (1 oz) tequila
45mL (1.5 oz) strawberry liqueur
20mL (0.66oz) Rubis
4 strawberries
30mL (1 oz) Cointreau
1 scoop crushed ice

Method
Blend until smooth and pour into a champagne saucer and serve.

SOMETHING SWAMPY

90mL (3 oz) blue curaçao
30mL (1 oz) parfait amour
90mL (3 oz) vodka
1 scoop crushed ice
30mL (1 oz) tequila
garnish:
3-4 jelly frogs
30mL (1 oz) Midori
lemonade (top up)

Method
Shake and pour over crushed ice in a very large brandy Balloon. Top with lemonade, add frogs, straws and serve.

SONJA

30mL (1 oz) yellow Chartreuse
fresh cream (float)
15mL (0.5 oz) blue curaçao
garnish:
nutmeg
15mL (0.5 oz) Galliano Liverno
garnish:
1 maraschino cherry

Method
Stir Chartreuse, curaçao and Galleon Liverno and strain into a 3 oz cocktail glass. Float cream and sprinkle with nutmeg, garnish with cherry and serve.

SOUTH PACIFIC

30mL (1 oz) gin
15mL (0.5 oz) Galleon Liverno
30mL (1 oz) blue curaçao
lemonade (top up)

Method
Place ingredients in a 10 oz highball glass. Top with lemonade and serve.

SOUTH SEAS

30mL (1 oz) Frangelico
60mL (2 oz) orange juice
20mL (0.66 oz) mango liqueur
1/2 banana

Method
Blend until smooth. Pour into a champagne glass and serve.

SOUTH YARRA SAMURAI

30mL (1 oz) Midori
1/2 banana
30mL (1 oz) banana liqueur
1 scoop crushed ice
30mL (1 oz) lemon juice
garnish:
1 strawberry

Method
Blend until smooth and pour into a brandy Balloon, garnish with strawberry and serve.

SOUTHERLY BUSTER

30mL (1 oz) brandy
dry ginger ale (top up)
15mL (0.5 oz) dry vermouth
garnish:
1 slice lemon
15mL (0.5 oz) lime cordial
cracked ice

Method
Half fill a 10 oz highball glass with cracked ice. Add liquid ingredients. Top with ginger ale. Garnish with slice of lemon and serve.

SOUTHERLY KISS

10mL (0.33 oz) gin
champagne (top up)
30mL (1 oz) parfait amour
1 sugar Cube

Method
Add gin to sugar cube in a champagne glass. Top with champagne. Pour parfait amour down the side of the glass and serve.

SOUTHERN FLAME SHOOTER

Method
Fill a shot glass with Southern Comfort, ignite and serve while flaming. Extinguish flames before shooting.

SOUTHERN PEACH

30mL (1 oz) Cointreau
15mL (0.5 oz) lemon juice
15mL (0.5 oz) brandy
garnish:
grated chocolate
15mL (0.5 oz) cherry brandy
1 Twirl cream
15mL (0.5 oz) pineapple juice
1 strawberry

Method
Shake and strain into a 3 oz
cocktail glass. Garnish with a
strawberry, grated chocolate and a
twirl of cream and serve.

SOUTHERN STRAWBERRY

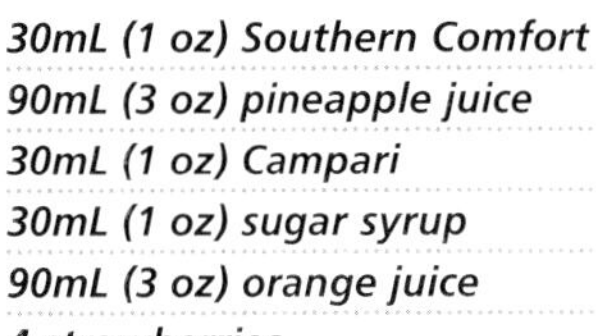

30mL (1 oz) Southern Comfort
90mL (3 oz) pineapple juice
30mL (1 oz) Campari
30mL (1 oz) sugar syrup
90mL (3 oz) orange juice
4 strawberries

Method
Blend with crushed ice until
smooth. Pour into a wine glass and
serve.

SOVIET COCKTAIL

30mL (1 oz) Smirnoff Vodka
10mL (0.33 oz) Cinzano Dry
Vermouth
10mL (0.33 oz) Amontillado

Method
Shake over ice and pour. Garnish
with a twist of lemon.

SPANISH MOSS

30mL (1 oz) Chambord
10mL (0.33 oz) Kahlúa
5mL (0.17 oz) Green Creme de
Menthe

Method
Shake with ice and strain over a
cube of ice. Garnish with a green
cherry.

SPECIAL CREAM CHOCOLATE

60g Plain chocolate
1/2 tsp cinnamon
20mL (0.66 oz) brandy
150mL (5 oz) whipped cream (float)
300mL (10 oz) milk

Method
Heat chocolate, milk and
cinnamon, add brandy and pour
into a 10 oz highball glass. Float
cream and serve with straws.

SPLICE

30mL (1 oz) Cointreau
15mL (0.5 oz) tequila
30mL (1 oz) Malibu
cracked ice
30mL (1 oz) Midori
1 scoop ice cream
15mL (0.5 oz) Margimix

Method
Blend until smooth and pour into a
colada glass and serve with straws.

SPRINGBOK

20mL (0.66 oz) Passionfruit Syrup
10mL (0.33 oz) Green Creme de
Menthe
5mL (0.17 oz) Aphrodite Ouzo

Method
Layer in order.

SPRITZER

60mL (2 oz) Still white wine
cracked ice
soda water (top up)

Method
Place white wine in a 10 oz
highball glass over ice. Top with
soda water and serve with straws.

SPUTNIK

75mL (2.5 oz) vodka
10mL (0.33 oz) lemon juice
30mL (1 oz) Fernet Branca
cracked ice
1/2 tsp sugar

Method
Shake and strain over ice in a 5 oz
cocktail glass and serve.

SPUTNIK NO. 2

30mL (1 oz) vodka
Sangrita
15mL (0.5 oz) brandy
1 shake cayenne pepper
15mL (0.5 oz) bourbon
cracked ice

Method
Shake and strain into a Tumbler
glass and serve with straws.

SQUASHED FROG

30mL (1 oz) Midori
30mL (1 oz) Bailey's Irish cream
15mL (0.5 oz) advocaat
15mL (0.5 oz) cherry advocaat

Method
In a 90mL port glass, place Midori.
Stir in advocaat and cherry
advocaat. Float Midori and serve.

STARS AND STRIPES

10mL (0.33 oz) blue curaçao
30mL (1 oz) strawberry liqueur
30mL (1 oz) Southern Comfort
4 strawberries
30mL (1 oz) Frangelico

Method
Pour blue curaçao in a 10 oz cocktail glass. Blend Southern Comfort and Frangelico with a scoop until frozen of ice and add to glass. Blend strawberry liqueur and 4 strawberries with ice Until frozen and add to top. Garnish with grated chocolate over top, add a strawberry with an American flag sticking out of it to the lip of the glass and serve.

STEROID BLAST

30mL (1 oz) O.P. rum
30mL (1 oz) vodka
15mL (0.5 oz) tequila
1 dash soda water (Last)
30mL (1 oz) Benedictine

Method
Shake and strain into a 5 oz cocktail glass, top with soda water and serve.

STIMULATION

30mL (1 oz) Bailey's Irish cream
30mL (1 oz) Cointreau
30mL (1 oz) Malibu
15mL (0.5 oz) cream

Method
Layer in order in a 5 oz cocktail glass and serve.

STINGER

60mL (2 oz) (1 oz) brandy
30mL (1 oz) white crème de menthe

Method
Shake with ice and strain into a 3 oz cocktail glass and serve.

STRAWBERRY BLONDE

30mL (1 oz) crème de cacao
Coca-Cola (top up)
1 splash grenadine
garnish:
1 maraschino cherry
fresh cream (float)

Method
Build over ice in a 10 oz highball glass, garnish with cherry and serve with straws.

STRAWBERRY COLADA

30mL (1 oz) white rum
30mL (1 oz) cream
30mL (1 oz) coconut cream
4 strawberries
30mL (1 oz) pineapple liqueur
1 scoop ice
90mL (3 oz) pineapple juice
garnish:
1 pineapple wedge

Method
Blend ingredients and pour into a
colada glass and serve with a
pineapple wedge as a garnish.

STRAWBERRY FANTASIA

30mL (1 oz) strawberry liqueur
30mL (1 oz) cream
30mL (1 oz) crème de Grand
Marnier

Method
Shake and strain into a 5 oz
cocktail glass and serve.

STRAWBERRY MARGARITA

30mL (1 oz) tequila
5mL (0.17 oz) egg white
15mL (0.5 oz) Cointreau
2-4 strawberries
15mL (0.5 oz) strawberry liqueur
ice

Method
Blend until smooth, pour into a salt
rimmed glass with a half 1/2
strawberry as garnish. Serve.

STRAWBERRY PASSION

30mL (1 oz) Bailey's Irish cream
60mL (2 oz) orange juice
30mL (1 oz) strawberry liqueur
30mL (1 oz) cream
30mL (1 oz) vodka
cracked ice
garnish: 1 strawberry

Method
Shake and strain into a Tumbler
glass, garnish with a strawberry
and serve.

STRAWBERRY ROYAL

30mL (1 oz) strawberry liqueur
2-3 strawberries
chilled champagne (top up)

Method
Blend strawberry liqueur and
strawberries with ice and pour into
a flute glass.
Top with champagne and serve.

STRAWBERRY SHORTCAKE

30mL (1 oz) strawberry liqueur
60mL (2 oz) cream
15mL (0.5 oz) Malibu
4-5 strawberries
15mL (0.5 oz) white crème de cacao
1 scoop ice
garnish: grated chocolate

Method
Blend until smooth and pour into
a brandy Balloon. Garnish with
grated chocolate and serve.

STRAWBERRY TANGO

30mL (1 oz) Tia Maria
10mL (0.33 oz) milk
30mL (1 oz) Kahlúa
2 strawberries
1 dash Grand Marnier
ice
30mL (1 oz) lemon juice

Method
Blend and pour into a 5 oz cocktail glass and serve.

STRAWGASM

15mL (0.5 oz) Malibu
3 strawberries
15mL (0.5 oz) strawberry liqueur
1/4 small banana
15mL (0.5 oz) Galliano Liverno
45mL (1.5 oz) cream
30mL (1 oz) crème de cacao
1/2 scoop ice

Method
Blend until smooth, pour into a colada glass and serve.

SUDANI'S SADNESS SHOOTER

10mL (0.33 oz) sambuca
10mL (0.33 oz) advocaat
10mL (0.33 oz) cherry advocaat
10mL (0.33 oz) Tai Maria
10mL (0.33 oz) blue curaçao

Method
Layer in a shot glass and serve.

SUMMER BREEZE

30mL (1 oz) mango liqueur
45mL (1.5 oz) orange juice
15mL (0.5 oz) Bacardi rum
45mL (1.5 oz) pineapple juice
30mL (1 oz) peach liqueur
20g mango
15mL (0.5 oz) gin
20g peach
garnish: 1 pineapple wedge

Method
Blend and pour into a colada glass. garnish with a pineapple wedge and serve.

SUMMER PASSION

30mL (1 oz) mango liqueur
60g fresh mango
30mL (1 oz) peach liqueur
1 tsp passionfruit pulp (float)
30mL (1 oz) cream

Method
Blend ingredients except passionfruit pulp. Pour gently into a champagne saucer, float passionfruit pulp over lop and serve.

SUMMER SHERBET

30mL (1 oz) mango liqueur
30mL (1 oz) lemon juice
30mL (1 oz) Galliano Liverno

Method
Shake and strain into a 5 oz cocktail glass and serve.

SUNBURST

45mL (1.5 oz) mango liqueur
orange juice (top up)

Method
Build over ice in a 10 oz highball
glass and serve.

SUNDANCER

20mL (0.66 oz) Bundaberg 0 P rum
1 dash egg white
20mL (0.66 oz) Bundaberg U P rum
15mL (0.5 oz) lemon juice
30mL (1 oz) amaretto
30mL (1 oz) orange juice
30mL (1 oz) pineapple juice
cracked ice

Method
Shake and strain into an Old
Fashioned glass and serve.

SUNKEN TREASURE

30mL (1 oz) gin
1 strawberry
15mL (0.5 oz) peach liqueur
apricot Conserve
champagne (top up)

Method
Place a dab of apricot Conserve in
the bottom of a champagne saucer
and push strawberry into it. Stir gin
and peach liqueur with ice and
strain over strawberry. Top with
champagne and serve.

UNKISSED

30mL (1 oz) Rubis
50mL (1.66 oz) blackcurrant juice
15mL (0.5 oz) Cointreau
1 tbsp Raspberries

Method
Blend until smooth and pour into a
champagne saucer and serve.

SUNSET

30mL (1 oz) cherry brandy
30mL (1 oz) fresh cream
30mL (1 oz) advocaat
lemonade (top up)

Method
Pour ingredients over ice in a 10 oz
highball glass, top with lemonade
and serve with straws.

SUNSET NO. 2

30mL (1 oz) Cointreau
5mL (0.17 oz) lemon juice
30mL (1 oz) peach tree
champagne (top up)
20mL (0.66 oz) peach nectar
garnish:
1/2 peach
5 drops grenadine

Method
Pour grenadine into bottom of a
10 oz highball glass and add other
ingredients over ice. Top with
champagne, garnish with sliced
peach half, straws and serve.

SUNSET SPECIAL

40mL (1.33 oz) sweet vermouth
garnish:
1 slice orange
40mL (1.33 oz) Cointreau
crushed ice
80mL (2.66 oz) gin

Method
Shake and strain into a 5 oz
cocktail glass, garnish with orange
slice and serve.

SUNSHINE SURPRISE

30mL (1 oz) Midori
30mL (1 oz) orange juice
30mL (1 oz) Kahlúa
30mL (1 oz) pineapple juice
15mL (0.5 oz) Cointreau
garnish:
1 pineapple wedge
1 dash cream

Method
Blend until smooth and pour into a
colada glass, garnish with
pineapple wedge and serve with
straws.

SUNTORIAN STAR

30mL (1 oz) Midori
pulp 1/2 a passionfruit
15mL (0.5 oz) banana liqueur
4 strawberries
4 pineapple Pieces

Method
puree strawberries and pour a swirl
in a 5 oz cocktail glass. Blend
Midori, banana liqueur, pineapple
Pieces and pour into glass. Top with
passionfruit pulp and serve.

SURFERS PARADISE

60mL (2 oz) vodka
10mL (0.33 oz) blue curaçao
40mL (1.33 oz) dry vermouth
1 maraschino cherry
20mL (0.66 oz) Galliano Liverno

Method
Stir and strain into a champagne
saucer, garnish with cherry and
serve.

SURPRISE

30mL (1 oz) gin
20mL (0.66 oz) apricot brandy
60mL (2 oz) orange juice
cracked ice

Method
Shake and strain over ice in an Old
Fashioned glass and serve.

SURPRISE KISS

30mL (1 oz) Galliano Liverno
15mL (0.5 oz) orange curaçao
20mL (0.66 oz) gin
30mL (1 oz) orange juice
15mL (0.5 oz) ouzo
1 dash egg white

Method
Shake and strain into a 5 02
cocktail glass and serve.

SWAMP WATER

30mL (1 oz) green Chartreuse
20mL (0.66 oz) lime juice (float)
pineapple juice (top up)

Method
Pour Chartreuse over ice in a 10 oz
highball glass, top with pineapple
juice. Float lime juice, add straws
and serve.

SWEET LADY JANE

30mL (1 oz) strawberry liqueur
30mL (1 oz) fresh cream
15mL (0.5 oz) Grand Marnier
15mL (0.5 oz) coconut cream
15mL (0.5 oz) orange juice
garnish:
chocolate Flakes
15mL (0.5 oz) Cointreau
1 sprig mint

Method
Shake and strain into a champagne
saucer, garnish with chocolate
Flakes, mint and serve.

SWEET SIXTEEN

30mL (1 oz) gin
1 dash pineapple juice
15mL (0.5 oz) Malibu
1 dash coconut cream
15mL (0.5 oz) white crème de cacao
1 slice pineapple

Method
Blend until smooth and pour into a
5 oz cocktail glass and serve.

SWEDISH SNOWBALL

30mL (1 oz) Advocaat
15mL (0.66 oz) lemon juice
top up with soda

Method
Build over ice then top up with
soda. Garnish with a lemon slice.

SWISS CHOCOLATE

30mL (1 oz) anisette
fresh cream (float)
30mL (1 oz) cherry brandy
garnish:
1 maraschino cherry
30mL (1 oz) green tea

Method
Pour ingredients into a 3 oz
cocktail glass, float cream, garnish
with cherry and serve.

T.K.O. SHOOTER

10mL (0.33 oz) Kahlua
10mL (0.33 oz) ouzo
10mL (0.33 oz) tequila

Method
Layer in order in a shot glass and serve.

T.N.T.

60mL (2 oz) brandy
2 dashes Pernod
30mL (1 oz) orange curaçao
garnish:
1 twist orange peel
2 dashes Angostura bitters

Method
Shake and strain into a champagne saucer, garnish with orange peel and serve.

TOBLERONE

30mL (1 oz) Frangelico
60mL (2 oz) cream
15mL (0.5 oz) Kahlúa
1/2 tsp honey
15mL (0.5 oz) white crème de cacao
garnish:
almond Flakes
5mL (0.17 oz) Bailey's Irish cream
nutmeg

Method
Blend with ice and pore into a 5 oz cocktail glass. Garnish with almond Flakes, nutmeg and serve.

TALISMAN

30mL (1 oz) Midori
15mL (0.5 oz) lime juice
30mL (1 oz) orange juice
1 slice lime

Method
Build ingredients in an Old Fashioned glass. Garnish with a lime slice in the glass and serve.

TAMOGOZAKE

180mL (6 oz) saki
1 tsp sugar
1 egg

Method
Bring saki to the boil and ignite with a match. Allow to burn for one minute and remove from heat. Add egg and sugar, whisk and serve in a cup.

TEDDY BOY SHOOTER

30mL (1 oz) Kahlúa
30mL (1 oz) Midori
30mL (1 oz) Bailey's Irish cream

Method
Layer in order in a shot glass and serve.

TEMPTATION

60mL (2 oz) rye whiskey
15mL (0.5 oz) Dubonnet
15mL (0.5 oz) Pernod
15mL (0.5 oz) white curaçao
garnish: 1 twist orange peel

Method
Stir and strain into a champagne saucer. Garnish with a twist of orange peel and serve.

TEN FURLONGS

30mL (1 oz) vodka
Bitter lemon drink (top up)
30mL (1 oz) apricot brandy
garnish:
1/2 slice pineapple
15mL (0.5 oz) white curaçao
1 maraschino cherry
3 dashes lime juice

Method
Stir ingredients except Bitter lemon drink, pineapple and cherry. Strain into a highball glass and top with Bitter lemon. Garnish with pineapple slice and cherry and serve.

TENNESSEE MANHATTAN DRY

45mL (1.5 oz) Tennessee whiskey
garnish:
1 twist lemon peel
20mL (0.66 oz) dry vermouth
cracked ice
2 dashes Angostura bitters

Method
Stir and strain into a 3 oz cocktail glass. Garnish with twist of lemon peel and serve.

TENNESSEE SNIFTER

Warm a brandy Balloon by pouring warm water over it. dry the glass, add 90 mL Tennessee whiskey and serve.

TENNESSEE SOUR

60mL (2 oz) Tennessee whiskey
garnish:
1/2 slice lemon
juice 1/2 lemon
1 maraschino cherry
1/2 tsp sugar
cracked ice
soda water (top up)

Method
Shake ingredients except soda water. Strain into a 5 oz cocktail glass, top with soda. Garnish with lemon slice and cherry and serve.

TEQUILA

60mL (2 oz) tequila
1 dash egg white
juice 1/2 lemon
garnish:
1 maraschino cherry
4 dashes grenadine
cracked ice

Method
Shake vigorously and strain into a 5 oz cocktail glass and serve.

TEQUILA CALIENTE

40mL (1.33 oz) tequila
15mL (0.5 oz) lime juice
15mL (0.5 oz) crème de cassis
soda water
2 dashes grenadine
cracked ice

Method
Stir ingredients and strain into a Tumbler glass. Add a shot of soda water and serve.

TEQUILA SLAMMER SHOOTER

30mL (1 oz) tequila
30mL (1 oz) ouzo

Method
Place ingredients in a shot glass and serve.

TEQUILA SLAMMER SHOOTER NO. 2

30mL (1 oz) tequila
20mL (0.66 oz) dry ginger ale

Method
Place ingredients in a shot glass and serve.

TEQUILA SPARKLE

20mL (0.66 oz) tequila
75mL (2.5 oz) milk
30mL (1 oz) coffee liqueur
75mL (2.5 oz) cream

Method
frost the rims of a margarita glass with salt. Stir ingredients and strain into prepared glass and serve.

TEQUILA SUNRISE

60mL (2 oz) tequila

soda water

30mL (1 oz) lemon juice

garnish:

1 slice lime

30mL (1 oz) grenadine

cracked ice

Method
Shake and strain into a 10 oz highball glass. Garnish with slice of lime and serve with straws.

TEQUILA SUNRISE NO. 2

30mL (1 oz) tequila

5mL (0.17 oz) lemon juice

15mL (0.5 oz) Galleon Liverno

cracked ice

15mL (0.5 oz) banana liqueur

garnish:

1 orange slice

5mL (0.17 oz) grenadine

1 maraschino cherry

Method
Shake and strain over crushed ice in an Old Fashioned glass. Garnish with a slice of orange and serve.

TEQUILA SUNRISE NO. 3

30mL (1 oz) tequila

orange juice (top up)

10mL (0.33 oz) grenadine

cracked ice

garnish: 1 orange slice

Method
Half fill a 10 oz highball glass with ice. Add tequila and top with orange juice. Float grenadine on top. Garnish with an orange slice and serve with straws.

TEST-TUBE BABY SHOOTER

30mL (1 oz) amaretto

30mL (1 oz) tequila

30mL (1 oz) Bailey's Irish cream

Method
Layer in a shot glass or test tube and serve.

THE BIG CHILL

30mL (1 oz) Midori

30mL (1 oz) Bacardi rum

15mL (0.5 oz) banana liqueur

90mL (3 oz) pineapple juice

Method
Build ingredients over ice in a 10 oz highball glass and serve with straws.

Toblerone
(Recipe page 221)

Traffic Light
(Recipe page 228)

Voodoo Child
(Recipe page 236)

Test Tube Baby
(Recipe page 224)

Atomic Bomb Shooter
(Recipe page 33)

Water-Bubba Shooter
(Recipe page 237)

THE DICK HEWETT

30mL (1 oz) cognac
glass water (on the side)
30mL (1 oz) Benedictine

Method
Shake with ice and strain into a 3
oz cocktail glass. Serve with glass of
water and serve.

THE ENFORCER SHOOTER

30mL (1 oz) Southern Comfort
30mL (1 oz) tequila
30mL (1 oz) grenadine

Method
Layer in order in a shot glass and
serve.

THE TIME WARP

20mL (0.66 oz) Midori
5mL (0.17 oz) blue curaçao
15mL (0.5 oz) Malibu
cracked ice
15mL (0.5 oz) pineapple juice
garnish:
1 maraschino cherry
5mL (0.17 oz) raspberry cordial

Method
Shake Midori, Malibu, pineapple
juice and strain into a 5 oz cocktail
glass. Add raspberry cordial and
blue curaçao, garnish with cherry
and serve.

THIRD DEGREE

90mL (3 oz) dry gin
8mL (0.27 oz) Pernod
30mL (1 oz) dry vermouth
garnish:
1 twist lemon peel

Method
Shake and strain into a champagne
saucer, garnish with lemon peel
and serve.

THIRD RAIL

30mL (1 oz) rum
20mL (0.66 oz) orange juice
20mL (0.66 oz) dry vermouth
cracked ice
20mL (0.66 oz) sweet vermouth

Method
Shake and strain into a 3 oz
cocktail glass and serve.

THREE ORBIT

30mL (1 oz) Drambuie
30mL (1 oz) vodka
30mL (1 oz) Cointreau

Method
Shake and strain into a 3 oz
cocktail glass and serve.

THREE SISTERS

45mL (1.5 oz) brandy
1 dash grenadine
45mL (1.5 oz) Galliano Liverno
garnish:
1 maraschino cherry
45mL (1.5 oz) orange juice

Method
Shake and strain into a champagne
saucer, garnish with cherry and
serve.

TIDAL WAVE

30mL (1 oz) Cointreau
30mL (1 oz) mango liqueur
30mL (1 oz) peach liqueur
30mL (1 oz) cream

Method
Layer in order in a 5 oz cocktail
glass and serve.

TOBLERONE

5mL (0.17 oz) Baileys Irish Cream
15mL (0.5 oz) Kahlúa
*15mL (0.5oz) White Crème de
Cacao*
30mL (1 oz) Frangelico
60mL (2 oz) cream
1/2 teaspoon honey

Method
Blend with ice and pour.
Garnish with sprinkled nut flakes
and ground nutmeg over top.

TIKI

30mL (1 oz) vodka
1/4 kiwifruit
30mL (1 oz) Midori
1 scoop ice
90mL (3 oz) pineapple juice
garnish:
1 pineapple spear

Method
Half fill a 10 oz highball glass
with cracked ice, blend the above
ingredients except the pineapple
spear and pour into glass. garnish
with pineapple spear, straws
and serve.

TIME BOMB

30mL (1 oz) vodka
30mL (1 oz) lemon juice
30mL (1 oz) Aquavit
garnish:
1 strip lemon peel

Method
Stir and strain into a 3 ?/ cocktail
glass, garnish with lemon peel
and serve.

TITANIC

30mL (1 oz) scotch whiskey
30mL (1 oz) Drambuie
30mL (1 oz) Grand Marnier
30mL (1 oz) green Chartreuse

Method
Layer in order in a 5 oz cocktail
glass and serve.

TOKYO JOE

45mL (1.5 oz) vodka
45mL (1.5 oz) Midori

Method
Layer in a 3 oz cocktail glass
and serve.

TOKYO ROSE

10mL (0.33 oz) tomato juice
10mL (0.33 oz) Smirnoff Vodka
10mL (0.33 oz) Gekkeikan Sake

Method
Layer in order.

TOM COLLINS

60mL (2 oz) gin
garnish:
1 maraschino cherry
60mL (2 oz) lemon juice
1 lemon wheel
1 tsp sugar
cracked ice
soda water (top up)

Method
Place ingredients in a 10 oz
highball glass and top with soda
water. Garnish with cherry, lemon
wheel, straws and serve.

TOP OF THE CROSS

30mL (1 oz) Pernod
ginger beer (top up)
30mL (1 oz) blue curaçao
cracked ice

Method
Quarter fill a 10 oz highball glass
with cracked ice. Add Pernod and
curaçao, top with ginger beer, add
straws and serve.

TOPPING

30mL (1 oz) gin
cracked ice
30mL (1 oz) dry vermouth
1 maraschino cherry
15mL (0.5 oz) crème de Violette

Method
Shake and strain into a 3 oz
cocktail glass, garnish with cherry
and serve.

T.Q. TORNADO

30mL (1 oz) T.Q. Hot Tequila
15mL (0.5 oz) Midori
5mL (0.17 oz) Blue Curacao
90mL (3 oz) pineapple juice

Method
Blend together T.Q. Hot and
pineapple juice with ice. Pour Blue
Curacao into bottom of glass, pour
blended mix on top, then float
Midori last. Garnish with a
pineapple leaf, lime wheel and
cherry.

TRADER VIC'S RUM FIZZ

30mL (1 oz) Whole Hog Rum
30mL (1 oz) lemon juice
10mL (0.33 oz) sugar
15mL (0.5 oz) cream soda
1 raw egg

Method
Shake over ice and pour. Garnish with an orange spiral.

TRAFFIC LIGHT SHOOTER

10mL (0.33 oz) strawberry liqueur
25mL (0.87 oz) green Chartreuse
10mL (0.33 oz) Galliano Liverno

Method
Layer in order in a shot glass and serve.

TRAFFIC STOPPER SHOOTER

30mL (1 oz) banana liqueur
30mL (1 oz) blue curaçao
30mL (1 oz) Bailey's Irish cream

Method
Layer in order in a shot glass and serve.

TRANSPLANT

30mL (1 oz) Bacardi rum
orange juice (top up)
1 dash Galliano Liverno
garnish:
1 spiral orange peel
1 dash crème de menthe
cracked ice

Method
Place ingredients into a 10 oz highball glass and top with orange juice.garnish with orange peel, straws and serve.

TRAVELEX

20mL (0.66 oz) kümmel liqueur
15mL (0.5 oz) lemon juice
15mL (0.5 oz) Galliano Liverno
garnish:
1 pineapple spear
10mL (0.33 oz) vodka
cracked ice
10mL (0.33 oz) crème de banana

Method
Shake and strain into a 3 oz cocktail glass, garnish with pineapple spear and serve.

TRIPLE BY-PASS

20mL (0.66 oz) Creme de Cassis
20mL (0.66 oz) White Creme de Menthe
20mL (0.66 oz) Cherry Brandy

Method
Layer liqueurs in order then float with cream.

TROPICAL

30mL (1 oz) vodka
60mL (2 oz) pineapple juice
30mL (1 oz) peach tree
1 dash cream
15mL (0.5 oz) Rubis
5 strawberries

Method
Blend and pour into a 10 oz highball glass, add straws and serve.

TROPICAL AMBROSIA

1 mandarin orange
1 apple
150mL(5 oz) coconut milk
15mL (0.5 oz) lemon juice

Method
Blend over ice and pour. Garnish with an apple slice.

TROPICAL DELIGHT

30mL (1 oz) dark rum
cracked ice
30mL (1 oz) cream
garnish:
nutmeg
20mL (0.66 oz) orange juice

Method
Shake and strain into a 3 oz cocktail glass, sprinkle with nutmeg and serve.

TROPICAL FIELD

30mL (1 oz) strawberry liqueur
cracked ice
15mL (0.5 oz) cherry brandy
garnish:
1/2 strawberry
30mL (1 oz) pineapple juice
1 maraschino cherry
30mL (1 oz) cream

Method
Shake and strain into a 5 oz cocktail glass, garnish with strawberry, cherry and serve.

TROPICAL PARADISE

45mL (1.5 oz) Bacardi rum
5mL (0.17 oz) lemon juice
45mL (1.5 oz) peach tree
1 slice mango
20mL (0.66 oz) mango liqueur
1 dash mango nectar

Method
Blend and pour into a 3 oz cocktail glass and serve.

TROPICAL SMIRNOFF

30mL (1 oz) Smirnoff vodka
90mL (3 oz) orange juice
15mL (0.5 oz) Grand Marnier
1 peach

Method
Blend and pour into a 5 oz cocktail glass and serve.

TROPICAL SUNSET

30mL (1 oz) Bacardi rum
60mL (2 oz) orange juice
20mL (0.66 oz) Grand Marnier
1 egg yolk
30mL (1 oz) pineapple juice
garnish:
1 pineapple slice
1 dash grenadine

Method
Shake and strain into a 10 oz highball glass, garnish with pineapple slice, straws and serve.

TRUE BLUE

15mL (0.5 oz) Bacardi rum
fresh cream (float)
15mL (0.5 oz) crème de cacao
garnish:
1 maraschino cherry
15mL (0.5 oz) maraschino
crushed ice

Method
Half fill a champagne saucer with crushed ice. Shake remaining ingredients except cream and pour over ice. Float cream and serve.

TROPICAL SURPRISE

30mL (1 oz) peach tree
30mL (1 oz) coconut cream
15mL (0.5 oz) vodka
5mL (0.17 oz) lemon juice
30mL (1 oz) Midori
30mL (1 oz) orange juice
30mL (1 oz) pineapple juice
cracked ice

Method
Shake and pour into a 10 oz highball glass, add straws and serve.

TURKISH DELIGHT

30mL (1 oz) Sabra
5mL (0.17 oz) grenadine
15mL (0.5 oz) parfait amour
cracked ice
30mL (1 oz) cream
garnish:
chocolate Flakes
120mL (4 oz) milk

Method
Shake and strain into a 14 oz colada glass, sprinkle with chocolate Flakes, add straws and serve.

TWILIGHT ZONE

60mL (2 oz) Bacardi rum
15mL (0.5 oz) fresh cream
30mL (1 oz) crème de menthe
garnish:
1 maraschino cherry
15mL (0.5 oz) parfait amour
cracked ice
15mL (0.5 oz) lime cordial

Method
Shake and strain into a champagne
saucer and serve.

U.S.S. ARIZONA

30mL (1 oz) Kentucky bourbon
15mL (0.5 oz) Bianco vermouth
30mL (1 oz) Malibu
Coca-Cola (top up)

Method
Pour ingredients over ice in a 10 oz
highball glass, top with Coca-Cola.
Add straws and serve.

TWO STROKE

30mL (1 oz) chilled Smirnoff Vodka
cracked pepper

Method
Layer in order.

TZEN WITH ENVY

15mL (0.5 oz) crème de menthe
15mL (0.5 oz) parfait amour
15mL (0.5 oz) sambuca
lemonade (top up)

Method
shake and strain into a 5 oz cocktail
class, top with lemonade and serve.

VALENCIA SMILE

30mL (1 oz) apricot brandy
30mL (1 oz) orange juice
4 dashes apricot brandy
champagne (top up)

Method
Shake and strain into a flute glass,
top with champagne and serve.

VAMPIRE

90mL (3 oz) Americano vermouth
30mL (1 oz) banana liqueur

Method
Shake and strain into a champagne
saucer and serve.

VAMPIRE'S PASSION

30mL (1 oz) red crème de menthe
30mL (1 oz) Opal Nera
30mL (1 oz) sambuca
30mL (1 oz) Bailey's Irish cream
15mL (0.5 oz) strawberry liqueur

Method
Layer in order in a 5 oz cocktail
glass and serve.

VELVET HAMMER

30mL (1 oz) Cointreau
30mL (1 oz) cream
30mL (1 oz) Galliano Liverno
crushed ice

Method
Half fill a 5 oz cocktail glass with
crushed ice. Shake ingredients,
pour over ice and serve.

VELVET HAMMER NO. 2

30mL (1 oz) Cointreau
30mL (1 oz) cream
30mL (1 oz) Kahlúa
crushed ice

Method
Half fill a 5 oz cocktail glass with
crushed ice. Shake ingredients and
strain over ice and serve.

VELVET HUE

30mL (1 oz) brandy
30mL (1 oz) Tia Maria
30mL (1 oz) Cointreau
60mL (2 oz) cream

Method
Shake and strain into a champagne
saucer and serve.

VERMOUTH CASSIS

90mL (3 oz) dry vermouth
soda water (top up)
40mL (1.33 oz) crème de cassis
garnish:
1 strip lemon peel

Method
Place a few cubes of ice in a Goblet glass along with vermouth and crème de cassis. Top with soda water, garnish with lemon peel and serve.

VIBRATOR SHOOTER

10mL (0.33 oz) Bailey's Irish cream
20mL (0.66 oz) Southern Comfort

Method
Layer in a 1 oz cordial glass and serve.

VICIOUS VERNON SHOOTER

30mL (1 oz) banana liqueur
30mL (1 oz) Bailey's Irish cream
30mL (1 oz) Kahlúa

Method
Layer in a shot glass and serve.

VIKING II

20mL (0.66 oz) Galliano
20mL (0.66 oz) Aquavit

Method
Layer in order.

VIOLET SLUMBER SHOOTER

15mL (0.5 oz) Malibu
10mL (0.33 oz) orange juice
15mL (0.5 oz) parfait amour

Method
Layer in a shot glass and serve.

VIRGIN

30mL (1 oz) gin
20mL (0.66 oz) Forbidden fruit
20mL (0.66 oz) white crème de menthe
garnish:
1 maraschino cherry

Method
Shake and strain into a 3 oz cocktail glass, garnish with cherry and serve.

VIRGIN MARY

150mL (5 oz) tomato juice
15mL (0.5 oz) lemon juice
teaspoon Worcestershire sauce
Tabasco sauce
salt and pepper to taste

Method
Blend all ingredients together, then serve in salt-rimmed glass with ice, garnished with celery stalk, mint sprig and slice of lemon.

VIRGIN'S DELIGHT

20mL (0.66 oz) Cointreau
20mL (0.66 oz) cream
20mL (0.66 oz) Galliano Liverno
garnish:
1 maraschino cherry
20mL (0.66 oz) orange juice

Method
Shake and strain into a champagne saucer , garnish with cherry and serve.

VIRGIN'S PARADISE

20mL (0.66 oz) gin
20mL (0.66 oz) cream
20mL (0.66 oz) Galliano Liverno
20mL (0.66 oz) orange juice
20mL (0.66 oz) almond liqueur
garnish:
1 maraschino cherry

Method
Shake and strain into a champagne saucer, garnish with cherry and serve.

VIRGIN'S PRAYER

30mL (1 oz) dark rum
80mL (2.66 oz) orange juice
30mL (1 oz) Bacardi rum
cracked ice
30mL (1 oz) Kahlúa
garnish:
1 lime wheel
40mL (1.33 oz) lemon juice

Method
Shake and pour unstrained into a 10 oz highball glass, garnish with lime wheel and serve.

VIVID RESOLUTION

30mL (1 oz) Rosso Antico
10mL (0.33 oz) lemon juice
30mL (1 oz) vodka
cracked ice

Method
Pour ingredients over ice in an Old Fashioned glass and serve.

VODKA COLLINS

30mL (1 oz) vodka
cracked ice
1 tsp sugar
1 slice lemon
juice 1 lime
garnish:
1 maraschino cherry
soda water (top up)

Method
Shake and strain into a 10 oz highball glass and top with soda water. Garnish with lemon slice, cherry and serve with straws.

V

VODKA GIBSON

30mL (1 oz) vodka
cracked ice
15mL (0.5 oz) dry vermouth
garnish:
1 cocktail Onion

Method
Shake and strain into a 3 oz
cocktail glass, garnish with Onion
and serve.

VODKA MIST

45mL (1.5 oz) vodka
1 twist lemon peel
cracked ice

Method
Shake and pour unstrained into an
Old Fashioned glass and serve.

VODKATINI

30mL (1 oz) vodka
cracked ice
1 dash dry sherry
garnish:
1 strip lemon peel

Method
Stir and strain into a 3 oz cocktail
glass, garnish with lemon peel and
serve.

VODKATINI NO. 2

40mL (1.33 oz) vodka
cracked ice
10mL (0.33 oz) dry vermouth
garnish:
1 twist lemon peel

Method
Shake and strain into a 3 oz
cocktail glass, garnish with lemon
peel and serve.

VOLCANO

15mL (0.5 oz) Bacardi rum
15mL (0.5 oz) blue curaçao
15mL (0.5 oz) Bundaberg rum
garnish:
green Chartreuse
orange juice
1/2 slice lime
pineapple juice

Method
Soak 1/2 lime wheel in a small
amount of green Chartreuse. Shake
Bacardi and rum with ice and strain
into a 10 oz Hurricane glass. top up
with equal parts of orange and
pineapple juices. Add blue curaçao
and float the lime slice. Ignite the
lime and serve with straws beside
the glass.

VOLTAGE

30mL (1 oz) Midori
30mL (1 oz) Cointreau
30mL (1 oz) vodka

Method
Shake and strain into a 3 oz
cocktail glass and serve.

VOODOO

15mL (0.5 oz) Frangelico
15mL (0.5 oz) Opal Nera
15mL (0.5 oz) strawberry liqueur
cracked ice
30mL (1 oz) cream
garnish:
grenadine
15mL (0.5 oz) Midori
3 jelly Babies

Method
Shake Frangelico, strawberry
liqueur and cream and strain into
a 3 oz cocktail glass. Layer Midori
and Opal Nera on top. Garnish
with jelly Babies dabbed in
grenadine on Toothpicks and serve.

VOODOO CHILD

15mL (0.5 oz) Midori
15mL (0.5 oz) Tia Maria
15mL (0.5 oz) Opal Nera
15mL (0.5 oz) cream
15mL (0.5 oz) Bailey's Irish cream
garnish:
green & black jelly Babies

Method
Layer Midori over Opal Nera in a
3 oz cocktail glass. Shake remaining
ingredients and carefully strain
over the top. Garnish with green
and black jelly Babies on a skewer
placed across the glass and serve.

VOODOO CURE

30mL (1 oz) Bacardi rum
1/2 banana
20mL (0.66 oz) banana liqueur
60mL (2 oz) orange juice
15mL (0.5 oz) Malibu

Method
Blend until smooth and pour into a
champagne saucer and serve.

WALDORF

30mL (1 oz) Jim Beam Bourbon
5mL (0.17 oz) Pernod
5mL (0.17 oz) Cinzano Sweet
Vermouth
2 dashes of Angostura Bitters

Method
Shake over ice and strain. Garnish
with an orange twist.

WARD

45mL (1.5 oz) Canadian whiskey
15mL (0.5 oz) Powdered sugar
30mL (1 oz) lemon juice
cracked ice
7mL (0.23 oz) grenadine

Method
Shake and strain into a 3 oz
cocktail glass and serve.

WARD EIGHT

45mL (1.5 oz) rye whiskey
10mL (0.33 oz) grenadine
15mL (0.5 oz) orange juice
cracked ice
15mL (0.5 oz) lemon juice

Method
Shake and strain into a 3 oz
cocktail glass and serve.

WATER BUBBA SHOOTER

15mL (0.5 oz) cherry advocaat
12mL (0.4 oz) blue curaçao
10mL (0.33 oz) advocaat

Method
Pour advocaat into cherry advocaat
in a 1 oz cordial glass. Layer blue
curaçao an serve.

WEST INDIES YELLOW BIRD

30mL (1 oz) white rum
30mL (1 oz) pineapple juice
15mL (0.5 oz) banana liqueur
1 1/2 scoops ice
30mL (1 oz) lemon juice
garnish:
1 pineapple wedge
30mL (1 oz) orange juice
1 maraschino cherry

Method
Blend until smooth, pour into a
brandy Balloon, garnish with a
pineapple wedge and cherry and
serve.

WESTMOORELAND

90mL (3 oz) bourbon
garnish:
2 sprigs mint
1 tbsp sugar
crushed ice

Method
Crush half the mint with half the sugar and ice. Place in a 7 oz Old Fashioned glass, add bourbon. Place remaining mint and ice into glass and serve with straws.

WET SPOT

30mL (1 oz) Midori
30mL (1 oz) cream
15mL (0.5 oz) Frangelico
30mL (1 oz) passionfruit pulp (float)
30mL (1 oz) apple juice
cracked ice

Method
Shake and strain into a 5 oz cocktail glass. Float the passionfruit and serve.

WHISKEY BOMB

60mL (2 oz) scotch whiskey
5mL (0.17 oz) sugar syrup
1 dash Angostura bitters
cracked ice

Method
Stir and strain into a 3 oz cocktail glass and serve.

WHISKY SOUR

30mL (1 oz) scotch whisky
30mL (1 oz) lemon juice
15mL (0.17 oz) sugar syrup
1/2 egg white

Method
Shake with ice and strain. Garnish with a red cherry at bottom of glass and slice of lemon on side.

WHITE LADY

30mL (1 oz) Gilbey's Gin
15mL (0.5 oz) lemon juice
15mL (0.5 oz) sugar syrup
1/2 egg white

Method
Shake with ice and strain. Garnish with a Twist of lemon.

WHITE MAGIC

bitter almonds
20mL (0.66 oz) Cherry Brandy
10mL (0.33 oz) vanilla ice cream

Method
Pour Cherry Brandy onto bitter almonds then float vanilla ice cream.

W

WIDOW'S KISS

30mL (1 oz) Apple Brandy
10mL (0.33 oz) Benedictine
10mL (0.33 oz) Yellow Chartreuse
5mL (0.17 oz) Angostura Bitters

Method
Shake over ice and strain. Garnish with a floating strawberry.

WOODSTOCK

30mL (1 oz) Gilbey's Gin
10mL (0.33 oz) lemon juice
10mL (0.33 oz) maple syrup
2 dashes Angostura Bitters

Method
Shake over ice and strain then add cubed ice. Garnish with a straw.

YORKER

30mL (1 oz) Midori
30g Avocado
30mL (1 oz) cream
garnish:
1 strawberry
60mL (2 oz) milk

Method
Blend ingredients and pour into a
colada glass. Garnish with a
strawberry and serve.

ZANDARIA

30mL (1 oz) brandy
cracked ice
30mL (1 oz) Tia Maria
garnish:
1 Pinch nutmeg
120mL (4 oz) fresh cream

Method
Shake and strain into a 6 oz
cocktail glass. Sprinkle with
nutmeg and serve.

ZED

30mL (1 oz) gin
1 tsp sugar
30mL (1 oz) Mandarin Napoleon
garnish:
1/2 slice lemon
90mL (3 oz) pineapple juice
1 sprig mint

Method
Shake and strain into a 3 oz
cocktail glass. Garnish with mint
sprig and lemon.

ZIPPER SHOOTER

15mL (0.5 oz) tequila
15mL (0.5 oz) Grand Marnier
15mL (0.5 oz) Bailey's Irish cream

Method
Layer in order in a shot glass
and serve.

ZOMBIE

30mL (1 oz) light rum
30mL (1 oz) apricot nectar
30mL (1 oz) Golden rum
15mL (0.5 oz) O.P. rum
30mL (1 oz) dark rum
5mL (0.17 oz) sugar syrup
30mL (1 oz) lemon juice
cracked ice
30mL (1 oz) pineapple juice
fruit for garnish

Method
Fill a Zombie glass 3/4 full with ice.
Shake and strain ingredients except
0 P rum into the glass. Gently add
rum. Garnish with fruit and serve.

ZOMBIE NO. 2

30mL (1 oz) dark rum
4 dashes passionfruit soda
30mL (1 oz) Jamaican rum
30mL (1 oz) lemon juice
4 dashes apricot brandy
garnish:
1 slice orange
30mL (1 oz) white rum
green and red Cherries
4 dashes cherry brandy
cracked ice
15mL (0.5 oz) Proof rum (top up)

Method
Fill Zombie glass with cracked ice. Add the above ingredients except 151 Proof rum. Stir and top with 151 Proof rum. Decorate with Cherries and orange slice. Serve with straws.

ZOOM

40mL (1.33 oz) brandy
20mL (0.66 oz) cream
15mL (0.5 oz) honey
cracked ice

Method
Shake and strain into a 5 oz cocktail glass and serve.

ZORBA THE GREEK

60mL (2oz) Bacardi rum
30mL (1 oz) orange juice
15mL (0.5 oz) ouzo
15mL (0.5 oz) grenadine

Method
Shake and strain into a 5 oz cocktail glass and serve.

ZULU WARRIOR

30mL (1 oz) Midori
garnish:
1 slice Rockmelon
30mL (1 oz) strawberry liqueur
3 strawberries
30mL (1 oz) lemon juice
1 1/2 scoops ice

Method
Blend until smooth. Pour into a brandy Balloon. Garnish with a slice of Rockmelon and serve.

Index

Index

Gin

Index